S0-BNI-278

DOING BUSINESS WITH
SPAIN

A NEARBY SPACE AT YOUR SERVICE

THE MOST TYPICAL EXHIBITION CENTRE IN MADRID
five minutes from Plaza de España

Nine Buildings: **39.000 m²**
- Exhibitions • Conventions • Theatre
- Valencia • Masía • IX, XI, XII
y **Crystal Pavillion**

Madrid Town Hall
Patronato de la Feria del Campo

Avd. de Portugal, s/n Casa de Campo
Tel.: 463 63 34 - Fax: 470 21 54, 28011 MADRID-SPAIN

DOING BUSINESS WITH
SPAIN

THE SPANISH CHAMBER OF COMMERCE IN GREAT BRITAIN

Consultant Editor:
Pablo Villaneuva

Forewords by:
Guillermo de la Dehesa,
Spanish Confederation of Chambers of Commerce

Anthony Nelson, Minister for Trade

This book was compiled on the basis of information supplied in January 1996. Kogan Page and the editor cannot assume legal responsibility for the accuracy of any particular statement in this work. No responsibility for loss or damage occasioned to any person acting or refraining from action as a result of the material in this publication can be accepted by the editor or publishers.

First published 1996

Apart from any fair dealing for the purposes of research or private study, or criticism or review, as permitted under the Copyright, Designs and Patents Act, 1988, this publication may only be reproduced, stored or transmitted, in any form, or by any means, with the prior permission in writing of the publishers, or in the case of reprographic reproduction in accordance with the terms of licences issued by the Copyright Licensing Agency. Enquiries concerning reproduction outside those terms should be sent to the publishers at the undermentioned address.

Kogan Page Ltd
120 Pentonville Road
E-mail:kpinfo@kogan–page.co.uk London N1 9JN

© Kogan Page 1996

British Library Cataloguing Data
A CIP record for this book is available from the British Library
ISBN 0 7494 1918 0

Typeset by Northern Phototypesetting Co Ltd, Bolton
Printed and bound in Great Britain by Clays Ltd, St Ives plc

382.0941046
D 65

97-6120
35599848

Contents

PART 13: USEFUL ADDRESSES

Foreword

Spain as a business partner for UK companies is not accorded the importance that it deserves. In fact, it is one of Western Europe's fastest growing economies and most rapidly industrialising nations. Many still view Spain as a favourite holiday destination. Of course it is, but the wide range of business opportunities in this large market continue to be overlooked.

When Spain joined the European Union a decade ago, the effect on our bilateral trade was dramatic. UK visible exports have almost quadrupled since 1985 and now stand at about £6 billion. By any standards this is impressive. In the opposite direction, Spanish exporters have also benefited from EU membership; the value of their sales to the UK has more than doubled over the same period.

My government places great importance on the development of closer business links with our European partners. But these links are not confined to the exchange of goods and services. The UK is a major foreign investor in Spanish manufacturing industry, in the Spanish tourist industry, in financial services and in property development. Many leading UK companies are operating in Spain through subsidiaries or in joint ventures with Spanish partners. Every year our bilateral trading and commercial ties are being strengthened and deepened. Long may that continue!

This guide on *Doing Business with Spain* deals with many different aspects of trade, commerce and international finance. I am sure it will be a valuable reference both for newcomers to UK–Spanish business circles and for those already benefiting from existing bilateral ties.

Anthony Nelson
Minister for Trade

BUSINESS IN EUROPE

Here's a Spanish package that could help your business

Spain is the UK's eighth largest export market. It offers excellent opportunities for British companies in all sectors.

If you are thinking about exporting to Spain, DTI and the Foreign and Commonwealth Office (FCO) offer a package of services that could help.

DTI's Spain Desk can provide you with advice on the market. General and sector specific information, including market summaries of major product sectors and tailor-made lists of potential agents and distributors, is also available.

Up-to-the-minute advice on market conditions for your product or service is provided by an experienced team of FCO Commercial Officers throughout mainland Spain and the Canary Islands.

If you would like to find out more about exporting to Spain please telephone:–

0171-215 4284 (capital goods)

or 0171-215 4724 (consumer goods)

Alternatively write to:
Spain Desk
Business in Europe
Department of Trade and Indu.
Bay 854, Kingsgate House
66-74 Victoria Street
London SW1E 6SW

Fax: 0171-215 4711

Department of Trade and Industry

Foreword

Information is an essential tool for doing business. This is the reason why *Doing Business with Spain* will be very useful to any British business person operating in the Spanish market and indispensable for those who are entering the Spanish market for the first time. Spain is well-known to foreigners, and especially to British citizens as many millions of visitors and tourists come to Spain each year. Since joining the European Union, the Spanish economy has rapidly embraced foreign trade and investment, now that the single market has abolished the remaining barriers among European Union members. Nevertheless, there is huge potential for increasing business with Spain. On the one hand, the Spanish economy remains one of the least open in Europe and its share of foreign investment is still not very high while Spanish investment abroad is small in relation to total output.

On the other hand, however, the Spanish market is the fifth largest in Europe, with a population close to 40 million and a high level of purchasing power. The quality of Spanish labour is excellent and wages are still reasonable, compared with European averages. This important factor, together with newly-built transport and communication infrastructures, a healthy environment and an agreeable climate make Spain one of the most attractive locations for foreign direct investment.

To exploit these business opportunities, a good practical knowledge of the Spanish legal framework of business practices and business culture helps to find the right partners, and provides a real insight into the Spanish market. These are the main objectives of this practical and very useful guide. I congratulate the Spanish Chamber of Commerce in the UK and Kogan Page for their initiative and for having compiled in this guide such an excellent group of leading experts on the different subjects on the Spanish market.

Guillermo de la Dehesa
President, Spanish Confederation of Chambers of Commerce

Do you **really** want to do business with Spain or Britain?

Then you should be in

HISPANIA

"the Anglo Spanish Fair of Business & Arts"

Every year, in London, a uniquely
Spanish marketing mix of business and pleasu
for entrepreneurs and investors in
Spain and/or the UK

For further details please contact

Bruno Giorgi,
HISPANIA Communications,

Correspondents for Gaceta de los Negocios,
Radio Intereconomia & Revista Dinero

Tel & Fax 0181 205 1168
Email:bruno@hispania.org.uk

You can start exhibiting <u>now</u> at our Internet site
http://www.hispania.org.uk

The Contributors

Aserplan is the Spanish member of Woodrow Milliman, an international network of actuarial and consulting firms represented in more than 90 offices in 21 countries.
Félix Soroa is managing director of Aserplan in Madrid.

Baker & McKenzie is the largest international law firm in the world, with more than 50 offices in key business centres worldwide.
José Arcila and *Cecilia Pastor* are partner and associate practitioner in the fiscal department at the Baker & McKenzie office in Madrid.
José Luis Stampa and *Ramón Fernández-Castellanos* are both practitioners in intellectual property law at the Barcelona office.
Alex Valls and *Fraser Young* are lawyers at the Madrid office.

The Confederation of Spanish Industry (CEOE) is an independent body which promotes and represents Spanish businessmen and women. It is involved in a large number of European projects and maintains a privileged relationship with its corresponding organisations in Latin America.

Deloitte and Touche operates in Spain as part of the international group Deloitte Touche Tohmatsu International, one of the world's largest accounting, auditing, tax and management consultancy firms.
Angel Salgado and *Fernándo Carvajal* work in the fiscal and legal department of Deloitte and Touche in Madrid.

Despacho Ramón Hermosilla is a well-established law firm in Spain, providing a wide array of legal services for business organisations.
Ramón Hermosilla Gimeno and *José Antonio González* are senior partners at the Madrid office.

Ernst & Young is one of the biggest organisations in the field of business services in the world. It specialises in auditing, accounting, legal and taxation advice, and management consulting.
William Field deals with international taxation issues in Ernst & Young's London office.

ESADE (Escuela Superior de Administración y Dirección de Empresas) is one of the oldest Spanish business schools. Based in Barcelona, it provides a business education and executive training for Spaniards and foreigners. It is a member of a large number of international associations of business schools.
Ramón Montaner lectures at ESADE and is the managing director of M&A personnel consultants.

ESTE is the business school of the Universidad de Deusto in San Sebastian, one of the most respected Spanish universities.
Dr Victor Urcelay Yarza and *Fernando Moroy Hueto* lecture at ESTE, and the latter is also deputy managing director of Banco Guipuzcoano.

Gaceta de los Negocios is one of the three most relevant economic journals in Spain. It is part of Grupo Negocios, which owns two other economic information media: the weekly magazine *Mercado* and the 24-hour economic radio channel Intereconomia.
Albert Recarte, Francisco Cabrillo, Jesús González, Lorenzo Bernáldo de Quirós and *Emilio González* are members of Negocios' task group.

L & A Garrigues is a well-established Spanish firm of solicitors which develops its activities in all areas of law, particularly in those relating to international operations.
Miguel Riaño is a lawyer in the administrative and environmental law section of L&A Garrigues.

Gómez Acebo & Pombo is a Spanish firm dedicated to all areas of law, providing services to businesses mostly in connexion with corporate law, banking, intellectual property, insurance and litigation.
Gonzalo Ulloa is managing partner of the intellectual property and media department.

Income Data Services Ltd is an independent research organisation providing a range of services to HR specialists. It publishes the monthly magazine *IDS Employment Europe*.
Caroline Welch is assistant editor of *IDS Employment Europe* with specific responsibility for covering developments in Spain.

The Instituto de Empresa is one of Spain's leading business schools. It provides postgraduate business education and executive training in all areas of management.
Fernándo Cortiñas teaches at the Instituto de Empresa school in Madrid.

Jones Lang Wootton is an international firm of chartered surveyors specialising in real estate.
James Preston is a manager in the investments department of the Madrid office.

KPMG is one of the largest professional services firms, with international headquarters in Amsterdam and 72,500 personnel, including 6,000 partners, based in 136 countries. KPMG provides services to more than a third of the world's top 1,000 commercial and industrial companies.
Nigel Cooper is Spanish liaison partner in KPMG's London office, and *Javier Jimenez*, based in KPMG's Seville office, is workiing in London at present.
David Adams and *Celso Garcia Granda* work in the personal tax department of KPMG in London and Madrid respectively.

Optimum Media España is the media buying and planning division of DDB/Needham, which is part of the international group Omnicom. Optimum Media has offices in Madrid and Barcelona.
José Antonio Llaneza is general manager at Optimum Media in Madrid.

Price Waterhouse is one of the six leading auditing, accounting and specialised management consulting firms worldwide.
Juan Ramón Ramos and *Enrique Aznar* are director of the international tax department in Barcelona and manager of the Spanish desk of the international tax services group in London respectively.

Richard Ellis is an international firm dedicated to valuation brokerage and investment in real estate.
Eduardo Fernández–Cuesta is managing director of Richard Ellis Residencial in Madrid.

The Spanish Chamber of Commerce in Great Britain is an independent, non profit-making organisation dedicated to the promotion of trade between Spain and Britain.

The Commercial Office of **the Spanish Embassy in London** is the branch of the embassy which specialises in assisting British investors with business opportunities in Spain, and in promoting Spanish exports in Britain.

Leslie Stern works for the DTI as export promoter for Spain.

Francisco Javier Suso is an advertising expert and independent consultant. He also lectures at Odec and at the business school CESMA in Madrid.

Uría and Menéndez is a leading Spanish law firm founded in the 1940s. It has offices in Barcelona, Madrid, Valencia and London, and is a member of the Alliance of European Lawyers.
Juan I González and *Gabriel Núñez* are currently working in the London office. Their main areas of practice are corporate law, banking and financial law, and capital markets.

Asturias, Nature and Industry

You may think of Spain as a recently industrialised country, based on agriculture and tourism. If you do, you may be surprised to know that the first steel mills were built in Asturias back in the early nineteenth century. From then onwards, Asturias has meant industry. For nearly two centuries, industry has shaped Asturias, filling its land with mills, pits and workshops. Industry has also moulded the Asturian people, forging an established working culture that accords with Asturias' historical links with Northern Europe.

Industrial heritage

Today, the region is clearly turning away from any previous concentration it may have shown in traditional industries. Services such as advanced engineering or software development, and industries such as environmental equipment or new materials, are growing fast in Asturias. The German conglomerate Thyssen, appreciating the existing infrastructure and wealth of qualified personnel in the metal transforming field, has decided to locate an escalator and an airport 'fingers' manufacturing plant.

The manufacture of automotive components will surprise few as a wise investment in Asturias. The region is situated in the automotive heartland of the north of Spain and has already attracted corporates like Suzuki. Right now, however, the sector most rapidly expanding in Asturias is chemicals, following major investments by Du Pont de Nemours, Bayer GMBH and Química del Nalón, SA.

Europe's gateway

One of the clear advantages of locating business or industry in Asturias is its strategic position. Direct highway links to the French border and to the south of Spain and five direct weekly flights to London and Paris make the rest of Europe easily accessible. Links with the rest of Spain are abundant, with six flights leaving for Madrid each day and a similar number for other major Spanish cities. Rail links in the region are excellent. The extensive national railway system offers comprehensive freight services. Two sea ports in Gijón and Avilés offer up-to-date cargo and roll-on/roll-off facilities.

Asturias' greatest force

The Asturian workforce is the region's greatest asset. Asturias' labour force is multifarious, and extensive training of the young has been a top priority of the regional authorities. Its 400-year-old university has a national reputation for excellence in sciences. It has more than 35,000 students, whereas over 20,000 youngsters and workers attend vocational training and retraining courses. Foreign companies have been impressed by the ease with which the Asturians have adapted to the company's corporate culture.

Advertising feature

A nice investment climate

Asturias is classified as an 'Objective 1' region by the EU. Companies interested in investing in the region can qualify for some of the highest grants available in the EU, extending to 50 per cent of the capital invested.

Industrial land and utilities prices are very competitive in Asturias. A number of industrial parks are spread throughout the region ensuring the availability of land at prices as low as $100 per sq m, the main example being the Technology Park of Asturias . You will find abundant water, gas and electricity supplies there and anywhere else in the region. The abundance of water in Asturias has reduced the price enormously compared with other regions in Spain.

A natural paradise

The quality of life in the region is rarely as important in influencing investment decisions as it is in Asturias. Any corporate investor asked why the area was selected will invariably mention the quality of life factor. As 80 per cent of the 1.1 million region's population live in its centre, the rest of Asturias forms largely 10,000 km^2 of unspoilt landscape, which has been labelled a 'natural paradise'.

Asturias falls into the 'Green Spain' area of the country. The countryside is ideal for outdoor activities. A 300-km coastline offers every possibility for all kind of nautical sports. Thanks to its long history Asturias has a rich culture heritage. Visitors can see historical sites, museums and exhibitions or attend cultural events such as opera and concerts. And lovers of the good life will be attracted by Asturias' reputation as the gastronomic centre of Spain.

As for Du Pont . . .

Du Pont de Nemours' greenfield site is an example of the new industrial profile of companies setting up in Asturias. The company needed 800 acres of unspoilt land, 1,000 suitably qualified and highly adaptable staff, and a strategically significant location in southern Europe. After the analysis of other possible locations in Italy, the South of France, Portugal and Spain, Du Pont found that Asturias met all these requirements.

. . . Asturias is ready to welcome you and your company

The response of the regional government and the Regional Development Agency (IFR) to foreign investors has been highly praised. 'Another factor in our coming here is that there is a very cooperative government in Asturias and we have also had a lot of support from the IFR', claims a representative of a multi-national located in Asturias. The IFR offers a tailor-made service to any company interested in locating in Asturias, providing specific information on legal and economic factors of such an investment IFR advice can help you to cope with the frustrating layer of bureaucracy which blight the establishment of large production plants.

Advertising feature

Asturias

or its nature

d down beneath the
ights of powerful
ountains towards the sea,
turias is blessed with
spoilt and astonishingly
autiful landscapes.

or its industrial
adition

turias long history is full
industrial development,
entreprising, of expertise,
business culture.
well doing. Traditional
ustries have been
structured into next century
tivities. Du Pont de
emours, Thyssen and
zuki have located their
ost updated plants among

or its investment
imate

turias offers competitive
ppliers, water and land
ailability, modern and
ways improving
rastructure, generous
ants up to 50% and an
tstanding quality of life.

sturias
ready for the future
d you.

Du Pont's Nomex® plant,
first project in Asturias ▶

$\mathcal{A}$sturias,

in the northern coast of Spain,
is an undoubtly privileged region,
ready to welcome you and your
company.

IFR

Instituto de Fomento Regional

Towards New Ways of Living and Working in the Twenty-First Century

We are witnessing a change of historic dimensions: a new economy, based on new technologies and information-processing activities, is relegating the industrial activity of the more developed countries to other parts of the world where it can be economically competitive.

Thus, a new global economic system is taking shape, and no country, region or city will be free of its effects. This change is not just economic; it has an impact on infrastructure, social structure, culture, urban development, lifestyles etc. To address this challenge, all regions must emphasise the competitive advantages which will enable them to remain competitive.

The Balearic economy in the twenty-first century must reflect these new circumstances. The economic model based on mass tourism, low wages and low costs has been virtually exhausted; and while traditional tourism still serves to maintain economic activity, it can no longer be relied upon to provide sustained and balanced growth over the long term. The region's future economic prosperity would be best served by the creation of innovative companies, and by the attraction of highly qualified professionals and knowledge-intensive activities, which would use the Balearic Islands as a platform for reaching the European market. This would complement efforts to upgrade the area's tourist industry.

To attain this goal, in the current information age it is necessary to develop a process of innovative economic growth, adapted to its social and territorial structure and based on a healthy, stable environment. This is the option that the Balearic Government is implementing, through strategic planning and actions, under the name of 'BIT Strategy' (Balearics Innovation and Technology), in the firm belief that the Balearics enjoy some of the best conditions in Europe (quality of life, an international airport, good telecommunications infrastructure, high standard of living etc) to make the most of the opportunities of the information age.

In this sense, it is clear that the Balearic Islands cannot choose between traditional and technological development. The region must invest in technology or it will be relegated to a marginal position in the new global economic system. Furthermore, technology (ie telecommunications) is the best way to both encourage more affluent tourists to extend their holidays in the Islands, and attract permanent or semi-permanent residents. The presence of businessmen and qualified professionals throughout the year would help balance the acute seasonality of tourism. It is intended that the ParcBIT project should be one of the main instruments of this strategy, following successful examples such as Sophie Antipolis in Nice and the Multifunctional Polis in Adelaide.

In conclusion, ParcBIT should be considered as:
• a symbol representing the aim of the Balearics to be in the forefront of the new information economy; • an example on both a local and an international level, of 'sustainable development', proving that it is possible to generate economic growth without sacrificing the environment • a catalyst to encourage innovative, advanced technological activities to establish themselves and grow in the Balearic Islands: this will complement tourism as the main economic activity.

Advertising feature

Quality of life, quality of work.

One day, the world will want to live and work this way. Here in the **Balearic Islands**, we are planning for it already. With an oustandingly **beautiful landscape**, warm seas, blue skies, a **prosperous economy**, and **no traffic jams or pollution**, the daily grind of working in the big city is a world away. **Investment** in **information technologies** and **communications** means that it is now possible **to work**, as well as **to relax** here.

The Balearic Islands

shaping the 21st century

 Ministry for Economy and Finance. Govern Balear
Palau Reial,17 . 07001 Palma de Mallorca (SPAIN) . Tel: +34 71 176751 . Fax: +34 71 176757

The Basque Country moves towards the XXI century

The Basque Country, made up of the historical territories of Alava, Gipuzkoa, and Bizkala, has enjoyed since 1979 a unique Statute of Autonomy, which confers a high degree of self-government based on two pillars: its own government and parliament.

By virtue of its self-government, the Basque Country has a broad fiscal autonomy which permits the collecting of taxes within its territory and the regulation of its own taxation system. The income obtained allows the Basque institutions to draw up budgets that establish investment and expense priorities in their different areas of concern, such as public health, citizen security (guaranteed by the Basque Autonomous Police Force or *Ertzaintza*), economic and industrial promotion, construction and maintenance of all kinds of infrastructures, and radio and television; to mention a few of their exclusive functions.

Proof of its financial capacity is the nearly one billion pesetas of its own resources administered by the Basque institutions in 1995, to a population of 2.1 million. This financial and tax autonomy permit the adoption in a given moment of the most appropriate and interesting incentive measures for the promotion of economic activity, within the guidelines defined by the tax structures of the Spanish State and the European Union.

Thus, Euskadi has notably modernised its transport infrastructures over the last ten years, which has required an enormous financial effort on the part of the Basque institutions. Besides an excellent network of roads, highways, and toll roads, the Basque Country has the largest port in Spain: the port of Bilbao. Of Euskadi's three airports, Bilbao's is of international importance, and Vitoria's has become the third largest freight-handling airport in Spain, behind those of Madrid and Barcelona.

Currently, the Basque Country is in the process of the full development of its telecommunications infrastructures. Its most ambitious project is the laying of a fibre-optic network, which will make possible the introduction of new telecommunications services, and so open new formulas for economic activity.

At the same time, Euskadi is dedicating 1.2 per cent of its GNP to research and development, both in business production centres and in the seven existing technological centres, promoted by the autonomous government.

With respect to training, the institutions, companies, and trade unions are undertaking the enormous task of permanent training of human resources. Every year, the Basque government earmarks approximately 650 million dollars for education. Furthermore, the conjunction of financial forces of Basque businesses, strengthened by fiscal incentives, together with the direct contribution of public funds, permits the design of a system of professional training of very high quality.

The concern for quality has been a constant during the last few years and has extended generally into the business fabric of the Basque Country. Today, several hundred companies have already accredited the quality of their products and manufacturing processes with the attainment of the corresponding quality certificates. For every 100 Spanish companies that have earned these certificates, 30 are Basque.

Over the last ten years, the internationalisation of the Basque economy has been consolidated, a fact confirmed by the constant increase in exports, the significant investments being made throughout the world by Basque businesses, and the increasing choice of Euskadi as the location for business projects in which multinational companies participate.

Advertising feature

THE BASQUE COUNTRY
A PARTNER OF PROMISE

10 TEN REASONS WHY THE BASQUE COUNTRY IS TODAY AN ATTRACTIVE, UP-TO-DATE PROPOSITION:

A STRATEGIC GEOGRAPHICAL SETTING

A vital link in the communications axis between Lisbon and Stockholm, the Basque Country has Spain's leading merchant shipping port and Europe's deepest docking facilities (32 metres). The region also has three airports, 322 kilometres of motorway and the only direct Spanish connection with Europe's high-speed rail network.

A NETWORK OF INTELLIGENT HIGHWAYS

The Basque Country has a latest -generation micro-wave network and a broad-band optical fibre trunk network covering 85% of the Basque population and all university campuses and industrial centres.

BROAD-BASED, DIVERSIFIED POWER INFRASTRUCTURE

Efficiency and savings programmes have enabled the Basque Country as a whole to reduce energy consumption by 14% since 1980. The area currently depends on oil for 36.7% of the energy it needs. Power sources have been diversified in recent years, with particular attention being paid to natural gas, which has its own gas field and modern distribution network.

SPAIN'S INDUSTRIAL POWERHOUSE

Much of Spain's production in a number of strategic sectors comes from the Basque Country: machine-tools, the automotive ancillary industry, capital goods and the iron and steel industry. The Basque Country is also home to the Mondragón Corporación Cooperativa (MCC), the world's largest industrial cooperative group, and Iberdrola, Europe's fifth largest power generating company.

INVESTMENT INCENTIVES AND GUARANTEES

Treasury bonds issued by the Basque Government have been given an Aa2 rating by American ratings agency Moody's and AA+ by Standard & Poor's. Of the incentives offered for investment, among the most attractive are the deduction of 20% on fixed assets and new materials and a 40% tax cut on production investments.

TECHNOLOGY RESEARCH APPLIED TO INDUSTRY

The Basque Country has seven Research Centres employing more than 900 professionals; the largest science and technology park in northeastern Spain; engineering firms and other companies involved in international research projects: LHC particle accelerator (CERN-Geneva); the European Space Agency and NASA; the EURECA (European Retrievable Carrier) Platform, currently in orbit and the Polar Platform, in collaboration with the International Freedom Station in Columbus.

ONE OF EUROPE'S LEADING FINANCIAL CENTRES

The Banco Bilbao Vizcaya, Spain's leading bank in terms of the volume of savings managed, the Bolsa de Bilbao, the country's second busiest Stock Exchange, Elkargi, the first mutual guarantee company in Spain, and Luzaro, the country's first mezzanine finance company, are all based in the Basque Country.

HUMAN RESOURCES, THE BASQUE COUNTRY'S MOST IMPORTANT RAW MATERIAL

There are two universities in the Basque Country, one of which, Deusto, is Spain's most famous seat of learning. Students can choose from 22 faculties, 8 technical and 3 Higher colleges and schools. The Basque Country also has 172 vocational training centres.

A UNIQUE, AGE-OLD CULTURE

Euskera, the Basque language. Part of mankind's linguistic heritage, *Euskera* is the oldest language in Europe, a survival from the pre-Indo-European era.

AN UNRIVALLED NATURAL SETTING

The UNESCO recently declared the Gernika estuary a "Biosphere Reserve". According to the 1992 Economic Report on the Spanish Autonomous Communities, the Basque Country has the most complete environmental protection infrastructure in all Spain.

For further information contact:

GOBIERNO VASCO-PRESIDENCIA
VITORIA-GASTEIZ / BASQUE COUNTRY, SPAIN. TLF: 34.45.18 80 92 • FAX: 34.45.18 80 81

SPRI-SOCIEDAD PARA LA PROMOCION INDUSTRIAL
BILBAO / BASQUE COUNTRY, SPAIN. TLF: 34.4. 479 70 12 • FAX: 34.4. 479 70 23

QUALITY MAKES THE DIFFERENCE
BASQUE COUNTRY

Galicia is a European region located in north-eastern Spain. It has an extensive, 1,300km coastline on the Bay of Biscay and the Atlantic Ocean, and shares a border with Portugal. Its 29,453 km² and oceanic, damp, European climate give it beautiful scenery and rich, fertile land where the introduction of modern life has respected history and old customs. Its 2,731,693 people are characterised by their outward-looking and enterprising nature.

Galicia is constantly growing, creating the foundations for the future and developing its communications network. Its roads provide excellent internal communication and links to the rest of Spain. Its four large ports with modern infrastructures enjoy a privileged position as doorways to the marketplace of Europe. Communication by air is covered by three airports which satisfy Spanish and international demand. In the field of telecommunications, the creation of institutional networks has been promoted, along with the installation of an optical fibre circuit to connect the largest Galician cities.

The main economic sectors of the Galician community are the automotive industry and related industries; the food, fishing, agricultural and fish-canning sectors; the textile sector; the wood-transformation industry; the granite and slate industries; and the ship-building and electricity sectors.

Galicia's beaches and scenery offer great opportunities for tourism, leisure and sport. The tranquility of its estuaries is perfect for water sports.

Galicia is one of the most popular regions for foreign investment. There has been a progressive increase in investment since 1990, and there are 68 firms in Galicia with foreign share capital, providing jobs for 22,000 people. The main investors come from the European Community, EFTA countries and the United States.

Galicia is an Objective No 1 region of the European Union and receives the maximum level of aid from structural funds. Business projects in Galicia are eligible for outright grants of up to 60 per cent of the investment. The regional government also offers low-interest loans to finance up to 70 per cent of the investment and up to 95 per cent of real estate purchases.

IGAPE can help you cut through the red tape to make your project a reality: anything from looking for a venture capital company to participating in your investment and providing information for your project, to offering special proposals for large investments in light of the fact that in Galicia the maximum limit allowed by the EU can be reached.

Advertising feature

LUIS CABBALO/VIGO

The Galician Institute for Economic Promotion, IGAPE.
An effective instrument for the development of Galicia.

The Galician Institute for Economic Promotion, IGAPE, is an effective instrument helping Galician companies to maintain a constant rhythm in innovation and competitiveness.

IGAPE provides services to companies by offering financial support to SME; promoting Galician companies and their products abroad; introducing the most innovative business techniques, developing new information services or helping young entrepreneurs to set up their business project.

To benefit from these and other services, contact IGAPE at:

IGAPE
INSTITUTO GALEGO DE PROMOCION ECONOMICA

XUNTA
DE GALICIA
CONSELLERIA DE
ECONOMIA E FACENDA

HEAD OFFICE:
Frei Rosendo Salvado, 16 bajo
15701 Santiago de Compostela (A Coruña) Spain
Tlf.: + 34 - 81 - 54 11 75
Fax: + 34 - 81 - 59 04 67

BRANCH OFFICES:
Príncipe, 43 - 2º E
36202 VIGO (Pontevedra) Spain
Tlf.: + 34 - 86 - 43 92 69
Fax: + 34 - 86 - 43 41 19

A Cabana, s/n
15590 FERROL (A Coruña) Spain
Tlf.: + 34 - 81 - 37 20 05
Fax: + 34 - 81 - 37 20 90

An Introduction to Extremadura

Extremadura is a region situated in the west of Spain. It has a long border with Portugal and comprises Badajoz and Cáceres, respectively the first and second largest provinces in Spain. A large region, it covers more than 42,000 Km^2 and represents 8 per cent of the total area of Spain, making it larger than some countries in the European Union, and similar in size to Holland.

From the economic point of view, current developments in Extremadura are very interesting and make it particularly attractive to investors. There are two reasons for this. First, the Extremadura region contains raw materials and certain production sectors which offer great potential for development. Second, in recent years Extremadura has overcome two of its greatest longstanding structural problems: emigration and the lack of communications. These historical circumstances have prevented Extremadura from becoming a prosperous region with a dynamic economy.

Until little more than 12 years ago the population of the Extremadura region was dwindling, and its inhabitants were emigrating to other areas in Spain and the rest of Europe with more robust economies. At the same time, any investment in production in the region risked incurring additional overheads, due to problems experienced in the transport and distribution of products. Today, the situation has changed dramatically. The inhabitants of Extremadura now have the resources and opportunities for progress within their own region and do not need to emigrate, so there has been an increase in population in recent years.

In addition to benefiting from good communications both inside and outside the region, Extremadura enjoys a privileged situation close to Portugal. It is located in the centre of a strategically important commercial triangle formed by Madrid, Seville and Lisbon, and lies between the capitals of Spain and Portugal and Seville, the most important city in the southern Iberian Peninsula.

As regards opportunities for economic growth, the region of Extremadura possesses certain strategic sectors which have enormous potential for future development. One of these is the agri-food sector, based on the traditional high quality and wide variety of Extremadura crop and livestock production. Many varieties produced here are market leaders, including: tobacco, soya, cherries, tomatoes, olives, asparagus and the famous Iberian pig meat products. Cork production deserves special mention; the product is

Advertising feature

transformed by means of industrial processes which are currently very successful and look promising for the future.

Another industrial sector offering great opportunities for Extremadura and its raw materials is mining in general, and particularly specialities such as slate and ornamental stones. In addition mining of nickel is about to start in the south of the region. Discovered recently, these deposits are unique in Europe.

In the important sector of energy production, Extremadura is a national leader, while tourism is another economic resource with great potential for Extremadura. This has become particularly important in recent years, due partly to the growing development and promotion of the Extremadura's well-favoured environment which has a large and valuable variety of plant and animal life and great opportunities for hunting; and partly to the recognition of the cultural heritage of the region, with its variety of landscapes and monuments, including the three cities of Cáceres, Guadalupe and Mérida which are designated World Heritage Sites.

The government of the region, the 'Junta de Extremadura' is making great efforts to develop industry and general economic activity in the region. It offers a number of measures to encourage investment, providing a wide range of subsidies and economic incentives to businesses, particularly industrial activities setting up in the area. This assistance covers all forms of corporate incentives offered in Extremadura, and includes subsidies for investment, job creation, interest payments and many other promotional measures, some funded locally and others directly from the European Union, which classifies Extremadura as an Objective 1 region.

In addition to institutional measures, research centres, and three technology centres which currently provide support for the strategic sectors of agri-food, cork, wood, and coal and ornamental stones also have a discount impact on economic activity. The Public Sector in Extremadura is also open to any joint participation formula which may make an economic project in the region interesting and viable.

The regional Government Department of Economy, Industry and Treasury collates, processes, coordinates and supplies information regarding all forms of support available to promote investment in this Spanish region, which offers many attractive inducements to all potential investors.

Consejería de Economía y hacienda, Avda. del Guadiana, s/n Puerias C y D, 06800 Mérida (Badajoz), Spain. Telephone: 924/38.51.61. Fax: 924//38.51.71

Advertising feature

There is a Spanish region situated in the geographical triangle which in the forthcoming years is going to experience a global development which will surpass all expectations, ...

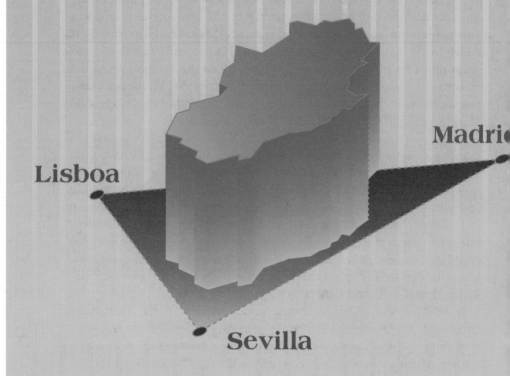

Lisboa

Madrid

Sevilla

... do you now realize why there are people who

INVEST IN EXTREMADURA?

JUNTA DE EXTREMADURA

Part 1

Doing Business in Spain

1.1

The Spanish Economy

Albert Recarte, Francisco Cabrillo,
Jesús González, Lorenzo Bernaldo de Quirós
and Emilio González, Gaceta de los Negocios

THE INTERNATIONAL SETTING

In 1995 the international economy experienced moderate expansion, less than had originally been predicted. All estimates indicated that the industrialised countries' 1995–96 growth rate would be approximately 2.5 per cent per annum, and that of the whole of the European Union (EU) was calculated at between 2.5 and 3 per cent. However, during the last months of the year these estimates were reevaluated and lowered.

The World Economic Institute of Kiel revised its forecast for the growth of industrialised nations in 1995, setting it at 2.1 per cent, as opposed to the initial estimate of 2.6 per cent. The International Monetary Fund (IMF) lowered its forecast from 3 per cent to 2.5 per cent for those same economies. The Organization for Economic Co-operation and Development (OECD) also changed its calculations and considered growth would be 2.25 per cent in 1995 instead of the 3 per cent which it had originally estimated, and 2.5 per cent in 1996 as opposed to 2.7 per cent.

There are various reasons which explain these revised figures. Monetary turbulence had a negative effect on the expectations for growth in the EU, while the effects of the prolongation of the Mexican crisis and the stagnation of the Japanese economy have been felt throughout the world. Nor are things going as well as expected in Germany, where a forecast for 3 per cent growth was lowered to 2.25

per cent according to the estimates of the 'six wise men', the principal German institutes (DIW of Berlin, the prestigious IFO of Munich, the HWWA of Hamburg, the IW of Kiel, the RWI of Essen and the IWH of Halle).

Economic observers have commented that the rate of growth in this second year of an upward economic cycle has been weaker than in previous cycles and have expressed their concern about the underlying reasons, such as a deceleration in the growth of the international economy or in problems directly related to Spanish imbalances and economic rigidities.

Efforts to reorganise public finances need to be strengthened despite a reduction of seven tenths of the public deficit figure in 1994, closing at 6 per cent of gross national product (GNP) in 1995. It has been noted that if we discounted income from privatisations, transfers from the EU and profits from the Bank of Spain, the underlying figure would fall in the region of 8 per cent. Growth in developed nations has fallen more than expected and at the beginning of 1996 it is uncertain whether this is a pause or a recession.

THE SPANISH ECONOMY

During 1995, the Spanish economy continued the recovery which was initiated in the last quarter of 1994. According to some estimates, GNP was close to 3 per cent in real terms, which is almost 1 per cent higher than in the previous year (2 per cent). This growth is due largely to investment and to a lesser degree to exports.

Nevertheless, this rate is low for a second year of an upward economic cycle. It can be said that the Spanish economy leaves each depression or recession with a lower growth rate and a higher rate of unemployment. This means that the weight of accumulated problems has increased, which prevents GNP from achieving its growth potential, 2 points above real growth according to the OECD reports.

Consumer spending was slow since the beginning of the recovery, increasing from 0.2 per cent in 1994 to 0.3 per cent in 1995, which has partially compensated for the weakness in private spending, but which also explains in part the fact that the public administration's deficit closed the year at 6 per cent of GNP, only seven tenths less than in 1994. This difference reflects the need to strengthen efforts to reorganise public finances, which maintained real budget debt above 8 per cent of GNP, if we discount extraordinary income arising from privatisations, transfers from the EU, profits from the Bank of Spain, or the second licensing of mobile telephones.

Investment experienced growth of 8.5 per cent as opposed to 1.0 per cent in 1994, while variation in stocks added 0.3 points to the growth of GNP, after having detracted 0.1 points in 1994. The thrust in investment appears to be tied fundamentally to the rise in exports, which showed a strong growth of 11 per cent, somewhat lower than 17.7 per cent during the previous year. The growth of imports also decelerated, being around 10.6 per cent as opposed to 11 per cent in fiscal year 1994. This drop, together with the sharp increase in the net balance of EU transfers to Spain, inverted the balance of the current account from a deficit of 0.8 per cent of GNP in 1994 to a surplus of 0.2 per cent in 1995.

The consumer price index dropped in 1995, finishing out the year at 4.5 per cent. From December to December the rate was lower (has been 3 per cent). Inflation, meanwhile was in the region of 5 per cent, as opposed to 4.6 per cent in 1994. Any data which place inflation above 4.5 per cent should be considered disappointing. On the other hand, the price disparity with the average of the three countries with the lowest inflation rate of the EU remains near 3 points, reflecting the need to reduce the differential further.

The unemployment rate, as defined by the Survey of the Working Population (see also Chapter 8.1), was reduced by a little over 1 point, dropping from 24.17 per cent to 22.7 per cent. This reduction was due in great measure to labour reforms and the growth of production. But this continued to be too high a percentage, due to a structural unemployment rate of 17 per cent, as measured by the Survey.

PRODUCTION

Industry

Industry experienced strong growth at the beginning of the year, supported by capital goods production. Throughout 1995, however, industrial production's pattern of growth has decreased, although with some fluctuation. This tendency sharpened from the third quarter on as a result of the slowdown in export demand, which was the secondary sector's principal motor during the whole fiscal year and which, combined with the persistent lack of private consumption, resulted in negative interannual rates and is in the origin of a more pronounced slowdown of industrial production growth.

Construction

Construction began the year with a strong growth rate but in mid 1995 decelerated; this can be appreciated both in the demand for public works as well as in the evolution of cement and construction materials consumption. The large construction companies felt the abrupt drop in civil works which resulted from a cut in public expenditure in that area. Housing, however, has given signs of reactivation.

Services

The services sector registered growth indicators similar to the last two quarters of 1994, due primarily to the growth of sales services.

Agriculture

Agricultural production continued to drop as in 1994, due to the effects of the drought. Over the course of the year it was reduced by close to 20 per cent. However, given the small relative weight of this sector, its contribution to GNP was reduced by one point from what it should have been. However, the repercussions for consumption have been less than expected due to the EU transfers.

DEMAND

Private consumption shows some weakness throughout the year. It is partly explained by the cut in the public transfers to families and the moderation in the costs of labour, resulting in a drop in the average earnings per hour. Other reasons are the uncertainty regarding unemployment and the rise in interest rates.

It is also explained in part by the temporary employment situation. Temporary contracts affect an ever greater percentage of salaried workers, at the same time that they receive a lower average wage than that of indefinite contracts. Likewise, an increase in savings is taking place, motivated by lower confidence regarding the future. All these factors have prevented private consumption growing more than 1.8 per cent (interannual rate), only nine tenths more than in 1994.

Public consumption's growth rate, however, increased by one tenth (to 0.3 per cent), as a result of the growth in public employment, which rose again after two years of stagnation, and the increase in purchases of goods and services.

The gross formation of capital continued to be tied to the growth of exports, with the double objective of defending market quotas and selling more beyond our borders. During the first half of the year, the gross formation of fixed capital increased to interannual rates superior to 8 per cent and 9 per cent. Nevertheless, the deceleration of export demand brought a parallel movement in industrial activity and, with it, in fixed capital investment, which did not find in the growth of consumption the support it needed to maintain the level of the first six months of 1995. The political uncertainty, manifest in a prime risk incorporated in interest rates, has also limited the growth of the gross formation of capital. Public investment has suffered, having carried the weight of the government's budget adjustments in January 1995, falling to minimum levels. (See Figures 1.1.1 and 1.1.2.)

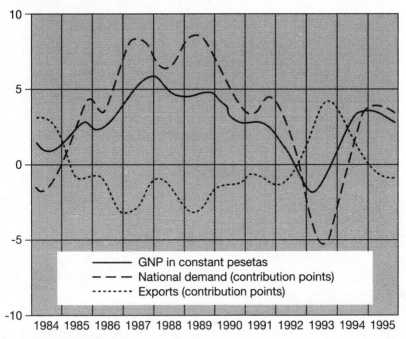

Source: INE, CNTR

Figure 1.1.1. *GNP and its components*

% annual variation rates

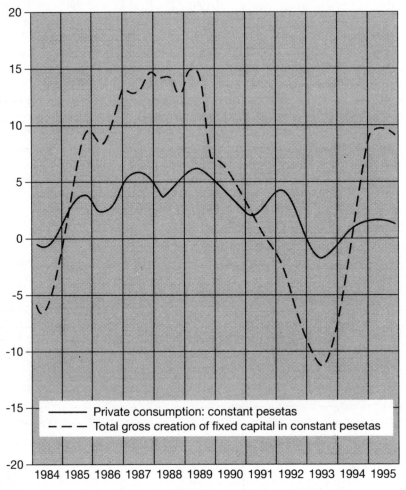

Figure 1.1.2 *Components of the national demand*

THE FOREIGN SECTOR

The current account balance shows a positive evolution on paper. With a deficit of 0.8 per cent of GNP in 1994, it will reflect a surplus of almost 0.2 per cent in 1995, mostly as a result of the deceleration in import growth which accompanies the weakness of consumption (see Figure 1.1.3). Foreign purchases are expected to grow to 10.6 per cent as opposed to 11 per cent in 1994. Exports are remarkable but still about

11 per cent, 6.7 points less than in the previous fiscal year, as a result of the drop in growth of the EU, where more than 70 per cent of Spanish foreign sales are destined. The other major factor that is contributing to the balancing of the trade figure is the increase in 650,000 million pesetas of Spain's net financial balance with the EU.

The favourable development of the tourist sector throughout the year also contributed significantly to balance the current accounts balance.

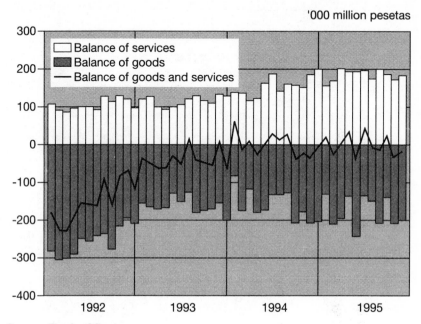

Source: Bank of Spain

Figure 1.1.3 *Balance of funds*

PRICES

In 1995 the rise in prices softened inflationary pressure, reflecting the low rates of private consumption.

However, the drought, which has pushed up the prices of non-processed foods, the extraordinary increase by 1 point in the three types of VAT and the increase in world prices for raw materials during the first part of the year, combined with some structural rigidity of the Spanish economy (particularly in the service sector) has prevented the consumer price index reaching its objective, which had been fixed by the government for this year at 3.5 per cent.

Industrial prices maintain an upward tendency which has been evident since 1993, until in April, achieving a maximum growth rate of 7.4 per cent in interannual terms. However, at that point in time the trend changed, starting a deceleration in the pattern of growth, although the level is still elevated. (See Figure 1.1.4.)

% annual variation rates

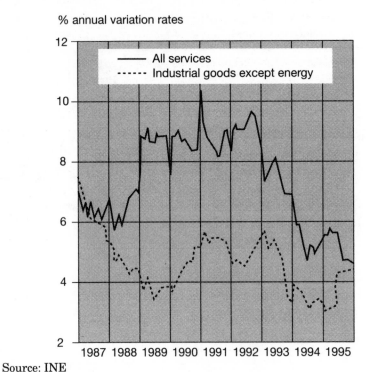

Source: INE

Figure 1.1.4 *Consumption price index by sectors*

As a result of this, the inflation rate remained at the same level as in 1994, at 4.8 per cent, although if taken from December to December it falls to 4 per cent. This figure needs to be improved (the government target is at 3.5 per cent) in order to reduce the price differential with the leading countries of the EU. (See Figure 1.1.5.)

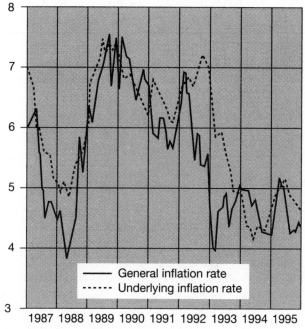

% annual variation

Source: INE

Figure 1.1.5 *Inflation*

THE LABOUR MARKET

In 1995 unemployment was reduced from 24.17 per cent to 22.7 per cent. The drop in unemployment was largely due to the effects of growth on job creation resulting from an enhanced dynamism in the economic production and also in part due to labour reform/ The decrease was maintained until September, when the trend curved. There is a rather worrying 17 per cent structural unemployment rate which has resisted reduction. During that period, there was a 1 per cent increase in the working population. (See Figure 1.1.6.)

The unit labour costs (ULC) are growing above 3 per cent due to an increase in mean monetary earnings per person to approximately 4.4 per cent, while apparent productivity will only increase by 0.3 per cent. In the European Union, ULC are only increasing by 1.5 per cent (UK

3.5 per cent), a difference which weakens Spain's competitive position in relation to the fifteen members of the EU. (See also Chapter 8.1.)

% of active population

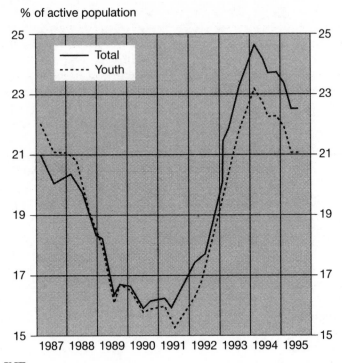

Source: INE

Figure 1.1.6 *Unemployment rate*

THE PUBLIC SECTOR

Although the public administration deficit was placed at 6 per cent of GNP, seven tenths lower than in 1994, this improvement should be carefully considered given that it is largely due to the increase in income tax which accompanied economic growth of 3 per cent. There has been an effort to reduce public expenditure substantiated in a cut of 150,000 million pesetas at the beginning of 1995 but if extraordinary income was subtracted, eg the 1,000,000 million pesetas net balance with the EU which grew during 1995 (a growth of 300,000 million pesetas), the extracts of selling government shares in Repsol and Argentaria, the 85,000 million pesetas received from the concession of the second licensing of mobile telephones and the 300,000 million pesetas profit of the Bank of Spain, the real deficit would fall in the region of 8 per cent.

Another figure which subtracts from the supposed 1995 deficit reduction has to do with the increase in GNP. In 1994 the deficit was 4.3 billion pesetas, which represents 6.7 per cent of GNP of 64.7 billion pesetas. In 1995 the deficit will be 4.2 million pesetas, representing a reduction of only a little over 100,000 million pesetas. However, if this figure is compared to the projected 1995 GNP of 69.7 billion pesetas, it represents a reduction of only 0.7 tenths of GNP (of which 0.5 points are due to the increase in GNP and only 0.2 points correspond to the real deficit reduction).

For their part, the regional governments contributed almost 1 point of GNP to the total deficit of public administration.

National debt continued to grow in 1995, ending the year at 65 per cent of GNP. This elevated level of debt maintains long-term interest rates over 10 per cent. Consequently, and due both to this high volume of national debt as well as to economic growth of 7.8 per cent in nominal terms, debt service has become one of the principal burdens contributing to the increase in public spending and in the budget deficit.

MONETARY POLICY

In 1995 the Bank of Spain introduced substantial variations in its monetary policy; instead of fixing an objective for annual inflation it established an objective for mid term price increases. The Bank's goal was that by March of 1996 inflation would be below 4 per cent, finishing the year with a rate of 3 per cent. In order to achieve this, monetary authorities raised interest rates at the beginning of the year to cushion inflationary effects both of a 1 point increase in the three types of VAT and the absence of a stronger deficit reduction policy. By April 1996 the Bank had discontinued this policy and interest rates were coming down.

The cost of money has benefited from the international financial market's normalisation process initiated in the second quarter. Together with the relative political stabilisation, it allowed for a reduction in cash interest rates negotiated in the monetary and public debt markets, although the Bank of Spain maintained the ten year intervention rate at 9.25 per cent in the face of certain persistent factors which could endanger the objective of mid term price stability.

The exchange rate of the peseta has evolved similarly. In March 1995 it was devalued for the fourth time since 1992 as a consequence of international monetary instability. The central exchange rate of the peseta against the deutschmark was devalued by 7 per cent. Since then, the Spanish currency has tended to appreciate, absorbing the relative gain in competitiveness achieved by the devaluations, which is starting to cause concern among exporters who fear the repeat of a situation similar to that of 1990 when the exchange rate tended to overvalue the peseta due to the high interest rates necessary to finance the public deficit. If this were to happen, it could result in significant internal price fixing and would have consequences for growth and employment. The peseta shows a small appreciation in relation to the ECU in 1995. (See Table 1.1.1.)

Table 1.1.1 *Spanish economy results in 1995*

	1994	1995(a)	1995 I Semester	1995 II Semester (a)
GNP and aggregates				
National private consumption	0.8	1.8	1.9	1.7
Public consumption	−0.3	0.9	0.6	1.2
Fixed capital creation	1.4	9.0	9.4	8.6
– Equipment	1.2	10.8	11.0	10.6
– Construction	1.5	8.0	8.5	7.5
Stock variation (b)	0.3	0.2	0.2	0.2
National demand	1.1	3.4	3.5	3.3
Exports	16.2	10.3	11.5	9.1
Imports	10.4	11.0	11.9	10.1
Trade balance (b)	1.0	−0.5	−0.4	−0.6
GNP	2.1	3.0	3.1	2.9
Employment and unemployment				
Active population	1.0	1.0	0.5	1.4
Total employment	−107	305	262	348
Change	−0.9	2.6	2.2	3.0
Unemployment (% of active population)	24.2	23.0	23.1	22.9
Prices and costs				
GNP deflactor	4.9	4.8	5.0	4.6
Consumer price index	4.7	4.7	5.0	4.4
Salaries under collective bargaining	3.5	3.6	Data not available	
Unit labour costs	0	3.2	Data not available	
Balance of payments (% GNP)				
Trading balance FOB–FOB (c)	−3.0	−3.1	−3.1	−3.1
Current account balance (c)	−0.8	1.0	0.3	1.7
National debt (% GNP)				
Total public administration	−6.9	−5.9	Data not available	
State cash deficit	−5.4	−4.5	Data not available	

(a) Projected without data for the third quarter for GNP and employment survey (EPD). Unit labour costs and total public administrations are estimates for the whole year based on partial indicators.
(b) % contribution to growth in GNP
(c) according to IMF methodology

Source: INE, IGAE, Bank of Spain, and DG Prevision y Coyuntura

Part 2

Establishing Your Company in Spain

INTRODUCTION

The decision to set up operations in a foreign country often involves the analysis of a complex variety of strategic issues. Given the advanced state of the development of Spanish industry and distribution sector, the decision may involve the capitalisation of the experience of existing market players. In this case it could result in a form of direct investment. We have selected four categories: merger, acquisition, joint venture and franchising.

Each one of these forms of setting up a business in Spain offers a variety of advantages which should be balanced against the problems that each one may raise. Independent of the strategic position of your company, they need to be considered from the fiscal and legal points of view. Chapters 2.1 to 2.3 will examine each of these key issues. Chapter 2.4, written by the Spanish Commercial Office, summarises the financial incentives to invest in Spain, providing practical advice in relation with the information sources, the requirements of the incentives and the application process.

It is important to note that the sources of financial aid that are available – the European Union, the national government and the 17 autonomous administrations or regional governments – could complement each other: they are not necessarily mutually exclusive. The amount and conditions applying to grants and subsidies are largely dependent on the interest that each individual project raises in the granting bodies and how well projects relate to their economic strategies. Since there is a great deal of decentralisation in Spain and many of the European funds are addressed to regions, it is important to bear in mind that the regional level is often the best one to contact first. We have provided contact details of the investment offices in Part 13, on useful addresses.

2.1

Mergers and Acquisitions

José Arcila and Cecilia Pastor
Baker & McKenzie

GENERAL LEGAL FRAMEWORK

Mergers

Under Spanish law two or more companies can merge either by incorporation or absorption.

A merger by incorporation entails the dissolution of the merging companies and the creation of a new company which will acquire all rights and obligations of the merging companies.

A merger by absorption entails the dissolution of one or more companies and the transfer of all their assets and liabilities to an acquiring company in exchange for the issuance of shares in the acquiring company to the shareholders of the dissolved companies.

In both cases all companies taking part in the merger will be dissolved (but not liquidated) except the absorbing or resulting company. The absorbing or resulting company succeeds to all the assets and liabilities of the dissolved companies and the former shareholders become the shareholders of the absorbing or resulting company in accordance with the share exchange rate agreed as part of the merger.

Shares versus assets

The most common procedure to acquire a company is through a purchase of shares, which sometimes is undertaken progressively. Nevertheless, an assets purchase may have important tax advantages which makes it attractive to purchasers. The differences between both options will be further examined in major tax considerations below.

REGULATORY FRAMEWORK

Exchange controls and foreign investment restrictions

In general terms, with certain exceptions, there are no exchange controls in Spain although transactions between residents and non-residents will be monitored. To the extent that such monitoring affects EU residents, it may not unduly hinder or delay practical and effective freedom to make payments or to transfer currency or assets. Authorities are entitled to request reasonable and essential information on transactions and that the relevant payments or transfers are carried out through appropriate financial entities.

Royal Decree 671/1992 provides that foreign investments are investments carried out in Spain by non-Spanish resident individuals or companies.

There are four kinds of foreign investments:

- direct investments are those undertaken by non-resident investors via (i) the participation in Spanish companies resulting in a foreign interest in the share capital over 10 per cent, or even less, should the foreign investor be able to influence the management or control of the company; (ii) the incorporation of Spanish branches; and (iii) the granting of loans to Spanish companies maturing more than five years as from the date thereof for the purpose of establishing or maintaining durable links;
- portfolio investments or the acquisition of securities which do not qualify as direct investments;
- investments in real estate situated in Spain;
- other forms of investment.

Portfolio investments are free and no prior clearance or approval is required. The remaining investments listed above are free, but may require previous clearance in certain instances.

The following investments will however require prior authorisation:

- investments of non-EU residents in certain areas (radio, television, air transport and gambling), all investments by non-EU foreign governments and any foreign investment in the defence industry;
- non-EU foreign governments and official foreign entities will, *ab*

initio, also require prior authorisation from the Cabinet of Ministers to carry out investments in Spain.

Any foreign investment in Spain must be legalised before a Spanish notary public, broker or consul. For such purposes the investor must submit evidence of (i) the relevant authorisation or clearance, (ii) the foreign contribution (ie: in the event of funds a bank certificate is usually required), and (iii) the non resident status of the investor. The foreign investment must be subsequently registered with the Foreign Investment Registry.

Any currency may be freely transferred to and from Spain, although certain declaration requirements may sometimes be required.

Competition laws

The 1989 Competition Act (Ley de Defensa de la Competencia) establishes a system for the control of economic concentrations (both mergers and acquisitions) which may affect the Spanish market, on the basis of the submission of a voluntary notice as opposed to mandatory filing. Further to the provisions of the Act:

- concentrations are defined as any project or transaction resulting in a concentration of business or in an assumption of control of one company or group by another which affects Spanish commerce and, in particular, which creates or reinforces a dominant position;
- any concentration may be voluntarily notified to the Competition Authorities by any company taking part in the merger or acquisition so as to determine whether or not the proposed merger or acquisition may restrict effective market competition in Spain. Notice may be filed by any party to the transaction, either before or after the merger within a certain time frame.

  Clearance of a notified merger will be presumed if no answer is given within one month as from the date of filing of the notice. Within this one month term the Competition Office may submit the proposed transaction to the Competition Court for review. The Court has three months to issue an opinion. Should the Competition Office fail to send the file to the Court within the one month term, or should the Court not issue an unfavourable opinion within the three month term, the merger will be deemed cleared;
- the government may challenge concentrations which affect the Spanish market if:
  - the market share acquired or increased equals or exceeds 25

per cent of the total Spanish market; *or*
- the aggregate Spanish turnover of both parties in the last fiscal year exceeds 20 billion pesetas;
- even if no voluntary notice should be filed with the Competition Office, the government may request a report from the Competition Court with regard to any proposed concentration affecting the Spanish market;
- in the event of voluntary notice, no penalties will be levied except in the case of failure to comply with the government's requirements.

The government's decision may be conferred by specific performance orders, and any breach may lead to a fine up to 10 per cent of the annual turnover of the parties in Spain.

Consequences of achieving different levels of investments

A purchaser may not always wish to acquire 100 per cent ownership of a company. Table 2.1.1 shows the levels of shareholding in a Spanish company will confer the following rights:

Table 2.1.1 *Levels of shareholding in Spanish companies, pursuant to the Spanish Companies Act of December 1989*

One share	The purchaser will become a shareholder and will be entitled to all rights afforded by the Companies Act and the company by-laws;
	to assist and vote at any shareholders' meeting unless the by-laws require a qualified interest;
	to obtain information from the company (including annual accounts prior to the ordinary shareholders' meeting, report from the auditing company, any document to be submitted to and discussed at any shareholders' meeting and all documents related to a merger);
	first refusal right;
	to request the directors to call an extraordinary shareholders' meeting for the purposes of passing a resolution to dissolve the company, when justified;
	to request the courts to call the ordinary shareholders' meeting to start a dissolution procedure (in certain cases);
	to request the resignation of a director when he/she holds interests which conflict with the interests of the company.
5%	To request the directors to call an extraordinary shareholders' meeting;
	to request the courts to call an ordinary or an extraordinary shareholders' meeting;
	to object to a director's or Board of Directors' resolution;
	to request the suspension of resolutions objected to;

	to start any action in the name of the company against a director for breach of duty;
	to request the Commercial Register to appoint an auditing company when such appointment is not required by law.
20%	To request the government to withdraw a shareholders' resolution dissolving the company, if justified due to economic or social circumstances of national interest.
25%	To request the extension of a shareholders' meeting;
	to invalidate the prohibition imposed by directors in certain cases to provide certain information about the company;
	to hold general shareholders' meetings at first call.
50%	To hold extraordinary general shareholders' meetings at first call, in order to approve special resolutions.

MAJOR TAX CONSIDERATIONS

Mergers

In the case of mergers, spin-offs, contribution of a business activity and share for share exchanges, Spanish regulations establish a 'tax neutrality situation' via the non-computation on the taxable base of the absorbed company of any capital gain or loss derived from the transfer of its net worth to the absorbing company. Similarly, there will be no change in the tax value of the assets received by the absorbing company as a consequence of the merger.

The above also applies to capital gains or losses obtained by the shareholders as a result of the exchange of shares undertaken. Said gain or loss (ie the difference between the real value of the shares received and that of the shares delivered), will not be included in the taxable base of the shareholder unless such shareholder is a tax haven resident company, or where the capital gain is obtained through a tax haven. These provisions give rise to a deferment of the taxation applicable to the transfer of the assets until a subsequent transfer is carried out.

In order to enjoy this tax neutrality, the Spanish authorities must be notified in advance of the transaction.

Shares versus assets

As far as indirect taxation is concerned, the purchase of shares is tax free for the purchaser, although if more than 50 per cent of the shares of a 'land company' (ie a company where real estate comprises more than 50 per cent of its total assets) are purchased, 6 per cent transfer tax will be levied.

On the other hand, the purchase of the totality of assets and liabilities of a company is regarded as an 'enterprise purchase' and will be VAT exempted.

Sellers' tax considerations

It is important for a purchaser to understand the seller's tax concerns if he is to persuade the seller to sell assets rather than shares or vice versa. It will normally be advantageous for an individual shareholder to sell shares in the target company rather than procure the sale by the target company of its assets.

When an individual sells shares he will generally be liable to capital gains tax (at his top income tax rate, currently up to 56 per cent). This capital gain will be gradually reduced as time goes by, in such a way that after a holding period of 15 years for non listed shares and ten years for listed shares the capital gain will be tax exempted.

When a company sells its assets, assuming it makes a capital gain, it will generally be liable to corporation tax (current rate 35 per cent). If the target company then distributes the proceeds to the shareholders by way of a dividend (assuming that it has distributable profits for company law purposes), the company must pay a withholding tax on the dividend, currently at the general rate of 25 per cent. The individual shareholder will be liable to income tax on the aggregate of multiplying the gross dividend by a certain percentage (currently 140 per cent on a general basis) and will enjoy a tax credit on the tax quota of a certain percentage of the gross dividend distributed (currently 40 per cent on a general basis). The corporate shareholder will be liable for tax on the gross dividend distributed although it will enjoy a tax credit offset against its tax quota (depending on the shareholding, the tax credit may be of up to 100 per cent of the dividend distributed).

In the case of an asset sale, once the business has been sold, another way for the shareholders to realise the proceeds of sale would be to liquidate the vendor company.

Purchaser's tax considerations

A purchaser may obtain capital allowances (tax depreciation allowances) on acquiring qualifying assets (principally plant and machinery). These allowances are not available if it purchases shares. Instead the target company continues to claim allowances by reference to the current tax written down value of assets.

Where a purchaser buys assets, its base cost in the capital assets for capital gains tax purposes will generally be the price it pays. By contrast, where a purchaser buys shares, the assets and business owned by the target company will be valued for capital gains tax base cost purposes at their book value. However, the purchaser will be able to depreciate its portfolio investment at the end of the year if the target company obtains losses.

After a share purchase, the target company and, therefore, indirectly the purchaser may be able to continue to use trading and capital losses of the target company for taxation purposes. On the sale of a business by way of an asset sale to an unconnected party, any right to carry forward trading losses against the business in question is lost.

Tax liabilities in share transactions

In a share acquisition, responsibility for taxation is not affected since the target company remains responsible for its own obligations.

Tax liabilities in asset transactions

In an asset acquisition, the Spanish General Tax Act (Ley General Tributaria) provides that the purchaser will be responsible for the tax liabilities arising from the economic activities and business operations of the target. In order to protect its position, a prospective purchaser of a business may, with the consent of the seller, petition the government for a detailed certificate of the tax liabilities arising from these economic activities and business operations, this applying to tax only and not to other debts. Unless the certificate is provided within two months, there are deemed to be no such tax liabilities and the purchaser is released from all liability for tax accrued for the target to date. However, the seller will continue to be responsible for the tax liabilities during the period provided as a statute of limitations. The Spanish General Tax Act provides for a period of five years, since the tax liability was accrued, after which the taxpayer will not be responsible for such liabilities.

Summary of tax advantages of a share sale for sellers and purchasers

- The seller avoids any possibility of a double tax charge which may arise when proceeds of sale are distributed to the shareholders;
- the individual seller may benefit from a tax exemption if the shares are held for a period of 10 to 15 years depending on whether they are listed or not;
- the target company and, therefore, indirectly the purchaser may

be able to continue to use trading and capital losses of the target company for taxation purposes;[1]

- no taxes will be payable upon the consideration payable for the shares except in the case of land companies where 6 per cent tax will be paid;
- on the sale of assets VAT will be payable except in a case where the ongoing business is transferred. Real estate will be subject to 6 per cent transfer tax, although in some cases it will not pay transfer tax but 16 per cent VAT.

Summary of tax advantages on an asset sale for sellers and purchasers

- The purchaser will qualify for capital or writing down allowances on certain of the assets. It will therefore be important to set out in the acquisition agreement an agreed allocation of the purchase price among the various assets;
- the purchaser's base cost for capital gains tax purposes will generally be the price paid for capital assets (including the goodwill of the business);
- if the proceeds of sale are to be reinvested in another business a seller of assets may be able to defer tax or obtain a tax exemption.

Specific issues for overseas purchasers

An overseas purchaser with no existing subsidiary in Spain could carry out an acquisition itself or through a new Spanish company it has established for the purpose.

In the case of an asset acquisition, it follows that the business will thereafter be carried on in Spain through a Spanish branch of the overseas company, if the purchaser is the overseas company itself. If, on the other hand, the business is bought by a new Spanish company established as a subsidiary of the overseas company, the business will be carried on by the Spanish subsidiary.

In deciding which of these two structures to adopt, the factors to be taken into account will largely be those to be considered when deciding whether to structure a start-up business as a Spanish branch or subsidiary of the overseas operation. In either case, there should generally be no difficulty in setting off the interest expense against the future profits of the business for Spanish tax purposes, although the borrowing should be carefully structured, particularly in the case where the business is acquired by the overseas purchaser itself (see thin capitalisation, below).

In the case of a share acquisition, the business will thereafter be carried on by a Spanish subsidiary of the overseas purchaser, whether or not a share acquisition is effected by the overseas company or by a new Spanish company established for the purpose by the overseas company.

If the overseas company purchases the Spanish target company, the overseas company's interest expense incurred in funding the acquisition is not deductible for Spanish tax purposes, but may be deductible against other profits in the country in which it is resident.

Tax grouping

If the purchaser has existing operations in Spain carried on through one or more Spanish subsidiaries, it will often be advantageous for the acquisition to be effected by an existing Spanish subsidiary. This will enable the future profits and losses of the newly-acquired business and the existing businesses effectively to be consolidated for Spanish tax purposes on a year-by-year basis. It would also facilitate a merger of the businesses if that were desired.

Thin capitalisation

Specific issues arise where a non-Spanish related company capitalises a Spanish company by means of a loan rather than share capital in order to finance an acquisition. In such circumstances, interest payments will be treated as divided payments if the Spanish company is thinly capitalised. If any such interest payments are treated as dividend payments this would have the effect that the interest would not be tax deductible for the Spanish company which may also be required to account for withholding tax.

Labour law considerations

The EU Business Transfer Directive 77/187 has been implemented in Spain by section 44 of the Workers' Statute. (For further details concerning labour law, see Chapter 8.2.) On the basis of section 44, the following principles will apply to both share and assets transfers to the extent that there is a transfer of an ongoing business activity:

- all employment rights and obligations undertaken by seller will be transferred to purchaser in the event of a change of ownership in an enterprise, work centre or production unit;
- purchaser will be jointly and severally liable with seller for a period of three years for compliance of all obligations undertaken by seller with regard to existing employees, including: (i) compliance with all relevant court decisions; (ii) employees on sick or disability leave or on leave of absence; (iii) any outstand-

ing social security contributions; (iv) any fines for breach of applicable regulations; and (v) pensions;

- seller (or purchaser if seller should fail to do so) must notify the employees' representative or Works Council of the proposed business transfer. Fines may arise for failure to comply with such notice. Trade unions must be similarly notified of any proposed business transfer. However, no consent is required to implement the transfer;
- seller and purchaser are jointly liable for liabilities arising after the date of transfer if the transfer is subsequently declared illegal;
- a change in ownership of the employer will entitle an executive to terminate his employment contract in the three months following the change of ownership and claim the severance compensation agreed in the contract or, in the absence of any such provision, to compensation equal to seven days' salary in cash for each year of service up to a maximum of six months.

Potential environmental liabilities

The acquisition of a company will imply undertaking all potential liabilities for possible breaches by the company of applicable environmental regulations. Environmental liabilities may arise under civil law provisions, criminal law provisions and administrative law provisions.

NOTES

1. However, tax loss carried forward will in some cases be reduced in order to avoid fraud, as in the case of dormant target companies purchased on account of their existing capital losses only.

2.2

Joint Ventures

Juan I González and Gabriel Núñez,
Uría & Menéndez, London Office

GENERAL LEGAL ASPECTS

Foreign investors may find that a joint venture (JV) with a Spanish company is strategically the most appropriate form of presence in Spain. This structure has been proven to be very useful for entering a new country since it allows the parties to share risks and combine resources and expertise.

The JV agreements may be purely contractual, or structural, ie a JV agreement as a result of which a JV company is incorporated. In this latter case, foreign investors must be familiar with Spanish rules applicable to Spanish companies in areas such as decision-making processes or transfer of interests.

Foreign investors who decide to set up a JV company must comply with the Spanish Foreign Investments Regulations requirements. In this respect, it must be noted that, as mentioned in the previous chapter, recent legislation (mainly Royal Decree 671/1992 of 2 July, 1992, on foreign investments in Spain) has almost completely abolished the restrictions affecting movements of capital, the only requirement in most cases being an obligation to report the investment to the Spanish authorities. This notwithstanding, investments in certain sectors, exceeding certain amounts or those coming from countries deemed as tax havens, will be subjected to a more burdensome regime.

LEGAL VEHICLE TO BE USED

Basically, there are three legal vehicles which can be used to set up a JV under Spanish law: (i) an Economic Interest Grouping (*Agrupación de Interés Económico* – EIG) or a European EIG (EEIG); (ii) a Temporary Business Grouping (*Unión Temporal de Empresas* – UTE); and (iii) a company. Each of them is briefly described below.

EIGs

EIGs are, to a certain extent, similar to Spanish unlimited liability companies (*sociedades colectivas*) and, in fact, the rules governing this type of company apply subsidiarily to the EIG's regulations. This type of corporate form is designed to structure cooperation between business companies, agricultural companies or independent professionals (eg lawyers). Under Spanish law, EIGs are separate legal entities but it must be noted that they cannot have a profit-making purpose. Consequently, any profit or loss of an EIG will be attributed directly to the partners in the proportion indicated in the notarial deed of incorporation. Furthermore, EIGs do not need to have a capital established and, accordingly, liability is unlimited and joint and several among the partners with respect to the EIG's debts, although it is a subsidiary liability, ie only exists if the EIG is unable to pay its own debts.

European EIGs are regulated under an EU Regulation that makes continuous references to the internal law of each of the member states. These entities have many similarities to the EIGs (eg no capital needed, unlimited liability for the partners) but they can be domiciled in any country within the EU. In this respect, it must be pointed out that, as far as Spanish law is concerned, only EEIGs domiciled in Spain are separate legal entities.

UTEs

Under Spanish law, UTEs are temporary cooperation instruments, for a fixed or unfixed period of time, conceived to develop or execute a particular project or service. UTEs are not separate legal entities and are managed by a sole manager in favour of which all the parties to the UTE must grant sufficient powers. These type of entities are granted certain tax advantages by virtue of law, for which reason they must be registered within a special Registry of the Ministry of Economy and Finance. In principle, UTEs have a maximum duration of ten years.

Companies

In general, leaving aside JVs with special purposes, foreign investors wishing to enter into a JV structural relationship have, to a large extent, opted for a limited liability company, either a public limited company, a *Sociedad Anónima* (SA); or a private limited company, a *Sociedad Limitada* (SL). For the purposes of this paper, we have assumed that this second type of vehicle is the one chosen. The main differences between both types of legal vehicle, SA and SL, are: (a) management and formal requirements are more cumbersome in an SA than in an SL and (b) transfer of interest is limited by law in an SL, and completely unrestricted in an SA unless otherwise stated in the by-laws. For a better understanding of this paper, it should also be borne in mind that the capital of an SL is divided into participations instead of shares and thus the holders of such participations are not shareholders but partners. Generally speaking, by offering greater flexibility than the SA, the SL appears to be a more attractive option for setting up JVs in Spain. This attraction has been increased with the recent Law 2/1995, of 23 March 1995, on *Sociedades de Responsabilidad Limitada*, which gives even more flexibility to the legal regime applicable to the SLs (eg there is now no limit as to the maximum capital permitted, nor to the maximum number of partners permitted).

This notwithstanding, the decision as to the appropriate vehicle to be used should be taken on a case by case basis depending mainly on the type of business to be carried out by the JV (some activities, particularly in the financial industry, are limited to SAs), the financing desired (SLs may not issue bonds), and the types of investors involved.

JOINT VENTURE AGREEMENT VERSUS BY-LAWS

It is of enormous importance to determine which agreements or commitments are to be included in the JV Agreement and which ones are to be included in the by-laws of the company to be incorporated. The reason is that clauses provided for in the by-laws will be binding for the company *vis-à-vis* third parties, whereas the JV agreement is merely a private contract between the parties and may only give rise to claims for damages between them (ie no third party is allowed to rely upon the JV Agreement).

The Spanish laws governing limited liability companies (SAs and SLs) leave a broad margin for the parties in order to determine the contents of the by-laws. In this respect, the by-laws may include any provision or condition that the shareholders deem appropriate, as long as it does not contravene the law or the principles governing the Spanish limited liability companies. For instance, it would be possible to include a blocking clause requiring a majority of 75 per cent (or even more) of the share-capital in order to increase the share-capital or amend the by-laws. With such a provision, the Commercial Registrar will not register any resolution passed without this majority. However, such provisions or conditions must be stated in an objective and impersonal form.

CONTRIBUTIONS TO BE MADE BY THE DIFFERENT SHAREHOLDERS

The JV agreement should determine the contributions to be made by the shareholders. It is advisable to have these contributions delivered at the time of incorporation in order to avoid possible future non-participative attitudes.

With respect to contributions in kind, it is worth noting that the legal regime would be different depending on whether the corporate vehicle chosen is an SA or an SL. Contributions in kind paid into an SA require the appraisal of an expert appointed by the Commercial Registry. The contribution is not valid if the expert determines that its value is 20 per cent less than the value of the shares. On the other hand, contributions in kind paid into an SL do not require a special report to be drawn up by an expert, but the partners will be responsible for the value attributed to such contribution.

RESTRICTIONS ON THE TRANSFERABILITY OF SHARES OR PARTICIPATIONS TO THIRD PARTIES

It is commonly known that JVs are usually construed on an *intuitu personae* basis, that is to say that the parties' personal features and skills are fundamental in order to enter into a JV agreement. Accordingly, it is not desirable to allow for an easy exit from the JV vehicle nor, equally, to allow for an easy entrance by third parties.

A possible legal remedy for such purposes is provided by the Commercial Registry Regulations which allows the prohibition of the transfer of registered shares of an SA or participations of an SL during the following two years after the date of incorporation.

In addition, it is possible to include restrictions in the JV company's by-laws, granting the rest of the shareholders/partners a first refusal right in order for them to acquire the shares or participations intended to be sold to a third party. If the JV company is an SL, these restrictions will apply by virtue of law even if they are not provided for in the by-laws.

The above notwithstanding, clauses prohibiting transfers of shares/participations or those restrictions which, in practice, render the transfer impossible, are deemed null and void under Spanish law.

Finally, it is possible under Spanish law and quite common in practice, to provide in the by-laws for an exclusion from the restrictions on the transferability in cases such as transfers between companies of the same group or between related parties (eg family). In fact, such relief applies by virtue of law in the case of SLs.

QUORUM AND MAJORITY VOTING TO PASS RESOLUTIONS

It is a clear objective for minority shareholders of a JV company to increase the quorum and the voting majority in the General Shareholders' Meetings in order to approve the crucial decisions of the company such as amendments to the by-laws, issue of bonds, mergers, split-offs, liquidation or appointment of directors. This purpose is quite easy to achieve when the minority shareholders hold between 30 per cent and 50 per cent of the company's share-capital: a 75 per cent or 51 per cent majority, respectively, would be enough for these purposes. However, in cases where the minority shareholders have less than 30 per cent, the majority reinforcement would be more difficult to be agreed upon, and would probably not be accepted by the majority shareholders.

With respect to the Board of Directors, the majority required could be increased for the approval of the following resolutions: appointment of a Board delegate, appointment of general officers, approval of the company's budget, sales of assets, decisions on relevant investments, granting and accepting of loans, etc.

PROCEDURE TO AVOID DEADLOCKS

Where a JV is set up with two 50 per cent shareholders, or has minority shareholders and statutory high majorities, deadlock situations quite often arise within the corporate bodies of the company, and these situations, if not solved, may give rise, under Spanish law, to the liquidation of the company at the request of any shareholder or partner. In order for the company to 'survive', it is necessary to avoid these deadlock situations, although such situations are inherent to JVs. Some solutions to the problem may be pointed out, although none of them are definitive.

First, the by-laws can provide rules by virtue of which the resolutions of the Board of Directors and the General Shareholders' Meeting will be adopted subject to the condition that they will not be executed until the deadlock has been resolved. At the same time, a 'Commission of Compromise' can be created in order to resolve the deadlock within an agreed time limit. If the Commission reaches a solution, the resolution conditionally adopted will become firm and will be executed. If a solution is not reached, any of the parties may submit the matter to an arbitration of equity that will render a decision in a short period of time.

It is important that these clauses are not used in order to reinforce the deadlocks rather than resolving them, that is to say that it will be necessary to provide that if no party submits the matter to an arbitration of equity the resolution will become firm. Likewise, in order to avoid continuous referral to an arbitration, it can be a requirement of the parties to deposit an amount of money on taking the matter to an arbitration. The deposit could be used to penalise the party whose conduct has been contrary to the general interests of the company. The danger of this system is that the company would not be operational, although the requirement of a deposit in advance would discourage unnecessary claims before the arbitration.

An alternative solution would be the use of a put option combined with a call option. One of the shareholders or partners offers a put option with a determined price and the other shareholder or partner would be obliged to accept the put and purchase the shares or participations for the price offered or sell its own shares or participations to the other for the same price.

2.3

Franchising in Spain

Gonzalo Ulloa, Gómez Acebo & Pombo

There is no specific legislation in the present Spanish legal system designed to regulate the franchise agreement.

Law 7/1996 of 15 January on Retail Commerce has recently been passed and covers general aspects of commercial activity, one of its articles being dedicated to franchise agreements. This is the first Spanish law which specifically regulates, albeit in a limited manner, franchise agreements.

The Passing of the Law of Retail Commerce, does not mean, nevertheless, that said contracts are subject exclusively to the Commerce Law, but that previous precepts will continue to be effective. This is due to the fact that the Commerce Law only refers to franchise agreements in its article 61a, which is of very limited scope, although it supposes an important novelty for all who are dedicated to establishing franchises in Spain.

This article is divided into three subsections:

1. The first defines the franchise agreement, describing it as 'the agreement by which a company, known as the franchisor, grants to another, known as the franchisee, the rights to exploit its own system of commercialisation of products or services.'
2. The second establishes the obligation on all physical persons or corporations who mean to carry out franchise operations in Spain to proceed to the inscription of the franchise in a registry to be decided by the competent authorities.
3. The third establishes the obligation of the franchisor to provide the franchisee with all information regarding the franchise net-

work in order for the franchisee to be able to decide 'freely and knowingly' on his incorporation into the franchise network.

This information should be given with a minimum notice of 20 days before the signing of the contract or precontract, or before the payment by the franchisee to the franchisor of any amount prior to the signing of the definitive contract.

The minimum information which the franchisor must give the franchisee is also established as follows:

- essential identification information regarding the franchise;
- description of the commercial sector subject to the franchise;
- exploitation, structure and extension of the franchise network;
- essential elements of the franchise agreement.

Lastly, it points out that the rest of the basic conditions for the exploitation of the franchise will be established in a regulation which is in preparation at the time of going to press. Therefore, the effect of said Law on franchise agreements is limited, the only really relevant part being:

- the obligation on the franchisor, before the signing of any kind of agreement, to give the franchisee the necessary information regarding the franchise;
- the creation of a franchise registry.

The lack of an exhaustive regulation of franchise agreements in the Spanish legal system does not mean, nevertheless, that these agreements can be called atypical, or that their legal regime is left to the initiative and autonomy of the contracting parties. On the contrary, as we shall see, the essential elements of the agreement are ruled by norms which are directly applicable to franchising contracts which effect the Spanish market.

These norms are those which are included in Regulation (EEC) 4087/88 of 30 November 1988. On affirming that the norms of Regulation (EEC) 4087/88 of 30 November 1988 are directly applicable to franchising contracts which affect the Spanish market, the following important explanation should be given; the norms of Regulation 4087/88 are applied not only in their character of community norms, but also in their character of norms which have come to form part of domestic Spanish legislation. In fact, through the Royal Decree of 21 February 1992, which amplifies on the Spanish Law of Defence of Competition of 17 July 1989, the norms of Regulation (EEC) 4087/88 are directly applicable to franchising agreements in which only two companies take part and which affect *only* the Spanish market. In spite of the fact that as they do not affect intracommunity trade, such franchising agreements are not susceptible, in theory, to Regulation 4087/88, the truth is that the norms of Regulation 4087/88 are applied by virtue of Article 1.1 of the Royal Decree of 21 February 1992, which states:

> 1. In accordance with article 5.1(a) of Law 16/1989 of 17 July, on Defence of Competition, those agreements in which only two companies participate and which, belonging to any of the following categories, affect only the Spanish market and comply with the conditions for each of them which are established below:
>
> (a) Franchise agreements, whenever the agreement complies with the dispositions established in Regulation (EEC) 4087/88 of 30 November, 1988.

When it comes to defining in Spanish legislation the nature of franchising and determining the relationship of the same with the Law of Industrial Property, the definitions which are set out in Article 1 of Regulation (EEC) 4087/88 become specially significant. Within the definitions contained in Article 1 of Regulation (EEC) 4087/88, the following two are of particular significance:

> (a) *Franchise* means a set of industrial or intellectual property rights regarding trademarks, commercial names, shop signs, utility models, designs, copyright, know-how or patents, which are exploited for the resale of products or the supply of services to the final users.
>
> (b) *Franchise agreement* means the contract by virtue of which one party, the franchisor, concedes to the other, the franchisee, in exchange for direct or indirect financial compensation, the right to exploit a franchise for the commercialisation of certain types of products and/or services; and which consists, as a minimum, of:
> – the use of a common name or sign and a uniform presentation of the premises and/or the methods of transportation object of the contract.
> – the granting of know-how by the franchisor to the franchisee, and
> – the continual supply by the franchisor to the franchisee of commercial or technical help during the period of effect of the agreement.

Of the two definitions contained in letters (a) and (b) of Article 1 of Regulation 4087/88 it should be noted that although the aim of franchising may be a variety of industrial or intellectual property rights, it is absolutely necessary for the franchisor to grant to the franchisee a licence of use of distinctive signs and know-how. Without forgetting the circumstance that the franchising may have as its aim other industrial property rights and copyrights, it seems appropriate to centre this report on the two industrial property rights which a franchising agreement necessarily deals with, that is: a trade mark or other distinctive sign (a commercial name and a shop sign in Spanish legislation); and the know-how (protected by Spanish legislation as an industrial or business secret).

As described, franchising assumes that the franchisor is owner of a product or service trade mark and that he concedes a licence to the franchisee for the use of the corresponding trade mark or trade marks. It is possible that, apart from a trade mark, the franchisor may be proprietor of another distinctive sign (a commercial name or a shop sign). As, by virtue of the allusions made by articles 81 and 85 of the Spanish Trademark Law of 1988, the norms of the Law of 1988 regarding trade marks are applicable, in principle, to the commercial name and the shop sign, the considerations made below in relation to the licensing of the trade mark, may be extended *mutatis mutandi* to the eventual licensing of a commercial name or shop sign.

Under Spanish legislation the right to a trade mark may be originally obtained in two ways: the inscription of the trade mark in the Trademark Office or the use which precipitates the notoriety of the trade mark (*see* Fernandez-Novoa, *Derecho de Marcas* (Trademark Law), p. 31 etc). But it is not less than the full right of exclusivity over the trade mark which arises by virtue of the inscription in the Trademark Office; and which by regulating the trade mark licence, current Spanish Law of 1988 only contemplates the license of the registered trade mark. For these reasons, it is advisable, whenever possible, for the franchisor to grant the franchisee a licence to use a registered trade mark.

Although Spanish Trademark Law of 1988 only briefly mentions trade mark licences, it should be pointed out that Article 42.1 compares various types of trade mark licence: exclusive and simple (ie not exclusive) licences, licences which cover either the totality or just part of the products or services for which the trade mark has been registered; and licences which are valid either in the whole or just part of Spanish territory. It is possible, therefore, at the moment of defining the clauses of the franchising agreement, for the franchisor and the franchisee to combine – according to the peculiarities of each particular case – the various types of legally possible trade mark licence.

In order for the trade mark licence to affect third parties (*erga omnes*), it is absolutely necessary for the licence to be set down in writing (strictly speaking, in a notary attested document) and for the licence agreement to be inscribed in the Trademark Office (see Article 43 of the Law of 1988). The inscription of the licence should be requested through an application in which the following information should be set out: the identity of the proprietor of the trade mark and that of the licensee; and the identity of the trade mark for which the licence is being granted (see Article 44 of the Law of 1988). The Spanish Office of Patents and Trademarks will examine *ex officio* if the document

which accredits the licence and the application fulfil the legal requirements. In the case of there being defects of form, the application will
be suspended and the interested party will be notified so that he can
rectify the defects within a term of two months (see Article 45.1 of the
Law of 1988). Once the licence inscription is agreed, the resolution is
published in the *Official Gazette of Industrial Property*, setting out the
information which is mentioned in Article 45.2 of the Trademark Law
of 1988.

Current Spanish Trademark Law does not impose on the licensor the
onus of controlling the quality of the products or services distributed
by the licensee under the licensed trademark. The defence of the goodwill inherent to the licensed trade mark and the very maintenance of
the uniformity and integrity of the franchising system will logically
induce the franchisor to establish in the contract the level of quality of
the products or services to be distributed by the franchisee. The clauses
which guarantee the quality of the corresponding products or services
are foreseen and authorised in Article 3.1 of Regulation 4087/88 which
– as we already mentioned above – has been explicitly incorporated
into Spanish domestic legislation by the Royal Decree of 21 February
1992.

If the franchisee does not comply with the stipulations of the contract
regarding the level of quality of the products or services, the franchisor
(as licensor of the trade mark) may bring against him the actions arising from the right of exclusivity to the trade mark under license: among
which probably the most important is an injunction which permits the
franchisor to prevent the franchisee from using the licensed trade
mark when the clauses of the contract relative to the quality of the
products or services are contravened. This may be deduced from Article
42.2 of the Spanish Law of Trademarks of 1988: which article should
be interpreted in agreement with Article 8.2 of the First Community
Directive on the subject of trade marks of 21 December 1988 (which
still has not been incorporated into Spanish domestic law). To this end,
the doctrine underlines the convenience of restrictively interpreting
Article 42.2 of the Trademark Law of 1988 (Fernandez-Novoa, *Derecho
de Marcas,* p. 233 etc).

The second basic service with which the franchisor must provide the
franchisee, as mentioned above, is the matter of know-how. Spanish
doctrine recognises that the industrial secret or know-how is a legally
protected immaterial good (see also Chapter 3.2). (Gomez Segade, *El
Secreto Industrial* [Madrid 1974] p. 82 etc). In fact, the holder of the
know-how enjoys a legal position which, in some ways, is similar or
parallel to that of the holder of a patent. Although at first it may appear

that the monopoly held by the owner of the know-how is eminently real, the fact is that in current Spanish law an indirect protection is granted to the know-how through the application of the Articles of the Unfair Competition Law of 1991. Under the auspices of Articles 13 and 14 of the Spanish Unfair Competition Law of 1991, the owner of secret know-how may bring the actions foreseen by this law against certain acts of acquisition, divulgation and exploitation of know-how.

Systematic interpretation of Articles 13 and 14 of the Spanish Unfair Competition Law reveals how the holder of secret know-how may bring the actions contemplated by Article 18 of the same law in three cases:

1. When a third party has acquired the secret know-how through espionage or similar (see Article 13.2 of the Spanish Unfair Competition Law).
2. When a third party has obtained the secret know-how through the conducts described in Article 14 of the Unfair Competition Law, which are: (i) the inducement of the workers of the company which holds the secret know-how to infringe basic contractual duties; (ii) the inducement of the workers at the natural end of the corresponding contract, in order to diffuse or exploit a business secret; or (iii) the taking advantage – for one's own gain – of the infringement committed by said workers in order to diffuse or exploit a business secret.
3. When a third party diffuses or exploits the secret know-how to which it had logical access but a duty to keep secret (see Article 13.1 of the Spanish Unfair Competition Law).

In order to enjoy the protection offered by the legal system, the know-how must include certain characteristics. These characteristics are established in Article 1 of Regulation 4087/88 which, as mentioned above, has been expressly incorporated into Spanish legislation by virtue of Royal Decree of 21 February 1992. In fact, Article 1.3.f of Regulation 4087/88 defines know-how as non-patented practical knowledge in which the following three requirements are combined: it should be secret; it should be substantial; and be defined. It may be convenient to summarise these three basic requirements of the know-how with which the franchisor should provide the franchisee.

1. The know-how should be secret. The secret or privileged nature of the information which constitutes the know-how implies that this should not just consist of information which is generally known in a sector of the market. However, in no way should the requirement referring to secrecy be interpreted as absolute, but relative: it is not possible to demand that the corresponding information should be known only by the holder of the secret and

his closest collaborators. On the contrary, it should be held sufficient that the information and the business experiences should form part of the reserved circle of a company, in such a way that third parties may only arrive at knowledge of such through unfair practices. The relativity of the secret nature of the know-how is reflected in article 1.3.g of Regulation 4087/88 which states that the secret 'is not strictly limited in that each individual component of the know-how should be totally unknown and unobtainable outside of the franchisor's businesses'.

2. The know-how should be substantial. This second requirement refers to the competitive value of the information contained in the industrial secret – an objective element which aims to limit the amount of rules which can be protected as know-how, (see Gomez Segade, op cit, p. 239). It may be stated generally that the know-how possesses competitive value when the exploitation thereof confers an initial competitive advantage upon the holder of the secret information. This happens, for example, if the information contained in the know-how is completely new and represents an undeniable advance in the corresponding commercial or technical sector. It may happen, paradoxically even, that negative know-how, that is that information which consists precisely in having found out that certain technical or commercial procedures are difficult to apply or confer very little profit, may have competitive value and therefore be defined as substantial.

    The considerations regarding the substantial nature of the know-how which are set out in Article 1.3.h of Regulation 4087/88 are very illuminating. On one hand, it is stated that the know-how should include important information for the sale of products or the supply of services to the final users. On the other hand, it is emphasised that 'the know-how must be useful to the franchisee, enabling him, when the agreement is signed, to improve his competitive situation, especially improving his results and helping him to enter a new market'.

    Undeniably, the requirement that the know-how be substantial aims to defend the interests of the franchisee; it is meant to be a means of preventing the latter from paying an important amount of money for know-how of an insignificant competitive value.

3. The know-how should be defined. According to article 1.3.i of Regulation 4087/88, this means that 'the know-how should be described in such a way as to enable it to be verified that it complies with the requirements of secrecy and substantiality. The description of the know-how may be made in the franchise agreement, in a separate document, or in any other appropriate manner'. It is likewise undoubtable that this requirement protects the interests of the franchisee.

The franchisor must grant the franchisee a licence to exploit the secret know-how envisioned by the franchise. However, as the law underlines (Massaguer, *El Contrato de Licencia de know-how* [Barcelona 1989] p. 165), the know-how licence does not merely consist of a mere authorisation of use, but imposes on the licensor the obligation of making: 'a full communication of the secret technical knowledge which makes up the know-how'. This same author adds (op cit, p. 177) that the licensor should guarantee the licensee that the exploitation of the know-how will not be disturbed by third parties: the licensor is obliged to maintain the licensee in the tranquil enjoyment of the licensed know-how.

2.4

Grants and Incentives in Spain

Embassy of Spain in London,
Commercial Office
Investment Department

Nowadays, competition among countries and regions across Europe to attract corporate investment is greater than ever. Most European countries have developed financial aid packages aimed not only to attract investment but also to keep the existing investors from relocating to other countries.

This implies that, although companies will rank first those sites which fulfil their project's strategic, financial and operational conditions, they will also weight more positively those sites offering better financial incentives as they will contribute to the profit expectations of the project. In that respect, Spain maintains its position as one of the main beneficiaries of inward investments from abroad due mainly to the good package that investors receive when they choose to locate in Spain.

Spain's highly-skilled workforce is increasingly productive[1] and unit labour costs in Spain (US$11.1), are 34 per cent lower than the EU average (US$17.19) and 24 per cent lower than in the US (see also Chapter 8.1). On the other hand, and perhaps the argument that best summarises the advantages of Spain, the rate of return on capital invested in Spain is higher than in any other OECD country (reaching 19.6 per cent for 1994 and is expected to continue through 1996, when the figure should reach 20.3 per cent).

In addition to this, Spain has an extremely dynamic domestic market made up of 40 million inhabitants with substantial purchasing power

(Spain has a per capita income of US$13,000 and is visited by more than 60 million tourists each year). Also, since the creation of the single market in Europe and the consequential reduction in the number of facilities run by multinationals operating within the EU, Spanish organisations are in a good position to supply the new market-place.[2]

With regard to financial incentives, Spain has one of the largest land areas in Europe (83 per cent) qualifying for regional incentives and the highest ceiling (up to 75 per cent in some areas).

REGIONAL INCENTIVES

Regional incentives are the major mechanisms whereby financial aid is provided for investment in Spain, both in terms of the amount of funds budgeted for such incentives and of the high incentives ceilings offered by most of these schemes. They are tailored to foster business activity and encourage location in certain allocated areas, reduce inter-regional economic differences, distribute economic activities more fairly throughout Spain, and reinforce local development potential in the various regions.

This scheme provides incentives for productive investment (new facilities, or expansion/modernisation of existing facilities) made in both eligible areas and sectors. Assistance is based on non-refundable subsidies which are established as a percentage of the eligible investment expenditure.

In most parts of Spain, these incentives may reach up to 50 per cent, but the maximum rates of award vary from one area to another, ie Type I areas: 75 per cent or 50 per cent; Type II areas: 45 per cent or 40 per cent; Type III areas: 30 per cent; Type IV areas: 20 per cent.

The main industrial sectors qualifying for this scheme are: transforming/manufacturing, extractive, food, certain services providing industrial support which improve trade structures, and specific tourist resorts and recreational facilities of particular interest to development areas.

The investment items that are considered eligible for incentives are: land, land development, buildings, capital equipment, planning works, project engineering and other tangible fixed asset investments and R&D and other intangible assets (up to 20 per cent of the total investment project).

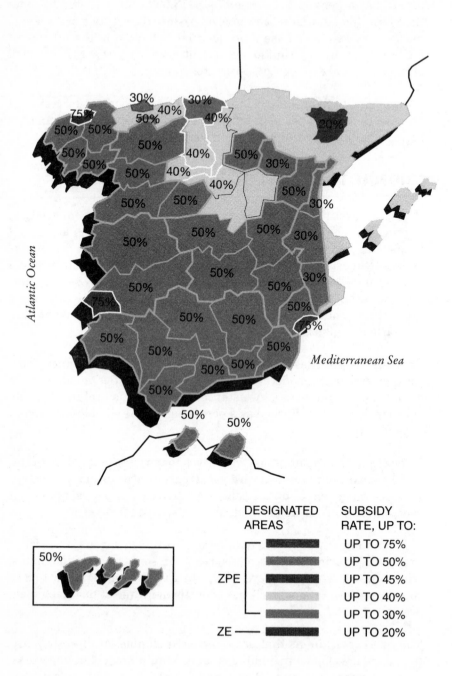

It is important to underline that as a general rule, and in order to be eligible, projects must comply with the following:

- start-up and expansion projects must involve an investment of over 15 million pesetas in fixed assets and lead to the creation of jobs;
- self-financing of at least 30 per cent of the investment;
- the project must be technically, financially and economically viable;
- the project should not start before submission of the application for regional incentives.

With regard to investment incentives offered by the governments of the 17 Autonomous Regions in Spain, it must be said that they are normally intended for productive investments and their aims are either to complement central government incentives, or to supplement the absence thereof. Incentives are usually financial in nature (non-refundable subsidies and soft loans). It should be mentioned that the sum of the aid granted by the two systems may not, however, exceed the ceilings set by the Spanish government in compliance with EU authorisation.

STEPS TO BE TAKEN BEFORE APPLYING FOR REGIONAL INCENTIVES IN SPAIN

First of all, you must draw up a detailed investment project (business plan), containing items such as: identification of the partners, analysis and description of the project, programmes of investment to be carried out (equipment to be acquired, period or phase of execution, timetable of payments, etc), labour report (employment creation, indirect employment, level of professional technical qualifications of employees, etc), financial plan, commercial activity report, etc. Normally, forecasting should be done for the first three to five years of the project's life.

In this initial stage, gathering up-to-date information on Spain is vital and can be readily obtained from the Investment Department of the Spanish Embassy Commercial Office in London on matters such as: macroeconomic indicators, market intelligence, regional development agencies, suppliers, etc, as well as an initial feed-back on Spain's potential interest in the project. The Department also offers unbiased regional advice when investors have not a clear idea on potential regional locations. (See contact addresses and telephone numbers in Part 13.)

Once the plan has been devised, it is advisable to contact the appropriate regional development agencies in order to gather further information, if necessary, making them aware of the project and, more importantly, to start developing relationships with regional authorities. Normally, the chosen agency will respond promptly, giving their initial opinion about the project. If this is a positive one, you should arrange meetings to discuss in detail your project, getting the interest of the authorities involved in the granting of subsidies and visit potential sites if appropriate.

The next phase is to work out a subsidy investment project, where the legal requirements and presentation of information compiled is processed using the Standard Application Form for Regional Incentives which can be obtained from the management office of the selected region (provincial delegation of the Ministry of Economy and Finance, Regional and Economic Incentives).

The application should be completed in Spanish and the amounts stated in Spanish pesetas. It is worth mentioning that although you may have put together a business plan, you should consider the application as a possible contract between your company and the Spanish government and, therefore, all the information requested in the application should be fully answered.

Figures should relate only to the project in Spain and not consolidated with your existing business.[3] This will allow them to assess your project fully and promptly. It is important to point out that the official application must be presented before any investment is made, otherwise all expenses incurred before the submission of the application will be excluded from investment subsidies. Once the Regional Delegation has received the application, they will prepare a report stating their opinion of the project as well as its economic interest for the region. Subsequently this report will be sent to the General Directorate of Regional Incentives in Madrid (the central government granting agency) together with all the documentation for their perusal.

Bear in mind that the decision on whether or not to support a project is of a reserved nature, as well as the determination of the percentage of aid, which is based mainly on the criteria expressed above. There is no such thing as an automatic granting of an 'x' percentage. Your project will be fully evaluated by the Administration.

In due course, a resolution is produced notifying the interested party by the managing office, stating the incentives approved, or the reasons for refusal of the application, and the rights and obligations of the recipient of the aid, commitments arising from the effective granting of the subsidies, etc. The beneficiary must accept or reject the subsidy granted within 15 working days, otherwise the resolution will be void.

With regard to the payment of the subsidies granted, the investors should be aware that, from the time the investment is justified until the subsidy is realised, there is a transitional period. However, there are certain provisions which facilitate part payments in advance of the subsidies being granted, as long as the investor can present sufficient guarantees. It is worthwhile mentioning that although the investor may divide up the execution of the project at his own convenience, establishing an investment timetable, payments will be made by the Administration only when the investor presents to the management office, the appropriate justification that the investment has been effectively carried out.

To conclude, we would like to mention that the Investment Department of the Spanish Embassy Commercial Office can assist potential investors in different ways. In terms of information, the Department can provide both general and tailored reports (the Department has direct access to all data held by the Industrial and Agricultural divisions of the Commercial Office in London, as well as different UK and Spanish on-line databases containing market research, company, financial and statistical information).

It can also help contacting both Central and Regional Offices (as we coordinate our activities with the General Directorate for Foreign Investment[4] and the network of Regional Development Offices in Spain), arranging meetings and visits to industrial sites in Spain and ensuring that each company's needs are borne in mind at all times.

The benefits of using our services are clear. Not only are they free and confidential but, also, potential investors in Spain can rely on the Investment Department's commitment to care for its clients, before, during and after their investment when selecting Spain as their investment location.

NOTES

1. A recent survey by Andersen Consulting, Cambridge University and the Cardiff Business School shows that, in the automobile components industry, only 13 plants worldwide reached the highest levels of productivity and quality established in the survey, two of which are located in Spain. There are five plants in Japan, three in the US, three

in France and two in Spain. Other countries with high technological industries, such as Germany or the United Kingdom, had none at all.

2. If we consider that nearly 21.7 per cent of the total foreign investment received during the period 1990–94 were projects submitted by affiliates of multinational firms already installed in Spain and this figure continued rising even during a recent period of economic stagnation, it is a sign of investor confidence in Spain's potential, since the projects in question were undertaken by companies with a good working knowledge of the Spanish domestic market.

3. Cash flows, P & L account and balance sheet consolidate forecast can be included in your business plan, as it may be useful for the granting agency to have an overall financial assessment of your existing business plus the project you intend to carry out.

4. The DGIEX is the Department of Spain's Ministry of Trade and Tourism in charge of the promotion of foreign investment in Spain.

HE CHANG PRACTICAL GUIDEBOOKS COLLECTION
RICHARD CHANG ASSOCIATES

ractical guidebooks to take you and your organisation into the next century!

he Chang Practical Guidebooks Collection comprises four exciting series, each of which
s geared to help you create a quality-focused work environment. Each book provides
roven tips, tools and techniques on a wide range of key management subjects which
an be applied immediately both in the workplace and on a personal level.

hoose from this great range of titles:

he Quality Improvement Series

ontinuous Improvement Tools vol 1
N 0 7494 1649 1

ontinuous Improvement Tools vol 2
N 0 7494 1650 5

ontinuous Process Improvement
N 0 7494 1652 1

nproving Through Benchmarking
N 0 7494 1655 6

leetings That Work!
N 0 7494 1656 4

atisfying Internal Customers First
N 0 7494 1653 X

ep-by-Step Problem Solving
N 0 7494 1651 3

ucceeding as a Self-Managed Team
N 0 7494 1654 8

lanagement Skills Series

oaching Through Effective Feedback
3N 0 7494 1657 2

xpanding Leadership Impact
N 0 7494 1658 0

astering Change Management
N 0 7494 1659 9

**ffective Induction
nd Training**
3N 0 7494 1660 2

ecreating Teams During Transition
3N 0 7494 1697 1

High Performance Teams Series

Building a Dynamic Team
ISBN 0 7494 1663 7

**Measuring Team
Performance**
ISBN 0 7494 1662 9

Success Through Teamwork
ISBN 0 7494 1661 0

Team Decision-Making Techniques
ISBN 0 7494 1664 5

New for Autumn 1995!

The High Impact Training Series

**Identifying Targeted
Training Needs**
ISBN 0 7494 1682 3

Creating High-Impact Training
ISBN 0 7494 1683 1

Applying Successful Training Techniques
ISBN 0 7494 1681 5

Measuring the Impact of Training
ISBN 0 7494 1680 7

Make Your Training Results Last
ISBN 0 7494 1684 X

Mapping a Winning Training Approach
ISBN 0 7494 1712 9

Producing High-Impact Learning Tools
ISBN 0 7494 1711 0

All books are in paperback with approximately 120 pages

KOGAN PAGE
120 Pentonville Road, London N1 9JN
Tel: 0171 278 0433 Fax: 0171 837 6348

Inter-regional competition for inward investment in Spain is mitigated by the fact that Spanish regions vary significantly from an industrial point of view and, therefore, have different things to offer to foreign investors. Nevertheless, there are three or four regions in which most foreign investment is concentrated.

The Valencian region – with a population of four million and direct access to a political group of 150 million – is one of these, Due to its highly diversified industrial sector, more than 200 multinationals are already based here. Foreign companies located in the Valencian region tend not to be relocations from elsewhere in Spain. Instead, they are mostly first-time implantations in the country, either in the form of new factories or establishments or as a result of acquisitions of existing Valencian firms. A strong regional industrial policy in re-allocation and greenfield promotion allows the development of enterprises in very competitive conditions. There is a great variety of available industrial sites with excellent productive conditions, as well as easy access to all markets.

Promotion of the Valencian region is entrusted to IVEX. Despite its regional focus, IVEX collaborates actively in all promotional activities with the government of Spain, especially in those markets considered by IVEX as prime targets. Inter-regional cooperation in foreign promotion is also undertaken in conjunction with other Mediterranean regions such as Cataluña or Murcia, which are all part of what is usually called the 'Mediterranean Arch.'

European countries have always been the natural export markets for the Valencian region. There are, however, other areas that have historical commercial links with Valencia, including the United States and a number of Latin American countries. As the second most important export region of Spain, its products are found today in numerous markets around the world.

Valencia's main selling point as a corporate location is its diversity. It offers a sound infrastructure serving a wide range of small- to medium-sized manufacturing enterprises and a pool of skilled labour with mass-production multinational companies and high-tech concerns. Incentive packages are available for up to 30 per cent of the project cost. On the one hand, the region has retained its traditional export base, derived from SME, in such diverse industrial sectors as furniture, textiles, ceramic tiles and marble, clothing and footwear, jewellery, and toys along with a dynamic argo-industrial sector. On the other hand, since the late 1980s major multinational manufacturers have further diversified Valencia's economic structure, expanding its production of electronic goods, medical equipment, biotechnology and food engineering, automobiles, and related metal and electrical components.

IVEX has its head office in Valencia, but operates an international liaison network throughout Europe, the Americas, the Pacific Rim, North Africa, and the Middle East. Through this international network, which now covers 17 countries, it is implementing a dual strategy.

Looking outward, it aims to provide its Valencian clients with an integrated range of services on an international basis. It works to raise Valencia's corporate presence in the world's largest markets by coordinating marketing strategies, distribution, after-sales policies, and direct investment. Simultaneously, IVEX acts as the regional investment office in Valencia for the further encouragement of industrial diversification. In this regard, it works to assist foreign manufacturers, particularly from Europe, the United States, and the Pacific Rim, in site selection and product manufacturing surveys; industrial procurement support and local joint ventures; investment incentives and business legislation; and a wide range of matters arising both before and after a foreign investment decision is made.

Plaza America, 2-8°, 46004 Valencia, Spain. Tel: (34) 63952001. Fax: (34) 63954274.

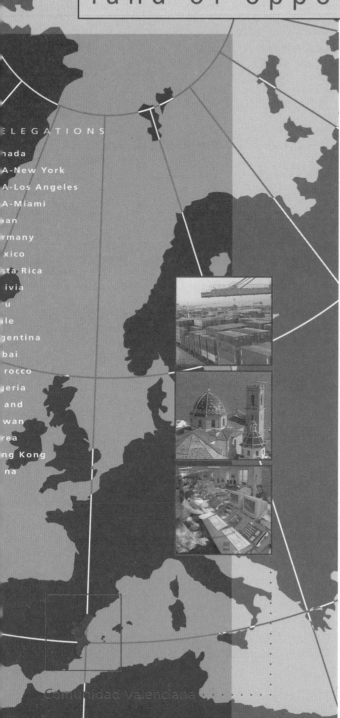

LAND OF VALENCIA

land of opportunities

- Located at the center of the Mediterranean Arch.

- Excellent platform for European, African and Latin American Markets.

- Gateway to 320,000,000 potential consumers.

- Regional leader in Exports.

- Highly diversified industrial base with unlimited subcontracting opportunities.

- Extensive availability of industrial grounds with direct access to maritime port, railroad and highways.

- Skilled and highly productive labour force.

- An incentive package and tax advantages for investment.

- Preferred place of residence for 25% of the foreigners living in Spain.

- Excellent quality of life, making the Land of Valencia a favoured place to live and to work.

This is a great opportunity for you!

I·V·E·X

Instituto Valenciano de la Exportación

GENERALITAT VALENCIANA

Plaza de América, 2
46004 Valencia (SPAIN)
Tf. (34.6) 395 20 01
Fx. (34.6) 395 42 74

IVEX TOKYO
Tf.(81.3) 5561 98 31
Fx.(81.3) 5561 98 30

IVEX DUSSELDORF
Tf.(49.211) 17 34 20
Fx.(49.211) 17 34 210

IVEX NEW YORK
Tf.(1.212) 922 90 00
Fx.(1.212) 922 90 12

Part 3

Operational Issues

INTRODUCTION

This part of the book is aimed at helping foreign investors to understand the intricacies of Spanish law regarding three important issues for any firm with operations in another country: the management of insolvency and bankruptcy of customers; the protection of intellectual property; and the duties of directors in that state.

When reading these chapters, it is important to note that the Spanish legal system provides two separate and complementary procedures which your company may use, ruled by the Civil and the Penal Code respectively.

The Civil Procedure is normally initiated by one party to the dispute. The role of the judge is limited here to the examination of the facts and evidence available without personally conducting an enquiry. The judge will then attend or deny the demands of the parties according to Law, but there is also room for the parties to reach an agreement among themselves or renounce their claims. In this case, the procedure will be terminated.

In Penal Procedures, there is no room for understanding between the parties. Once the facts have been established, and it is accepted, there must be a resolution settled by a judge. Normally, this procedure is initiated by a judge and is divided in two parts, the instruction and the hearing. During the instruction, the judge investigates all relevant facts. When the case reaches the hearing, a different judge will examine the facts and issue a resolution.

The outcome of a case could be rather different depending on the procedure enforced. The reader will find in these articles continuous references to what the Civil and the Penal code rule is in each case. There is limited room for party discretion in the enforcement of the Penal Code, but you will find that in practice it will be useful to consider the potential outcomes of all possibilities available.

3.1

Insolvency and Closure of Companies

Angel Salgado and Fernando Carvajal,
Deloitte & Touche

CHARACTERISTICS OF THE SPANISH LEGAL SYSTEM WHICH HAVE AN EFFECT ON THE LEVEL OF BAD DEBTS IN THE SPANISH MARKET

As is the case with most of Spain's neighbouring countries, there is a general lack of confidence within Spanish business circles with regard to the speed and efficiency of the Spanish legal system when it comes to solving the problems which arise in relation to business activity. This general impression is not entirely unfounded, and there are some very sound reasons for it: the age of Spanish substantive and procedural laws and the fact that they have not been adequately adapted to business practices which are constantly changing; a succession of partial reforms giving rise to problems in the functioning of our legal system; the relatively recent impact of EC Law and its insufficient or inadequate integration into internal Spanish legislation, and so on.

Perhaps the common complaint among companies operating in the Spanish market is the ineffectiveness of the different legal actions which may be brought (under both civil and penal legislation) in cases of insolvency, non-payment, and financial crises in general. The Spanish legal system does in fact provide a number of different mechanisms designed to ensure that any direct action taken by the state at the instance of one private party against another reflects a legitimate interest and does not lead to damages (to persons or property) which the party affected is not obliged to suffer. There are therefore a number of ways in which any debtor who acts in bad faith and with intent to elude its financial obligations may delay, undermine, or even prevent altogether the effects of legal actions brought against it by its creditors. The impression gained by the business creditor is therefore that the bad debtor often enjoys a certain impunity.

Despite the above, and while admitting that the Spanish legal system has its weaknesses, it must be said that it is perfectly comparable with the systems of the other countries which make up the European Union (especially those systems which derive, although indirectly, from ancient Roman Law, ie the so-called 'continental systems' as opposed to the Anglo-Saxon 'Common Law' system). It offers a series of procedural and substantive guarantees which are sufficient for the smooth running of business activity. This includes those guarantees which come into play in the verification of any non-payment or general insolvency of any kind. The functional weaknesses in the system of which the business person is aware are mostly due not to theoretical or conceptual faults in Spanish law, but to the insufficiency or inadequacy of the human and material resources available in the courts. We should also mention the efforts which have been made recently to eliminate these weaknesses.

SOURCES OF INFORMATION AVAILABLE TO BUSINESSES FOR THE PURPOSE OF EVALUATING COMMERCIAL RISK

It is clear that the best way in which a business can avoid the problems deriving from non-payment or insolvency is by obtaining sufficient and adequate information concerning the financial situation of the companies with which it intends to enter into contract. In Spain, this information may be obtained from two kinds of sources: the 'legal or official sources' and the 'private sources'.

The foremost official source from which information may be obtained concerning the financial situation and book results of a company is the Mercantile Registry (*Registro Mercantil*). This is an administrative body and all businesses structured as companies are under the obligation to be registered with it. Individual business people may also be registered on a voluntary basis. The public has access to information on record at the Mercantile Registry. It is possible to find out the date on which a company was set up, its share capital and the names of the members of its administrative body and founder shareholders. The public also has access to the annual accounts, directors' report and audit report, where appropriate.

In view of the importance that a company's accounting information may have for third parties in general (particularly the audit report in the case of companies which are obliged to have their accounts audited), it was made obligatory in 1990 for companies to deposit their annual accounts for each year with the Mercantile Registry. The obligation to deposit annual accounts has recently been reinforced with a view to ensuring effective compliance.

The information supplied by the Mercantile Registry is nevertheless of limited value (there is a Central Mercantile Registry which has basic information and a series of provincial Mercantile Registries). This is because many companies fail to comply with the obligation to deposit their accounts each year with the Registry (this in itself is very revealing). Also, the accounting information that is available is often not sufficiently up to date.

For information concerning the situation of real property assets, we have the Property Registry (*Registro de la Propiedad*). This is the administrative body which gives the public access to information on the ownership of and possible charges and encumbrances affecting the properties registered. There is also an Indices Service which is dependent on this Registry and provides basic computer-generated information on possible real properties registered in Spain in the name of any individual or legal entity (the party making the enquiry is then referred to the corresponding provincial Registry for further details).

Another of the 'official' sources from which relevant information may be requested for the purpose of evaluating the solvency of a business is the Registry of Unpaid Acceptances (*Registro de Aceptacomes Impugadas*, the RAI), which is dependent on the Bank of Spain. This Registry records all unpaid bills formalised through banks, savings banks and credit institutions operating in Spain, indicating the amount of the bill and the name of the individual or legal entity obliged to make the corresponding payment.

Due to the limitations of the information available through what we have termed the 'official' sources, business people are turning ever more frequently to private sources. These may be periodicals and yearly publications, databases to which access is obtained through payment of a subscription fee, and, lastly, private investigation agencies specialising in solvency studies.

PREVENTATIVE MEASURES DESIGNED TO MINIMISE THE RISKS OF NON-PAYMENT

Apart from obtaining sufficient reliable information concerning potential customers, to reduce the risks of possible insolvencies a business should also adopt a series of preventative measures and policies aimed at minimising commercial risk. Such measures and policies should be adapted to the Spanish market and to the generally accepted practices of each particular sector in question. It is essential that they be based on:

- strict mechanised procedures regulating the treatment and receipt of orders, the issue and filling out of delivery notes and invoices, and duplicates and general commercial correspondence with customers. Such procedures should ensure proper control and follow-up of all operations, including any incidences which may affect their conclusion;
- the use of trade bills (bills of exchange, promissory notes, cheques etc) suitable for the documentation of operations and which maximise the chances of collection in the event of non-payment for whatever reason;
- in cases in which the amount or risk involved is particularly high, the conclusion of a business operation may be made subject to the provision by the customer of either real guarantees (pledges or mortgages) or personal guarantees (deposits or avals).

PRIVILEGED TREATMENT OF CERTAIN INSTRUMENTS

For the proper implementation of the preventative measures summarised above, it is vital that the business has knowledge of certain commercial instruments to which Spanish law (as do the laws of most Western countries) attributes a 'privileged' effectiveness. These are the so-called notes or bills of exchange. They carry a credit right which the holder or bearer can enforce against the person named in the instrument through a special procedure characterised by the advantaged position attributed to the claimant and the limited means of defence available to the defendant.

The notes or bills for which Spanish legislation envisages a special, privileged procedure in the event of non-payment are the bill of exchange as such, the promissory note and the cheque. These three types of documents are defined and regulated in a 1985 law which sets out the special privileges attributed to the holder or bearer of any of these instruments in the event of non-payment (the so-called 'exchange procedure' in which the debtor's means of defence against the creditor are restricted.) Precisely because of the 'privileged' nature of these documents and the remedies available to their holders, it is necessary to make a distinction between instruments of this type and other commercial documents which fulfil similar functions but lack the same effectiveness since they do not fulfil the same formal requisites. These are the straightforward bills or drafts etc. They are commonly used and are not lacking in practical usefulness. They carry, however, no special privileges over and above all the other commercial documents used in business operations (orders, invoices, delivery notes, claims etc).

SPANISH JUDICIAL PROCEDURES FOR MONETARY CLAIMS

Civil procedures

The information provided above leads directly to a few brief comments on the two main groups of civil procedures envisaged in Spanish law for claims relating to compliance with payment obligations: the 'ordinary declaratory' procedure and the 'executory procedure'.

In the declaratory procedure (which is that used generally for civil claims of all types), the debtor has all legal means available to it in its defence against the action brought against it by the creditor. The judge (unless it is an exceptional case) cannot take any action against the property of the defendant (the attachment of assets and rights) until there is a judicial ruling in which the defendant is ordered to pay a certain sum.

In the executory procedure, the defendant's possibilities of opposing the claim are considerably restricted (there are specified, limited cases in which opposition is possible). The claimant also has a considerable advantage in that the procedure commences with the attachment of the assets and rights of the defendant to an extent which gives reasonable coverage to the amount of the claim. In view of the privileged nature of the executory procedure, only certain documents entitle their holder to make use of it. They include the bills of exchange referred to above: the bill of exchange as such, the promissory note and the cheque (provided that they fulfil the legal requisites necessary to be regarded as such).

Any company which documents its commercial operations with third parties using properly issued bills of exchange is therefore entitled to claim the corresponding amounts, in the event of non-payment, using the 'exchange procedure' (in which the delinquent debtor's means of defence are restricted) and through an executory procedure (which commences with the attachment of the assets of the defendant to an extent giving reasonable coverage to the amount of the claim).

Apart from the increased effectiveness attributed to bills of exchange by Spanish law in cases of non-payment, it should be added that there are certain advantages deriving from their negotiation and circulation (endorsement, negotiation through discounting facilities with credit institutions etc) which may also imply considerable benefits from the point of view of cash and banks' management.

Cases in which it is advisable to bring action under criminal law

The comments set out above refer solely to monetary claims through civil law procedures, which are the most common. Sometimes, however, the circumstances of the events which have given rise to the loss may constitute a criminal offence (fraud, misappropriation, concealment of assets, issue of uncovered cheques etc). In such cases, the company suffering the loss must choose between a civil action and an action under criminal law in an attempt to recover the corresponding amount. It is not possible to carry on civil and criminal procedures simultaneously in relation to the same events. The advantages of a criminal procedure include the fact that it is possible to request that the judge adopt certain precautionary measures against property or persons which cannot be adopted in a civil procedure. These measures, such as the search of offices, taking control of the accounting records or operations of a company, orders for the provision of guarantee deposits, imprisonment of those responsible etc, can be aimed at preventing the continuation or worsening of the events which gave rise to or facilitated the committing of the offence in question. Alternatively, they can be aimed at obtaining financial security which will make it possible for the party suffering the loss to obtain finally the corresponding compensation.

The recent reform of the Spanish Penal Code, which came into force in the spring of 1996, envisages greater criminal liability, in certain cases, for the administrators (*de jure* or *de facto*) of commercial entities. This will undoubtedly give rise to an increase in the number of claims for compensation of damages made through criminal procedures.

Recently, however, there has been a tendency to make improper use of criminal procedures in cases based merely on the non-payment of a debt which should have been the subject of a civil action. There can be serious consequences for any company wrongly seeking compensation under criminal law. It is therefore essential that a detailed examination be made of each case before deciding which course of action to take.

LEGAL POSITION OF THE CREDITOR IN DIFFERENT CASES OF INSOLVENCY

There are two different procedures envisaged in Spanish law to which general insolvency of a business may give rise: the *suspension of payments* and *bankruptcy proceedings*.

Suspension of payments

The suspension of payments is a procedure designed to protect businesses affected by situations of insolvency which are not irreversible. Its purpose is to favour the continuation of the business, insofar as this is possible, and avoid damages deriving from different actions taken individually by each of its creditors against its assets. The entire procedure for the suspension of payments is carried on before a judge, its aim being to bring about an agreement between the insolvent company and its creditors. The declaration of suspension of payments can only be requested from the judge by the insolvent business itself.

As soon as the business presents to the judge a request to be declared in suspension of payments and the judge considers such request to have been duly filed, the creditors lose their right to take individual actions against the assets of the business. Any procedure being executed against its assets must be halted immediately.

From this moment onwards, and once the report on the insolvent business's financial situation drawn up by the referees appointed by the judge has been released, the procedure continues in an attempt to bring about an agreement between the business and its creditors. If such an agreement is reached (for which it must receive the support of the majorities stipulated in applicable legislation in accordance with the reductions of amount and extensions of time required), both parties are bound by it. In the event that the insolvent business fails to comply with the agreement, any creditor may request the lifting of the suspension of payments and apply for the business to be declared bankrupt.

Bankruptcy

The purpose of bankruptcy proceedings is to distribute the assets and rights of an insolvent business among its creditors. The main aim in the case of bankruptcy is therefore to ensure not the continuation of the company but the ordered distribution of the bankrupt's assets among its creditors.

The bankruptcy is termed *voluntary* when it is the insolvent business itself which requests the declaration of bankruptcy from the judge. The bankruptcy is classed as being *by court order* when it is declared by the judge at the request of a creditor, provided that the conditions required by law for the fruition of such a request are fulfilled (attempt made unsuccessfully to proceed individually against the assets of the insolvent business, delay in payment or non-fulfilment of payment obligations by the business, disappearance of the business or person responsible for it, failure of the suspension of payments etc).

A declaration of bankruptcy means that the creditors lose their right to take individual actions for the collection of the amounts owed to them (except in the case of creditors whose credits are secured by real or chattel mortgage guarantees). The insolvency of the bankrupt is classified in the bankruptcy procedure. If it is classed as fraudulent, a bankrupt business person is prevented from engaging in any future business activity, even if the business's debts are eventually settled.

Spanish law envisages two procedures for restoring to the property of the bankrupt business assets which should never have been transferred:

- on the one hand, the judge may set a date preceding the declaration of bankruptcy to which the effects of the bankruptcy are to apply retroactively. All transactions performed by the business as from this date are therefore annulled, implying the recovery of the assets and rights transferred through them, including, in some cases, assets acquired by third parties in good faith;
- on the other hand, in certain cases the creditors are entitled to request the restoration to the bankrupt business's property of assets and sums of money transferred by the business prior to the declaration of bankruptcy, when there are grounds for believing that such operations were performed with a view to defrauding creditors.

Bankruptcy proceedings normally end with the distribution of the bankrupt business's assets among its creditors. It may, however, end in an agreement between the bankrupt business and its creditors for the payment of its debts (although such an agreement is not possible when the bankruptcy has been classed as fraudulent).

From a practical viewpoint, a creditor which is studying the possibility of requesting that a debtor be declared bankrupt should consider very carefully whether the net worth of the insolvent business is sufficient. It must decide whether the value of the assets which may eventually be allotted will offset the considerable expense incurred in any bankruptcy proceedings.

Petition for trading companies to be wound up by court order

In the case of trading companies, there is another way creditors can collect their debts in situations where their debtors are financially unstable: they can file a petition for the company to be *wound up by court order*. This possibility is envisaged by Spanish law for cases where a company's accumulated losses have reduced its net worth to less than half of its share capital. In such cases, and if the company's directors fail to call a general meeting of shareholders to resolve to dissolve the company, or if the general meeting, after it has been called, fails to effectively adopt such a decision, 'any interested party may file a petition for the company to be wound up by court order'. Evidently, the company's creditors are to be included among the parties interested in calling for the company to be wound up (for the purpose of attempting to collect their debts during the relevant liquidation period).

Furthermore, in the event that the company's directors fail to fulfil their obligations in this regard (ie to call a general meeting of shareholders to resolve to dissolve the company or to file a petition for the company to be wound up by court order, in the event that such a resolution is not passed), the law provides that the company's directors shall become severally liable for the company's debts.

OTHER LEGAL ACTION THAT CAN BE TAKEN IN THE EVENT THAT THE DEBTOR COMPANY BECOMES INSOLVENT

As is unfortunately often the case in other countries, it has become recently more common in Spain for the status of a trading company to be used as a cover for businesses that are completely insolvent, which disappear as easily as they were set up, leaving behind them a large amount of unpaid debts. In such situations, which are by no means uncommon, and once it has been found that the company owns no assets and that no recourse can legally be made to complex and costly procedures such as petitions for the company to be declared bankrupt, creditors may still attempt to recover their losses by suing the directors of the company. Spanish law expressly lays down a set of specific rules regarding the liability of company directors (see Chapter 3.3) with regard to the company's creditors 'for any damage they may cause by acts that are unlawful or are in breach of the company's Articles of Association or by acts performed without the due diligence with which they must perform the duties of their position'. This notwithstanding, the limits of the liability of directors as regards company debts need to be defined by the courts over the next few years.

The possibilities available to company creditors to take action in order to collect their debts do not end here, because in recent years an authorised trend in doctrine and case law has appeared which defends the right to claim payment of company debts even from the property of the shareholders, whenever the legal status of the company has been fraudulently used as a barrier between the shareholders and third parties, for the sole purpose of not having to fulfil the obligations formally entered into by the company. The requirements and conditions for such a claim against the shareholders of a trading company for debts contracted by that company to be successful are still being elaborated by the courts. Even so, this option, called 'lifting the veil of trading companies', is a definite method that can be used in certain cases to claim collection of debts formally contracted by the company.

CONCLUSION

To sum up, repeating what has been said at the beginning of these commentaries, it can be concluded that the Spanish legal system provides adequate and sufficient guarantees for protecting companies that become involved in the financial crises of third parties with whom they have relations in the market. Furthermore, the practical deficiencies of the working of the system are gradually being corrected by increasing expenditure aimed at bringing more human and material resources into the judicial system.

3.2

Forms of Intellectual Property

José Luis Stampa and Ramón Fernández-Castellanos, Baker & McKenzie

Spain, with a population of 40 million, has a modern legal system offering a wide variety of effective means to protect intellectual property (IP), ranging from patents, through industrial and artistic models and designs, to trade marks. The Spanish legal system is complemented by a number of international treaties offering further protection and extending availability of protection to foreign individuals and companies.

CONFIDENTIAL INFORMATION

The Spanish legal system protects business secrets (including commercial data, know-how, technological information and manufacturing processes) against use by unauthorised parties, by means of Spanish unfair competition law.

It is considered unfair competition for managers, employees, directors or third parties to disclose or use business secrets without the owner's authorisation, to obtain a competitive advantage, or to cause prejudice to the owner. Spanish law reverses the burden of proof so that in the absence of authorisation from the owner there is presumed to be unfair competition unless proved otherwise.

To be protectable, business secrets must usually comply with two essential characteristics: (i) they must have been kept confidential by the company; and (ii) the secret information should not be readily available in the business sector where the company is engaged nor be publicly disclosed. A company is responsible for taking adequate measures to protect its business secrets and for notifying recipients of information that the information is confidential. If the information becomes generally known in the profession or business circle, there will no longer be any scope for obtaining damages or an injunction. However, as long as confidential information is not disclosed and is kept secret, it can be perpetually protected.

COPYRIGHT

Requirements for protection

Any original literary, artistic or scientific creation capable of being recorded in some form may be subject to copyright under Spanish law. Ideas and styles do not qualify for copyright. In order for a work to be considered original, the work should somehow evidence the personality of its author (subjective originality), or demonstrate objective novelty (objective originality). However, Spanish case law has not yet developed a consistent originality threshold.

Protection available

The author of a copyright work is granted both moral and economic rights in such works. (The author is always deemed to be an individual; only for works of collective authorship, so-called 'collective works', may corporations be considered as the authors.) Moral rights receive greater recognition in civil law countries. They include the right of the author to decide whether the work may be disclosed and the manner of disclosure, to demand acknowledgement of authorship, to demand respect for the work's integrity, and even to withdraw the work from commercial use (upon compensation). None of the moral rights may be waived or assigned by the author.

Economic rights include rights to reproduce, to distribute, to communicate publicly and to transform the works. Only economic rights may be assigned to individuals or entities; however Spanish law imposes restrictions on such assignments.

Duration

Generally, copyright protection lasts for the author's life and for 70 years subsequent to the author's death; in the case of neighbouring (moral) rights, protection may last for 25 or 50 years from the year following first exploitation.

Software

Original software materials, including computer programs and their preparatory documentation, are protected under the copyright as literary works. The exclusive economic rights granted to the software owner include the rights to its reproduction, translation, adaptation, public distribution or leasing. Exceptions include the making of backup copies, reproduction by proper use and decompilation when obtaining information necessary to interoperate the software.

PATENTS

In 1986 Spain adopted a new patent system in accordance with the European and Community Patent Conventions, which encompasses two different forms of protection: (i) patents (Spanish and European); and (ii) so-called petty patents (*modelos de utilidad*).

A Spanish patent and a European patent designating Spain give the exclusive right to exploit an invention industrially in Spain for 20 years. Patents can be granted for inventions which (i) do not fall into any excluded category; (ii) are novel at a worldwide level in accordance with the state of the art; (iii) involve an inventive step; and (iv) are capable of industrial application. Excluded categories include methods of doing business and computer programs (unless the program has a technical effect such as in operating a machine).

Filing

Foreign applicants for Spanish patents are required to submit patent applications with the Spanish Patent and Trade Mark Office (*Oficina de Patentes y Marcas*) (SPTO) through any of the officially appointed agents (*Agentes de la Propiedad Industrial*). European patents designating Spain are obtained via the European Patent Office in Munich. Patent law operates on a 'first-to-file' principle, meaning that decisions on rights in conflict are based on who filed a patent first. Obtaining priority is therefore essential. The Spanish national application procedure includes all oppositions (it is possible to oppose the grant of a patent) and reports on the state of the art, and there is provision that it should not last for more than 14 months.

Who can apply for a patent

The patent is granted to the inventor or those to whom the inventor has assigned his or her rights, unless the invention occurred within the scope of an employment relationship. In that case, the employee is compelled by law to disclose the invention, under penalty of losing his or her rights in it, if any. If exceptional results arise from the invention and the invention did not fall within the normal scope of work, the employee may be entitled to claim compensation.

Rights and duties

Patent proprietors have the right to prevent third parties from manufacturing, offering, marketing and importing, without authorisation, the patented product or a product directly obtained by the patented process, and from using a patented process. The proprietor is entitled to assume that third party products were manufactured by the patented procedure unless the third party proves that it followed a different procedure.

Petty patents

Tools, instruments, devices and parts thereof containing a configuration or structure which results in practical advantage for its manufacture or use, may be protected by means of a petty patent. As long as these show some inventiveness and are novel in accordance with the Spanish state of art, protection is granted for a non-renewable term of ten years.

DESIGNS

Spanish Law distinguishes between industrial models and designs and artistic models and designs.

Industrial models are creations of shape, ornament, structure or representation that do not add anything technical to the product or increase its utility function; industrial designs are design features (lines, colours or both) or ornaments to be applied to an industrial product. No previous novelty or utility examination is required by the SPTO for their registration.

Artistic models and designs are those exploited with an industrial aim which include a reproduction from a work of art (thus requiring the authorisation of the work's author when registering). They may additionally be subject to copyright as plastic works, provided they have artistic value and are considered original; copyright is however only granted to the primary work produced by the author and not to reproductions, since these do not meet the requirement of manifesting the author's personality.

Protection of models and designs is granted upon their registration with the SPTO for ten years, renewable for an additional ten-year term. Registration is granted for a particular industrial use or ornamental type only.

TRADE MARKS

A trade mark is a sign distinguishing the goods or services of a person or company from goods or services of other undertakings. It may consist of mere words, a combination of words and a device, or a device alone. A sign is registerable as a trade mark provided it is distinctive with respect to the goods or services to be protected (eg, the sign 'SHOES' for footwear would not be registerable as a trade mark since it is not distinctive of the goods of one shoe manufacturer over another). Trade mark registrations are obtained for particular classes of goods or services. Registrations in more than one class are possible but require separate applications.

Other industrial signs related to trade marks are trade names, which identify a company in the practice of its business activities, and trade signs, which make a certain business (eg, store, shop, restaurant) known to the public.

Trade marks which may lead to confusion in the market or give rise to a risk of association with an earlier trade mark, trade name or trade sign may not be registered. Thus, a trade mark application for 'MUSICIANIA' for musical instruments may be refused because of the prior existence of a trade mark registration 'MUSICALIA' for services of a concert promoter.

Application

A trade mark's protection lasts for ten years and may be renewed indefinitely for further ten-year periods, provided the requisite fees are paid and the trade mark is used. Trade mark applications must be published, publication marking the start of the period during which third parties may oppose grant of the application. Once this period lapses, the SPTO examines whether the application is confusingly similar to prior trade marks, trade names or trade signs or falls within the prohibitions set out by the Trade Mark Act. If oppositions are filed or any objections are raised by the SPTO, the application will be provisionally refused and the applicant may reply to said provisional refusal. If registration is refused, it is possible to file an appeal before the SPTO which in turn may be reviewed before the court.

If no oppositions or objections are raised, and the SPTO does not issue a decision within ten months from the application date, the trade mark will be considered granted. If oppositions and/or objections are raised and the SPTO does not issue an express decision within 20 months from that date, the trade mark will also be considered as granted.

The Community Trade Mark

A European Community Trade Mark has been available from 1 January 1996. The trade mark can be obtained by registering it with the appropriate office in Alicante (Spain) or with any trade mark office in an EU state, and will be valid in all EU countries. The mark must be one which would be registerable in each member state if applied for through the national systems. All EU nationals can apply for registration. Nationals of other countries offering reciprocal trade mark protection can also apply.

UNFAIR COMPETITION

The Unfair Competition Act 1991 offers a variety of remedies against so-called unfair competition practices (any activity that might be considered unfair in accordance with current Spanish standard trade practices).

These practices must have, or be likely to have, an effect within Spanish territory. Remedies (interim and permanent injunctions to stop unfair practices) are only available to Spanish companies or foreign companies active in the Spanish market.

BRINGING AND DEFENDING INFRINGEMENT PROCEEDINGS

The Spanish legal system provides a wide range of remedies to bring and defend the IP rights. As far as trade marks and like signs are concerned, the system is as a general rule based on registration. The only exception is in the case of a trade mark considered as well-known in Spain, in which case registration is not necessary to enforce the right.

No registration is required for copyright and similar rights. It is only necessary to provide evidence of the creation of the original work by the author to enforce the rights.

Nature of trial and court venue

IP infringement claims are usually assigned to the standard civil procedure for smaller claims. Spanish legislation does not provide for an expert or special jurisdiction with respect to IP rights issues. The hearing of civil actions arising in connection with IP rights is within the competence of the courts of first instance. The judgment of the court may be appealed, and the outcome of the appeal can be revised at second instance and in the Supreme Court. The owner of the IP right must act before Spanish courts represented by a court liaison (*procurador de los tribunales*) and an attorney-at-law.

Challenging the validity of IP

Trade marks or related industrial signs may be cancelled totally or partially by the courts upon request by the SPTO or by any other interested party, whenever (i) they are not distinctive for the goods or services; (ii) the sign falls into the absolute prohibitions set forth by the Trade Mark Act; (iii) they may lead to confusion to the public with respect to any other signs; (iv) they are deemed to be a misappropriation of the reputation of other signs, a reproduction or an imitation; (v) they have not been used according to law; or (vi) when the trade mark has become the common name in the trade for the product or service.

Patents and petty patents are also capable of being declared invalid when (i) they do not meet with the conditions of patentability; (ii) the invention is not described in a sufficiently clear and comprehensive manner to allow a person skilled in the art to carry it out; (iii) the subject matter goes beyond the content of the application as filed; or (iv) the patent owner is not the person entitled to the patent according to law.

Assessment of damages and accounts of profit

The owners of IP rights may obtain compensation in the form of damages and an account of the infringer's profit comprising not only losses already sustained but also future profits which will no longer be earned.

Enforcement

In general, both permanent and interim injunctions are available as means of enforcing IP rights. The owner or the exclusive licensee of a trade mark, a related sign, a patent or a petty patent whose right is infringed may apply for the cessation of the acts infringing his right in civil proceedings, including compensation for damages, adoption of the necessary measures to prevent continuation of the infringement and publication of the judgment at the expense of the unsuccessful party.

Furthermore, the owner or licensee of patents or petty patents may seek the seizure of objects and means used for infringement and for the attribution of the ownership of the objects and means seized.

The Intellectual Property Act provides similar measures for copyright and neighbouring rights.

Legal costs can be awarded against unsuccessful litigants.

Criminal law

The Spanish criminal legal system provides for three main criminal offences with respect to IP rights: (i) faking (outright copying), (ii) usurping (unauthorised use) and (iii) imitation use likely to cause confusion. These offences, enforced by quick and flexible proceedings before the ordinary criminal courts, generally require title of registration and may be initiated by the proprietor of the title or directly by the police.

In criminal proceedings, the judge may adopt a wide range of measures to prevent the offender from pursuing the criminal offence (among others, the seizure of goods or means to pursue the offence or the destruction of the faked goods), which can lead to the imprisonment of the offender and the imposing of a fine.

A new Criminal Code, which came into force in May 1996, provides a wider protection to the owner of IP rights.

EXPLOITATION OF IP

Trade marks and patents must be used in order to be preserved. A patent owner is required to exploit the patent directly or through an authorised party within three years of it being granted; the patent owner may otherwise be compelled to grant compulsory licences. A trade mark owner is required to exploit the trade mark within five years of it being granted; if there is continuous non-use for more than five years the SPTO and any third party may challenge the registration of the trade mark.

Patents, trade marks, industrial and artistic designs and copyright (economic rights) may be transferred or assigned freely, provided the transfer or assignment is in writing; however, the transfer or assignment must be registered with the SPTO (except for copyright). All IP rights may be used as financial security.

Licenses can be granted for all or part of the patent rights and are non-exclusive and for the whole patent validity term, unless agreed otherwise.

IP law overlaps with competition law because of the competitive advantage of the IP owner. Spanish competition law follows EU jurisprudence; for instance, it prevents IP owners opposing importation of IP-protected goods if those goods were sold in another EU country with the IP owner's consent. This applies, for example, even where the goods bear an identical trade mark to the mark protected in the country of import.

3.3

The Liability of Directors

Ramón Hermosilla Gimeno and
José Antonio Salgado González, Despacho
Ramón Hermosilla

INTRODUCTION

In the period from 1988 to 1995 the laws governing joint-stock companies have been radically reformed. The new rules on the auditing of accounts, stock markets, the commercial code, public limited companies (*sociedades anónimas*), the companies' registry regulation and private limited companies (*sociedades de responsabilidad limitada*), now adapted to European Union directives, have undergone modifications of varying degree, according to the area regulated, but as a whole they have substantially transformed the legal framework in which these companies carry on their activities. With respect to directors and, specifically, the system of civil liability to which they are subject, the reform introduces stricter rules which put an end to the permissive system which existed under the previous legislation.

Of the various types of companies existing in Spain, the majority are private limited companies (*sociedades limitadas*), followed by public limited companies (*sociedades anónimas*) and finally, forming a tiny, practically insignificant proportion, are general and limited partnerships, with or without shares (*sociedades colectivas y comanditarias, simples y por acciones*). However, the weight of public limited companies, due to their size and tradition, continues to make them the most significant despite the large number which have altered their status to that of private limited companies due to the requirements of the reform. This chapter focuses on the regulation of public limited companies.

DIRECTORS' OBLIGATIONS

It would seem to be appropriate, before studying the liability of company directors, to reflect briefly on directors and their obligations. The word 'director' is used here to refer to those of public limited companies and, by extension, those of other joint-stock companies, specifically private limited companies and limited partnerships with shares. Managers, executives and attorneys are not included.

The management of a public limited company may be the responsibility of one single person, as sole director; various persons, each acting individually; two persons jointly; or more than two, also jointly, in which case they make up the Board of Directors. A director is a company organ, a necessary instrument to make the decisions and actions of the legal person possible.

Directors' duty of care is expressed in Spanish law in a general clause, of an abstract nature, on the basis of concepts defined by the Act as the 'responsible businessman' and a 'loyal representative'. Together with this general reference the law, in a broad sense, imposes on directors a large number of specific obligations, the majority of a formal nature, nonperformance of which gives rise to liability. There is not, therefore, a list of obligations. Indeed the functions of directors make it difficult to define the limits, which also depend on the sector in which each company is active, there being many obligations of an administrative nature.

The obligations established by the articles of association themselves are also a source of directors' obligations, provided that they are not against the law and they do not contradict the principles which shape the type of company concerned. The resolutions of the company in general meetings are also a source of obligations.

The care which directors are required to exercise in the performance of their duties, ie in the management (internal) and representation (external) of the company, must be specified with reference to the characteristics of the entity and the duties and the knowledge and participation of the directors in the acts or omissions concerned.

An innovation introduced by the Consolidated Text of the Public Limited Companies Act (*Texto Refundido de la Ley de Sociedades Anónimas*, hereafter the LSA) is the imposition of a duty to keep information of a confidential nature secret, even after vacating office. This obligation was legally recognised before the passing of the Act, which now refers to it specifically.

CIVIL LIABILITY

The system for the liability of directors which existed until the current Act came into force only made them liable 'for damage caused by malice, abuse of powers or serious negligence', without there being any express reference to infringements or non-performances of the law or the articles of association. The requirement for serious negligence was an exception to the general law principle under art 1 of the Civil Code (*Código Civil*) .

This standard of the repealed Public Limited Companies Act 1951 (*Ley de Sociedades Anónimas*), which lawyers considered excessively benevolent, had little or no effect in practice, and resulted in legislation significantly tightening the laws regarding directors' liability.

This tightening of the system can be summarised in three points: (a) elimination of the privilege implied by relieving directors of liability for ordinary negligence, returning to the standards of civil liability established in the Spanish legal system as general norms; (b) introduction of joint and several liability between directors; and (c) limitation of the grounds for exoneration from liability.

The liability of directors to the company is dealt with in art 133 of the LSA which states that they shall be liable to the company, the shareholders and the creditors of the company for any damage they may cause through acts contrary to the law or the articles of association, or acts carried out without the care with which they ought to perform their duties; and that all the members of the governing body which performed the act or passed the injurious resolution shall be jointly and severally liable, except those who prove that, since they did not take part in its passing and implementation, were not aware of its existence or, if they were aware of it, did everything appropriate to avoid the damage or at least expressly opposed it. The said provision ends by stating that the fact that the act has been passed, authorised or ratified by the company in general meeting shall under no circumstances cause exoneration from liability.

As we can see, in addition to the reference to the duty of care, the transcribed provision expressly mentions damaging acts contrary to the law and the articles of association. This could not be otherwise, in so far as the basis for the liability of the directors is specified precisely as the non-performance of obligations imposed by law and the articles on those who perform duties.

From the above it follows that for liability to exist it is not sufficient for damage to have been caused to the company, since important losses may occur to the net worth of the company without the directors being liable for this reason alone, since it is obvious that the risk is incidental to the business, and therefore the company directors are not responsible for all losses.

The following prerequisites are essential for liability to attach:

1. The acts of directors must be concerned, carried out in the exercise of their duties, by either action or omission, although in the latter case a legal duty to act must exist. These acts may be either individual or collective.
2. There must be damage. It must directly affect the company and only indirectly the shareholders and/or the creditors. If it affects the shareholders and/or third parties directly the individual's action to enforce directors' liability comes into play (art 135 LSA) instead of the company's action for liability.
3. The acts of the directors causing the damage must have been carried out in infringement of the provisions of law or the articles of association or their duty of care.
4. There must be a relationship of cause or effect between the unlawful act of the directors and the damage.

An interesting aspect to consider is the weight of the interest of the company in relation to the duty of care, in so far as company directors should not focus their attention exclusively on the shareholders or the capital, but also on the workers and even the general interest, which introduces very diverse and sometimes conflicting factors.

The Act does not pronounce on the burden of proof, a question of great practical importance. Legal commentators perceive that when the liability arises from infringement of the duty of care the plaintiff will have to prove the existence of fault; if it arises from non-performance by the director of the law or the articles of association, it shall be sufficient to prove the damage and its connection to the unlawful conduct, without proving fault, the defendant director having to prove that there was no fault to be free from liability.

On the other hand, the joint and several nature of the liability implies a presumption of fault by all the directors and involves a shifting of the burden of proof in that only the person who shows that he or she acted with due care is released from liability.

Company's action to enforce directors' liability

We have seen that the civil liability of directors may be enforced through the company's or the individual's action.

The company's action for liability, to which we have referred up until now, is specifically regulated in art 134 of the LSA, according to which it shall be filed by the company, after a resolution of the company in general meeting, which may be passed even when it is not included on the agenda, with a majority fixed by the Act which cannot be modified by the articles of association. The said article establishes that the company in general meeting may settle or waive exercise of the action, unless shareholders representing at least 5 per cent of share capital oppose the same, and that a resolution to institute the action or settle shall cause the removal of the directors involved.

Shareholders (holding shares with or without voting rights) who hold at least 5 per cent of capital, may requisition the calling of a general meeting for the company to decide whether to bring an action for liability and may file the action if the directors fail to convene the general meeting or when having passed a resolution to institute it, the company fails to file the action within one month. The shareholders may also bring an action if the resolution was against doing so.

Finally, the said provision contemplates the possibility that the creditors may bring the action when neither the company nor the shareholders have done so, provided that the net worth of the company is sufficient to satisfy their claims.

It is important to point out that the standing to bring the action is held by the company, in so far as it is the company which suffers the direct damage, and therefore any damages which the court may determine shall be paid in all cases to the company, even if the action has been brought by the shareholders or the creditors, since they are defending the company's interests, not their own. The action must be brought against the liable directors, either claiming against all of them, or only against one or more, since the joint and several nature of such liability authorises this. As regards the possibility of a conflict of interests between the company and the director in the voting of a shareholder director, the Act does not impose any duty to abstain from voting. The Act does not determine any specific proceeding for the hearing of this action so that the general regulations contained in the Civil Procedure Act (*Ley de Enjuiciamiento Civil*) shall apply.

Neither does the Act stipulate a period of limitation for the action for liability so that in accordance with the rules of art 949 of the Commercial Code (*Código de Commercio*), the right of action against the shareholders, managers and directors of firms or companies shall lapse four years after they have ceased for whatever reason to perform management duties.

As regards settlement and waiver of the action, the relevant agreements may only be approved by the company in general meeting after it has been resolved to file the action, irrespective of whether it has actually been instituted or not.

The standing of the shareholders to file the company's action for liability is not granted to them on an individual basis but as the right of a minority possessing a certain percentage holding in the share capital (which does not mean to say that if one single shareholder possesses that percentage he may not bring the action). However, a necessary requirement to bring the action, although the Act does not expressly mention it, is that this same minority shall have voted at the meeting in favour of the resolution to bring the action, even if they have not managed to pass the same.

As we have mentioned above, the standing of the shareholders and the creditors to bring the company's action for liability is a standing in default but the judgment which decides the litigation shall have the nature of *res judicata* and the company may not simply bring the same action on the same grounds.

The bringing of the action by the creditors requires that the company shall have failed to pay its debts upon their maturity. However much the net worth of the company has fallen, if that circumstance does not exist they have no standing. Another prerequisite follows from this: that the debts must be due and payable. On the other hand a judicial declaration of definitive insolvency is not necessary.

A case worthy of special consideration is that of a *de facto* director, ie, a director whose term of office has expired but who continues to perform activities of management or representation, or both. There is no doubt that liability may be enforced against him in the same way as against the lawful directors, as they have exactly the same obligations.

The regulation of groups of companies is spread over a number of provisions in the Spanish legal system which makes its study and the coherence of its legal treatment problematic. The characterising feature of these groups is the control of the controlled company by the controlling company, the existence of an actual unity of decision, whether through the votes of the shareholders or through the directors. The Public Limited Companies Act does not regulate the case of the liability of directors in groups of companies, that is to say the damage caused to the controlled company as a consequence of the illegal or abusive exercise of the power of decision of the directors of the controlling company. It seems that in such a case the liability of the directors of the controlling company will be a liability based on breach of duty and they will be jointly and severally liable with the directors of the controlled company. If unjust enrichment of the controlling company may be inferred from the facts, proceedings may be brought against that company to obtain compensation for the damage to the net worth of the injured controlled company.

Under Spanish law legal persons may be directors, but for registration of their appointment at the Companies' Registry it is necessary to state the identity of the natural person who the former has appointed as its representative to perform the duties corresponding to its position. Moreover, the liability of a civil nature acquired by the representative acting as the director shall be enforceable against the represented entity, and not the former, without prejudice to the director company's entitlement to recover subsequently from its representative for not having followed the instructions received.

The rules on liability of directors are not applicable to general managers.

Individual's action to enforce directors' liability

Art 135 of the LSA provides that the provisions of the preceding articles shall be understood without prejudice to any actions for liability which may be available to shareholders and third parties as a result of the acts of directors which directly harm their interests. The preceding articles referred to by the provision cited are those which regulate the company's action for liability, while this one contemplates the individual's action. The *raison d'être* for this distinction is the different legal interests protected: the net worth of the company in the case of the company's action; and the net worth of the shareholders and third parties in the case of the individual's action.

The prerequisites for bringing the individual's action are similar to those set out for the company's action, namely: (a) an act of the directors, by action or omission of a legal duty, carried out in their capacity as such; (b) direct damage to the interests of the shareholders or third parties; (c) illegality or fault in the director's behaviour; and (d) a causal link between the fault and the damage caused.

The individual's action arises only when the directors cause direct damage to the shareholders or third parties, although it may also have been caused simultaneously to the company, as would be the case of preparation of false accounts. In this case both actions, the company and the individual, could be filed at the same time, seeking to obtain compensation for different net worths.

The main problem raised by the individual's action is to delimit the factual cases contemplated in art 135, that is to say the circumstances in which it operates, distinguishing it from the company's action to determine the legal system applicable to it. We have said that the legal interest protected is different in the two cases and also the persons entitled to bring the action are different (leaving aside the standing by default for bringing the company's action mentioned above).

The problem arises of determining when the director and when the company is liable, since, as the director is a company organ, the consequences of his acts are attributable to the company, without prejudice to the latter's right to recover from the former. The solution must come from the distinction between management and representation; whenever the directors act with powers of representation their action shall be directly attributable to the company, even if the results are *ultra vires*, while if they act outside this representative capacity, even if they hold their office, they shall be liable personally through the individual's action.

The existence of joint and several liability between the directors is a matter of dispute, since art 135 does not pronounce in this respect. There are people who maintain that there is joint and several liability in the event of contractual liability to the shareholders. Others tend to consider that there is joint and several liability in relation to fault but not in relation to the compensation of damage.

There is no agreement either as regards the period of limitation of the individual's action, although the majority opinion distinguishes between where the action is brought by the shareholders, with a four-year period, and by third parties, when it is one year.

TAX LIABILITY

Among administrative liabilities perhaps the most important, at least in general, is liability to pay tax. The General Taxation Act (*Ley General Tributaria*) establishes vicarious liability on the part of the directors of legal persons for the infringements of taxation provisions where the former is the taxpayer, whenever the directors have not carried out the necessary acts, for which they were responsible, for performance of the infringed tax obligations, have adopted resolutions which make such infringements possible or have consented to the non-performance by those who report to them. The period of limitation in the field of taxation is, in general, five years.

For vicarious liability to come into play it is necessary for there to exist an assessed tax liability which has not been paid by the company within the period stipulated by the Act and for the proceedings for collection of the debt to have been exhausted without the debt having been fully paid. In such case the tax authorities must make a 'bad debt declaration' and subsequently decide to direct the administrative action against the directors, which must be duly notified to them.

CRIMINAL LIABILITY

The new Spanish Penal Code (*Código Penal*), which came into force on 24 May 1996 provides in art 31 that whoever acts as a *de facto* or lawful director of a legal person or on behalf or legally or voluntarily representing another shall be personally liable, even if the conditions, characteristics or relations which the relevant definition of the crime or offence require in order to commit the same do not apply to him, if such circumstances do exist in the case of the entity or person in whose name he acts or who he represents.

Chapter XIII of the new Spanish Penal Code comments on so-called 'corporate crime' (*delitos societarios*), particularly regarding liability created by the misbehaviour of directors. Due to the limited extent of this chapter, it is not possible to examine this in detail; suffice it to say that is has increased the liability of directors.

CONCLUSION

The reform of Spanish company legislation mentioned in the introduction has involved an improvement in the regulation of liability, adapting it to the criteria established in the proposal for a Fifth Community Directive on companies, and a tightening of the system applicable. The exclusion of the requirement for a *special degree of negligence*, with the result that from now on any negligence will qualify for liability, the explicit establishment of joint and several liability, and the shifting of the burden of proof, stand out. If we add to this the changes which have occurred recently in the rules regulating tax offences and the criminal liability of directors, we can conclude that there has been a significant change of direction in legislative policy, from a position of unjustified benevolence to one of increasing strictness, aiming to reinforce and make effective the liability of directors. This situation is reflected in the courts in which actions for liability were hardly ever filed in the past; in contrast, they are now much more frequent and sometimes of such economic importance that they are heavily reported in the media.

Part 4

The Fiscal and Accounting Framework

INTRODUCTION

Taxation is a key issue for those investing abroad. Chapter 4.1 is an introduction to how business taxation works in Spain. It reviews the key issues that will be encountered in daily practice, offering guidance for foreign investors about the special opportunities available for them. Chapter 4.2 is dedicated to a number of more specific fiscal issues for foreign companies operating in Spain. Finally, in Chapter 4.3 the reader will find a comparative study of the Spanish accounting standards (mainly the *Plan General Contable*) *vis à vis* the UK. It is constructed around specific issues which allow the reader to easily find guidance on any kind of accounting subject.

4.1

Business Taxation*

Juan Ramón Ramos and Enrique Aznar, Price Waterhouse

TAX SYSTEM

Legislative framework

According to the Constitution of 27 December 1978 and the General Tax Code of 28 December 1963, national taxes can only be imposed by law. Local taxes are imposed by the autonomous communities and the local administration and represent an important source of revenue for them. However, the principal revenues of the autonomous communities are derived from national taxes which are transferred totally or partially by the state (see also Chapter 12.1). In such circumstances, irrespective of who collects the taxes, the tax administration remains the same and governs both the national taxes and those transferred to the autonomous communities.

Case law is an important source of interpretation of tax legislation. However, its effect is limited, in principle, to the facts and circumstances of the particular case.

---

* This publication is designed to provide accurate and authoritative information in regard to the subject matter covered. It is made available with the understanding that neither the authors (nor the publisher) are engaged in rendering legal, accounting, or other professional services. If legal advice or other expert assistance is required, the services of a competent professional person should be sought.

The Spanish tax system recognises the principle of substance over form. In particular, there is one anti-avoidance rule in the General Tax Code, which basically extends the application of the tax laws to those acts and transactions which take place with the proven intention of avoiding taxes.

Under the rules of the tax code, potential foreign investors may request advance rulings before carrying out a significant transaction or investment in Spain. These advance rulings are generally binding, subject to subsequent law changes. Resident taxpayers who wish to request advance rulings are also entitled to consultations but these rulings are not binding. In both cases, however, such rulings are not easy to obtain and the process can be time-consuming. If the tax code has been changed since the time of the ruling, the responses given will not be applicable.

Charge to tax – corporations and individuals

Both corporate tax and personal income tax are unitary systems governed respectively by the corporate and the personal income tax laws. Income of all kinds is generally aggregated and subject to a single tax, with a flat rate in the case of corporate tax and progressive rates in the case of personal income tax. (See also Chapter 9.2.)

There are two types of taxpayer: legal entities or individuals resident in Spain, who are taxed on a worldwide basis (ie, Spanish and foreign-source income), and non-resident legal entities or individuals, who are taxed on Spanish-source income only. For both types of taxpayer, taxable income includes, in general, income and capital gains from all sources.

For individuals, the tax year is the calendar year. Businesses file their tax returns on the basis of their accounting year. The chargeable accounting period of a business cannot exceed 12 months and therefore commencement, termination or change of year-end of a business gives rise to a chargeable accounting period of less than one year. A corporate entity's financial year may end on any date established by its statutes. If no date is specified, the year-end is 31 December. The statutory closing date in the case of banks and certain other financial institutions is the calendar year-end. Under Company law the period of accounts may not exceed 12 months.

The corporate tax return is submitted 25 days after the approval of the accounts and this should not exceed six months from the closing date if penalties are to be avoided.

Tax returns for each calendar year are filed for personal income tax during the period 1 May to 20 June (30 June for refunds), together with the wealth tax return if the taxpayer is subject to the latter.

The Canary Islands are currently developing a reduced tax area called *Zona Especial Canaria* (ZEC) but, at the time of writing, the favourable regime is not yet in force.

There are no general tax-free zones, but temporary suspension of customs duties and some excise taxes is applicable in free-trade zones and ports, enterprise zones, bonded warehouses and customs clearance areas.

Legislation provides unilaterally for the possibility of deducting the tax paid abroad as a tax credit against Spanish tax subject to limitations, and in certain conditions for the deduction of the underlying tax, when related to dividends. A tax credit not applied in a tax period because of lack of tax quota can be carried forward for seven years. In addition, Spain has a comprehensive network of tax treaties following the Organization for Economic Co-operation and Development (OECD) model (see also Chapter 9.2). Under these tax treaties, several methods have been established to avoid double taxation; the main one being the traditional deduction of the tax credit from the tax effectively paid, subject to limitations.

As a general rule, there are few tax advantages in locating company headquarters for international operations in Spain. However, interest paid to overseas affiliates is generally deductible up to a ratio of 3:1 in relation to equity. In addition, there are tax incentives for Spanish corporations set up with the exclusive objective of holding shares in foreign entities. These benefits consist of the exemption from taxation in Spain of any dividends paid to the Spanish holding company and exemption from taxation of any capital gains arising from the transfer of shares of the participated companies, provided certain conditions are met.

TAX ADMINISTRATION

Corporate tax is governed by the recent law no 43/1995 of 27 December 1995, which came into force on 1 January 1996 and is applicable to tax periods starting on or after that date. It replaced law no 61/1978 and its regulations of 15 October 1982. Individual income tax is governed by law no 18 of 6 June 1991, which is effective from 1 January 1992, and the regulations developing it under Royal Decree 1841/1991 of 30 December 1991 (see also Chapter 4.2).

All Spanish entities, branches of foreign entities, and non-resident entities that have Spanish-source income must file a corporate tax return. An assessment is raised on profits disclosed by the taxpayers' books and declarations. The system is one of self-assessment, with periodical audits by the tax authority. The laws have been changed in an attempt to obtain an improved compliance. In particular, recent legislation has reduced penalties but the number of tax inspectors has increased to help enforce compliance.

Resident individuals with net assets of more than 17 million pesetas are required to file a wealth tax return as at the end of the previous calendar year, together with the personal income tax return. However, non-resident individual taxpayers are required to file returns on the basis of remittances and are required to designate a tax representative in Spain to discharge their tax obligations. However, non-residents owning only one residence in Spain do not have to appoint a tax representative if they designate such address as appropriate for notification purposes.

All partnerships and joint ventures must file a corporate tax return even though the partners, members or participants may be assessed individually through the imputation system.

TAXATION OF CORPORATIONS

Scope of the charge to tax

Corporate tax is levied on the taxable income from all sources that accrues to a legal entity. Subject to the exceptions mentioned below, tax is withheld on dividends distributed to shareholders. Dividends must then be grossed up as taxable income of the corporate shareholders but the withholding tax may be taken as a tax credit for intercompany dividends. Nevertheless, dividends normally escape tax for the most part after taking advantage of various tax deductions available.

Corporate tax is levied on all resident legal entities or non-resident entities with a permanent establishment in Spanish territory. All entities established in Spain or whose registered office is located in Spain or have the place of management in Spanish territory are residents subject to corporate tax on their worldwide income.

The basic rate of corporate tax on net income determined in accordance with the above rules is currently 35 per cent. However, the government is authorised to propose modifications to the rates of corporate tax in its annual budget proposal.

Relief for losses

All tax losses may be carried forward to the tax periods ending during the seven years following the year end in which they originated, but they cannot be carried back. However, losses of a company which has been inactive for more than six months prior to the acquisition of the majority of its shares by a new shareholder cannot be carried forward. Unrelieved losses are carried forward and applied in the same order as incurred. Losses incurred by companies under the imputation system cannot be imputed to the shareholders; instead, they must be offset by the company against future profits. Losses arising from the scrapping of assets are allowed as deductible expenses if certain conditions are met. Newly created businesses can carry forward losses to the seven years following the period in which they obtained taxable profits.

Measurement of gross taxable income

Income and expenditure should be consistently allocated to a financial period on the accrual basis following accounting principles accepted in Spain. However, income from instalment sales can be recognised on the cash basis, at the discretion of the taxpayer.

Asset valuations for tax purposes must not exceed historical cost, except when a revaluation of fixed assets has taken place by law.

Increases in asset value arising from simple book entries (eg reflecting increases in asset value over historical cost) are not taxed. However, decreases are not deductible except when there is a reduction in the value of an asset as permitted by Company law.

The starting point for determining taxable profits is the company's accounts prepared by following accepted accounting principles. Most costing methods for arriving at profits are generally acceptable for tax purposes if the method is consistently applied.

All kinds of income are treated as ordinary income. Other items, such as releases from reserves and other non-trading income, are also taxable as ordinary income. The presumption is that the use of property, the transfer thereof and the performance of services are remunerated, unless the contrary can be proved, on commercial terms.

Intercompany transactions attract thorough scrutiny by the tax authorities. Transactions between associated entities must be at arm's-length prices. This concept is extended to intercompany financing where interest is not charged or not charged at market rates.

Inventory (stock-in-trade) is valued for tax and accounting purposes at the lower of cost and market value. Any valuation methods accepted by accounting principles (those include the average, FIFO and LIFO methods) are accepted for tax purposes.

For tax purposes, inventories are normally valued at the lower of cost or market value at the close of the financial year. Any write-down from the original cost is normally tax deductible but subject to specific rules. The write-off of obsolete inventories is also permitted provided it is substantiated.

Capital gains are normally taxable in the tax period in which they arise. They are treated as normal income.

Interest, dividends, royalties, and service fees must be included gross for the purpose of determining taxable income. A related tax credit is then normally granted against the corporate tax liability equivalent to the tax withheld at source (if any). Dividends paid by a resident subsidiary to a resident company will not be subject to withholding tax if the shareholding in the subsidiary is higher than 5 per cent throughout the year prior to the day in which the dividend is due. For other resident entities and non-resident entities (other than entities resident in other European Union (EU) member countries) in non-treaty countries, the grossing-up withholding tax rate is 25 per cent. Reduced rates apply for those entities residing in treaty countries. Interest paid to non-resident entities, resident in other EU member states, is not subject to withholding tax. In certain cases, dividends paid to parent companies, resident in another EU member state, which own at least 25 per cent of the shares in the Spanish company during one complete year prior to the date the dividend is due are not subject to withholding tax. Otherwise, the withholding rate is 25 per cent, unless differently stated by a tax treaty, and is available as a tax credit.

Except in the case of members of the same tax consolidation group, in addition to tax credits available for dividend withholding taxes, if applicable, a further tax credit is available when a resident corporation receives dividends or profit participations from another; such credit is equivalent to 50 per cent the amount that results from applying the 35 per cent corporate tax rate to such dividends or profit participations concerned. The credit is increased to 100 per cent where the dividends are distributed by a corporate entity, controlled directly or indirectly by the recipient corporate entity holding more than a 5 per cent interest in the capital of the subsidiary, if such control has been exercised without interruption throughout the previous complete year.

Stock dividends received from second and third tier foreign subsidiaries are entitled to a tax credit of the foreign taxes paid including
the underlying taxes paid by their subsidiaries.

Deductibility of expenditure

Business expenses deductible for corporate tax purposes are those
expenses 'necessary' for the purpose of producing income. The meaning of 'necessary' is not always clear. However, necessary expenses generally include expenses that are compulsory, whether for legal or
contractual reasons, as well as expenses that are incurred for the purposes of producing income. The latter type of expense is deductible,
even though not theoretically essential for the production of income.

Interest is deductible on an accruals basis. Deductibility of the interest on loans by a foreign parent are subject to the formal debt/equity
ratio restrictions shown in the corporate tax law.

The new law no 43/1995 establishes that interest paid by a resident
entity to a non-resident entity directly or indirectly related is
deductible up to a debt/equity ratio of 3:1. Interest paid in excess of
such ratio, and only the excess, will be treated as a distribution. Some
tax treaties (ie the treaty between Spain and the UK) prohibit the
application of thin capitalisation rules (see also Chapter 2.1).

To be deductible for tax purposes, charges for royalties and technical
service fees must be supported by a written contract meeting specific
requirements, and preferably signed before a notary public, and the
effectiveness of the services has to be proven. Payment of such
expenses and any other to non-residents are subject to presenting
Form 210 for making payments to non-residents.

All wages, salaries, bonuses, and commissions paid or payable to staff,
whether foreign or local, are deductible.

There are no current restrictions on deductibility on bonuses paid to
staff, other than directors. However, it is advisable that bonuses be distributed in a uniform manner or be defined in contracts of employment.

All social security costs incurred by a company are deductible.
Amounts paid to third parties for personnel benefits or services are
generally deductible.

Certain donations and investments, bad debt and doubtful accounts
receivable, repairs and overhauls, and entertainment and travel
expenses can also be deducted subject to specific circumstances.

Non-deductible items include dividends, corporate income tax, service fees paid to tax havens, penalties and gifts. Expenses for public relations, incurred with suppliers, clients and personnel, are deductible expenses.

Taxes, other than corporate income tax and VAT, are deductible expenses, and in some cases they may be included in formation expenses and written off over a period of up to five years, such as stamp duty paid on capital increases.

All fixed assets, except land, are depreciable for tax purposes. Guideline rates of depreciation, by both industry sector and asset type, are usually established by orders issued by the Ministry of Economy and Finance, expressing a maximum per annum rate (straight-line method and a maximum number of years). The annual maximum depreciation rate for second hand assets is double that for new assets.

The rules governing amortisation of particular types of intangible assets are as follows:

1. Formation expenses, start-up expenses, and capital increase expenses – company law requires their write-off within five years of incurring the expense; this is acceptable for tax purposes.
2. Trademarks and intangibles – these must be amortised over a period of ten years if acquired from an unrelated party, unless otherwise established by law.
3. Costs incurred in unsuccessful research and development – such costs for new products or industrial processes may be amortised as intangibles with no limitations.
4. Goodwill – goodwill is deductible for tax purposes over a period of ten years when it has been purchased from an unrelated party.

Consolidation

A tax group for consolidation purposes comprises a controlling corporation and one or more dependent subsidiaries, irrespective of the activities of each. The controlling corporation must be a resident entity in Spain that owns, directly or indirectly, more than 90 per cent of the dependent corporation or corporations for a minimum period of one year prior to making the request for tax consolidation and this participation is not reduced during the period in which the group is in tax consolidation. The subsidiaries must also be resident in Spain. The new law has removed the requirement of obtaining authorisation to consolidate from the tax authorities.

Consolidation is for a minimum period of three financial years. Only the consolidated net income is subject to corporate tax and tax is not withheld in the case of dividends, interest or royalties paid between corporations of the group. However, indirect taxes are payable on transactions between corporations in the group.

Losses prior to consolidation can be offset only against subsequent profits earned by the same corporation, and consolidated losses cannot be carried forward into a subsidiary corporation when it is no longer consolidated. The consolidation has to be approved at the annual general meetings of each of the corporations involved.

CORPORATE TAX PLANNING STRATEGIES

Branch versus subsidiary

Foreign investors usually carry on business in Spain through a subsidiary or a branch. Subsidiaries are considered 'Spanish' for tax and legal purposes. Branches are not treated as 'Spanish' legal entities. Subsidiaries are subject to corporate tax on worldwide taxable income and branches pay tax on Spanish-source income only. Head office general and administrative expenses are deductible expenses in the case of a branch, provided the recipient pays the withholding tax on such expenses. Subsidiaries may only deduct management charges if the effectiveness of the service is proved and the amount of the charge is set at market value, providing certain requirements are met.

Generally, the distribution of profits of a subsidiary or a branch, after payment of the corporate income tax, is subject to withholding tax of 25 per cent unless a relevant double taxation treaty is applicable. Usually, no withholding tax will apply when:

(i) in the case of subsidiaries, the parent company resides in another country of the EU and the participation in the Spanish subsidiary is, at least, 25 per cent in a complete year prior to the distribution, in addition to the compliance of other anti-abuse clauses; or

(ii) in the case of branches, the head office is situated in another country which is member of the EU, subject to the reciprocity clause.

Exchange losses and interest payable by a subsidiary are deductible for tax purposes. They are not deductible when payable by a branch.

Mergers and acquisitions

Reorganisations usually have little tax effect. Mergers usually enjoy tax benefits and have no tax costs. The acquisition of shares is simple. The purchase price must be capitalised and it is not possible to increase the tax basis of assets to reflect the purchase price. The basis for tax purposes in asset acquisitions is the purchase price between arm's length parties. The buyer would be entitled to claim depreciation allowances. In addition, acquisitions of new fixed assets may qualify for tax credits.

Spain encourages investment in certain localities and regions. The basic incentives are subsidies. These subsidies are generally considered for tax purposes as income; however, the taxpayer can opt to be taxed on the subsidy over the life of the asset.

For further information, see Chapter 2.1.

Taxation of foreign corporations

Foreign corporations (non-resident entities) with no taxable presence in Spain are subject to corporate tax on the following payments made to them by resident persons or entities:

1. Income from all types of services rendered, technical assistance, loans, or any other type of work performed or capital used in Spain.
2. Income derived from property in Spain.
3. Income from securities issued by Spanish companies or by foreign companies with a permanent establishment in Spain. The tax would normally be applicable to dividends distributed by foreign companies with a permanent establishment in Spain; however, as a practical matter, no taxation is collected because the law has not established how taxable income is to be determined. It should be noted that foreign corporations are not subject to corporate tax on income and capital gains derived from securities issued in Spain by non-resident entities without permanent establishment, in spite of payments being made by resident agents.
4. Capital gains on the disposal of any type of property located in Spain.

All non-resident entities without a permanent establishment in Spain are required to appoint a representative in Spain for tax purposes. If a tax representative is not named, the resident paying entity is considered liable to tax. The taxpayer and the tax representative are jointly and severally liable for the payment of the related taxes.

Note: The above information is based on the law as stated on 1 January 1996.

4.2

Special Issues in Fiscal Strategy for Foreign Companies Operating in Spain

William Field, Ernst & Young

Spanish corporate tax has undergone significant changes in the last few years in an effort to modernise the approach of the tax authorities to the increasing cross-border nature of Spain's economy. This has led to a more sophisticated approach to the taxation of multinationals and to investment into Spain and transactions with Spanish resident companies.

The new corporate tax law which took effect from 1 January 1996 revises the treatment of certain areas of taxation (such as loss relief) and introduces new rules in respect of certain key areas (such as transfer pricing). Set out below is a discussion of certain of the key areas.

INTRA GROUP CHARGES

Until the appearance of the changes set out in the new law, charges to a Spanish company from a non-resident, connected party were only subject to a general provision that all transactions should be at arms length. Other than this the only constraints were what the local tax inspector might insist upon if and when the accounts were subjected to a tax audit.

The new law has clarified and tightened the requirements in respect of costs sharing arrangements on research and development and from management charges.

Costs on research and development, which are shared with a connected party, will only be deductible where they are in accord with a written contract that was agreed prior to the costs arising. The contract must:

(a) specify the projects and authorise the use of the results of any research;

(b) ensure that the basis of sharing the expenses is rational and in accordance with the rights to utilise the results by the paying entity.

Management charges from a connected party will only be deductible where they are in accordance with a pre-existing written contract which set out the basis for the charging of such charges to the Spanish company. The contract must:

(a) specify the nature of the services provided;

(b) set out on a consistent and rational basis the methods of allocating costs.

In both cases the term 'connected' is as defined for transfer pricing matters. This definition includes:

(a) all shareholders and directors of a company;

(b) the relatives of such individuals;

(c) group companies (as defined for accounting purposes);

(d) two companies where one holds at least 25 per cent of the share capital of the other;

(e) two companies where common shareholders hold at least 25 per cent of both companies;

(f) companies and their overseas/Spanish branches;

(g) two companies where one company exercises decision-making powers in the other.

In dealing with intra group charges which are made to a company resident in a 'tax haven' additional rules apply. These require that for such a payment to be deductible the tax payer must show that the transaction has taken place.

TRANSFER PRICING

Transactions between connected parties as defined above are now subject to specific rules. Where a transaction occurs that results in a loss of tax revenue for Spain, the Spanish tax authorities may substitute 'market value' for that used by the Spanish tax payer.

In order to determine 'market value' the law specifies four acceptable methods based upon the OECD models:

(a) comparable profit method;
(b) resale price minus normal profits method;
(c) cost plus normal profits method;
(d) profit split method.

Taxpayers may apply to the tax authorities for a binding advance pricing agreement. Such an agreement with the authorities will last for three taxable periods.

PARTICIPATION EXEMPTIONS

Under Spain's new corporate tax law a Spanish holding company will be exempt from Spanish taxation on dividends received from overseas subsidiaries. The Spanish holding company will also be exempt from capital gains on the transfer of shares in such subsidiaries. To enjoy these exemptions the following conditions have to be met:

- the Spanish holding company's sole purpose must be the holding and management of such investments;
- each holding must be at least 5 per cent held directly or indirectly;
- the holding company is not a transparent company for Spanish tax purposes;
- the companies do not form part of a Spanish tax group.

Dividends will be exempt provided that the Spanish holding company has maintained its share holding without interruption for the year preceding the date of payment of the dividend.

The subsidiary company (ie the dividend payer) must be subject to (and not then exempted from) a tax similar to Spanish corporation tax; nor can it be resident in a tax haven. The subsidiary's profits, from which the dividends are paid, must be derived from the carrying on of a business activity. There are specific rules as to what constitutes business activities both in terms of the nature of the activity as well as to whom and where services are rendered. The subsidiary company must not be party to financial operations with Spanish residents. Gains arising on disposal of a participation will not be taxable provided that the disposing company meets the requirements set out above and the acquirer is not a Spanish resident and connected to the disposing company.

There is a counterweight to the benefit of the participation exemption. The Spanish holding company will not be entitled to a tax-deductible write-down for a fall in the value of its investments arising from the distribution of the dividends (a 'dividend strip') unless those profits had been subject to taxation on a previous occasion prior to the participation arising. Dividends received by a company enjoying the participation exemption will not be entitled to credit for underlying taxes paid in overseas jurisdictions.

CONTROLLED FOREIGN COMPANIES

Spain introduced Controlled Foreign Company (CFC) legislation from 1 January 1995. This was based upon a study of CFC legislation in other major economies and unsurprisingly contains many familiar characteristics. For these purposes a CFC is one in which:

- at the end of an accounting period more than 50 per cent of the share capital, assets, profits or voting rights of a non-Spanish resident entity are held, directly or indirectly, by one or more connected Spanish resident individuals or entities;
- the tax paid by the non-Spanish resident company, in respect of a tax analogous to Spanish corporation tax, is less than 75 per cent of the tax that would have been paid in Spain on the same income.

Connected for these purposes is the same as set out for transfer pricing above.

Where a company qualifies as a CFC the appropriate share of its profits are added to any Spanish resident company's taxable income for the year. However, there are exclusions for certain types of income such as that from trading activities of the CFC, income arising from the CFC acting as a holding company or income arising from finance or insurance activities where more than 50 per cent of such income derives from unconnected parties. There are *de minimis* limits for excluding income from rental, investment and financial activities from the profits of the CFC.

In calculating Spanish tax due on the allocated part of the CFC's profits, the Spanish shareholder is entitled to a credit for the underlying tax paid by the CFC and any withholding taxes suffered on any distributions. However no taxes paid in a tax haven will be allowed as a credit for Spanish tax purposes.

SPAIN AND INTERNATIONAL TAX TREATIES

At the present time there are 35 treaties between Spain and other nations covering the avoidance of double taxation. Of these 11 have been agreed in the 1990s with the majority being concluded in the 1960s and 1970s. Spain has treaties with all its European Union partners except Greece.

Generally, Spain's treaties follow the OECD model but those agreed in recent years have included some very restrictive articles. The treaties generally give more favourable treatment to items such as dividends, interest and royalties than Spanish domestic law. Under domestic law withholding taxes on these items would be 25 per cent; under most treaties withholding taxes are reduced to 15 per cent or 10 per cent for dividends, 10 per cent or 0 per cent for interest and 10 per cent, 6 per cent or 5 per cent for royalties. In this last category it is worth noting that the Spanish tax authorities would include most types of lease payments to overseas lessors.

Perhaps the most difficult treaty is that between Spain and the United States. Not only does this have a restriction of benefits clause but also includes provisions for the taxing of both branch profits and the further taxation of the remittance of the profits from a Spanish branch to its US head office (and vice versa). There is also a provision for Spanish taxation of capital gains arising on the disposal of shares in a Spanish subsidiary.

Of Spain's other more recent treaties there has been a move towards specific restrictions on enjoyment of benefits given by treaties. Generally such restrictions are of the form whereby the income or benefits have to be beneficially owned to the extent of at least 51 per cent by a resident of a contracting state. The clear intention is the avoidance of the use of Spain or its contracting partner states as a conduit for certain types of income or gains, thereby reducing withholding taxes.

SPAIN AND THE EUROPEAN DIRECTIVES

The principal directives of the European Community concerned the payment of dividends between parent and subsidiary companies (parent/subsidiary) and the merger, division and share exchange transactions (mergers) between companies (see Chapter 2.1).

Spain has enacted these directives into its domestic legislation virtually word for word. The main difference is that it has extended the benefits of the mergers directive to all such transactions both domestic and cross-border; in the latter case the cross-border element does not have to include another party resident in a member state of the European Union. The only real restriction is that transactions involving a tax haven will not benefit from the directives.

As a result where a parent/subsidiary relation exists (where one company holds more than 25 per cent of the other for more than two years prior to the day a dividend is paid) payment of a dividend will not give rise to Spanish withholding tax where a dividend is paid out of Spain. Equally a Spanish parent company will not be taxable on dividends received from qualifying subsidiaries resident in the European Union. To qualify for these benefits the subsidiary company has to comply with conditions relating to its incorporation and taxation.

For mergers and divisions of companies, the transfer of branches and the exchange of shares in companies, relief from Spanish taxation is available provided that certain conditions relating to the transaction are met. These conditions generally require that the assets comprising the transaction remain within the Spanish tax net at the same tax cost as they were before the transaction. The real benefit from these laws is that reorganisation and restructuring of companies can take place without prohibitive tax costs.

Spain has also effected what was the draft European Union directive on interest. Any lender resident in a European Union country, which does not have a permanent establishment in Spain to which the loan can be attributed, can receive its interest tax-free of withholding tax from Spain. This is again subject to the usual provisos relating to the transactions not involving the use of tax havens.

LOCAL TAXES

A number of taxes at the local or municipal level exist in Spain. Of these, two are more significant – the *Impuesto sobre el Incremento de Valor de los Terrenos de Naturaleza Urbana* (Incremento) and the *Impuesto sobre Actividades Economicas* (IAE).

The *Incremento* is essentially a form of capital gains tax on the transfer of developed land levied by the local tax administrations rather than as a national tax. The tax arises at the point of transfer of title of land by legal deed and so even non-monetary transfers can give rise to this tax. There is also provision for the tax to be charged on a ten-yearly basis even where no transfer of title occurs.

The IAE is an annual tax based upon the type of activity a business undertakes and to an extent on the population size of the area in which it operates.

4.3

Accounting Principles and Reporting Requirements: A Comparative Study of the UK and Spain

Nigel Cooper and Javier Jimenez, KPMG

INTRODUCTION

This chapter describes the significant differences in the accounting principles and reporting requirements in the UK and Spain. It is not intended to be a fully comprehensive list of all the differences between the two countries, but, rather, a summary of those areas most frequently encountered in which UK and Spanish practices differ significantly or in which there is a difference in emphasis between the two. For an in-depth analysis of a given area it is essential that the authoritative literature be consulted.

EU HARMONISATION

The Fourth and Seventh EU Directives

The EU's aim has been to harmonise and integrate European legislation and reduce the differences in accounting and auditing standards in the member states. The main mechanism for this is Directives, which are drafted by the Commission, adopted by the Council of Ministers and implemented by the Parliaments of the member states. There are several Directives on company law, of which the Fourth and the Seventh are of greatest importance for financial reporting. The Fourth concerns format of financial statements, accounting principles and requirements for disclosure, publication and audit. It was notified to the member states on 25 July 1978. The main aim of this Directive is to protect the shareholders' and third parties' rights, to ensure that information included in the financial statements is comparable and these documents show true and fair view of a company's financial situation. This Directive was brought into force as follows:

United Kingdom

Companies Act 1981
(now included in 1985 Act)

Spain

Law 19 of 25 July 1989

The Seventh Directive concerns consolidated accounts and was notified to the member states on 13 June 1983 and brought into force as follows:

United Kingdom

Companies Act 1989

Spain

Law 19 of 25 July 1989

Local legislation

United Kingdom

Company law provides a framework (Companies Act 1985 with 1989 amendments) and is supplemented by accounting and reporting standards. Individuals and partnerships (other than limited partnerships) are not required to present financial statements in any prescribed format.

In addition to the principles set out in Company Law, the ASB has issued a draft statement of principles which seeks a theoretical basis to support the empirical approach of the legislation. The ASB has already issued FRS 5 which required that the substance of transactions dictate their accounting treatment.

This applies in particular to:

- debt factoring;
- sale and repurchase agreements;
- consignment stock.

Spain

In the past, Spanish accounting practices were significantly influenced by tax considerations. To correct this situation and bring Spanish standards into line with the 'true and fair view' concept, the existing accounting standards were significantly modified by law in 1989. This law established certain basic accounting, valuation, disclosure and presentation principles which were further developed in 1990 through the enactment of a revised 'General Accounting Plan' (GAP).

The General Accounting Plan is set out in five parts:

- accounting principles;
- accounts detail;
- definition and accounting relations;
- annual accounts;
- accounting standards.

The GAP is mandatory for all

The aim is to avoid companies keeping liabilities (and assets) off balance sheet.

enterprises regardless of their legal status (whether individuals or corporate).

Accountancy bodies and issuers of standards

United Kingdom

The accountancy profession in the UK is governed by a number of professional bodies. These include:

- The Institute of Chartered Accountants in England and Wales (ICAEW);
- The Institute of Chartered Accountants in Scotland (ICAS);
- The Institute of Chartered Accountants in Ireland (ICAI);
- The Association of Chartered Certified Accountants (ACCA);
- The Chartered Institute of Public Finance Accounts (CIPFA);
- The Joint Monitoring Unit (JMU) which reviews the work carried out by auditing firms to ensure that they are complying with professional standards.

Until 31 July 1990 accounting rules were developed by the Accounting Standards Committee which issued Statements of Standard Accounting Practice (SSAP). Since then:

- accounting rules have been developed by the Accounting Standards Board which issues Financial Reporting Standards (FRS);
- accounting issues which require immediate resolution have been resolved by the Urgent Issues Task Force which issues abstracts setting out mandatory treatments.

Spain

The *Instituto de Contabilidad y Auditoria de Cuentas* (ICAC), was created by the 19/1988 law of 12 July and is the equivalent to the Accounting Standards Board in the UK. Its main functions are:

- the development of accounting standards and their sectoral adaptation in the *Plan General de Contabilidad*;
- to monitor the audit work carried out by the auditing firms;
- the issue of accounting standards and questions posed by third parties in its own quarterly publication BOICAC (*Boletin Oficial del Instituto de Contabilidad y Auditoría de Cuentas*);
- to set up the organisation in charge of Chartered Public Accountants, ROAC (*Registro Oficial de Auditores de Cuentas*).

FINANCIAL STATEMENTS

Contents of financial statements

The financial statements must include the following:

United Kingdom

- Profit and loss account

All gains and losses recognised in the financial statements for the period should be included in the profit and loss account or the **statement of total recognised gains and losses**. Gains and losses may be excluded from the profit and loss account only if they are specifically permitted or required to be taken directly to reserves by some accounting standard or by law. Results should be analysed between continuing and discontinued activities.

- Balance sheet

A statement of assets and liabilities of the entity, identifying the shareholder's funds.

- Earnings per share

The profit in pence attributable to each equity share, based on the profit of the period after tax, minority interests and extraordinary items and after deducting dividends on preference shares, divided by the number of equity shares in issue and ranking for dividend in respect of the period.

- Note of historical cost profits and losses

A memorandum item, the primary

Spain

- Profit and loss account

All gains and losses recognised in the financial statements for the period should be included in the profit and loss account. There is no requirement to analyse the results between continuing and discontinued activities.

- Balance sheet

There are no significant differences.

- Earnings per share

No equivelent in Spain.

- Note of historical cost profit and losses

No equivelent in Spain.

purpose of which is to present the profits or losses of those reporting entities that have revalued assets on to a more comparable basis with those that have not. It adjusts the reported profit or loss, if necessary, so as show it as if no asset revaluation had been made.

- Statement of total recognised gains and losses

This primary statement shows how shareholders' funds have been affected by all gains and losses recognised in the period. It therefore shows, in addition to gains and losses recognised in the profit and loss account, those which are permitted or required by law or standards to be taken directly to reserves – eg revaluation surpluses on fixed assets.

- Reconciliation of movements in shareholders' funds

Brings together the performance in the period, as shown in the statement of total recognised gains and losses, with all the other changes in shareholders' funds in the period, including capital contributed by or repaid to shareholders.

- Cash flow statements (FRS 1, FRED 10)

A primary statement which is required for all companies with certain exemptions – ie for small companies and wholly owned subsidiary undertakings of an EU parent.

- Notes to the accounts

There are exemptions from some of the above requirements for certain small and medium sized companies.

- Statement of total recognised gains and losses

No equivelent in Spain.

- Reconciliation of movements in shareholders' funds

The contents are the same as under UK GAAP.

- Statement of source and application of funds

This is not a primary statement and is presented as a note to the accounts. It is required for all companies with exemptions for small companies.

- Notes to the accounts 'Memoria'

Similar exemptions apply to small companies in Spain.

Timetable

United Kingdom

A company's annual accounts must be approved by the board of directors. The directors must lay copies of the company's annual accounts and related directors' and auditors' reports for that year before the company in general meeting. Common practice is for a company's accounts to be laid at the annual general meeting (AGM) and some companies' articles actually specify that the accounts must be presented at the AGM.

A company must hold an AGM in each calendar year and not more than 15 months may elapse between the date of one AGM and that of the next.

- Filing and publication of the accounts

A copy of the full accounts must be delivered to the Registrar of Companies within seven months of the end of its accounting reference period for a public company, and within ten months for a private company. An extra three months can be claimed by application to the Registrar where a company carries on business or has interests, outside the UK, the Channel Islands and the Isle of Man.

Spain

Approval of the annual accounts and the annual directors' report by the company's board of directors. The annual accounts must be approved by the company's board of directors within three months of the end of the company's financial year. After this three month period has expired, the company's auditors have at least one month to issue their report.

The annual accounts and the annual directors' report are approved by a general shareholders' meeting which must be held within six months of the end of the company's financial year.

- Filing and publication of the accounts

Within one month after the annual accounts have been approved by the general shareholders' meeting, the following information must be filed in the Mercantile Registry corresponding to the company's corporate address:
- the certificate of the general shareholders' meeting in which the annual accounts and distribution of earning were approved;
- a copy of the annual accounts and directors' report;
- the related audit report on the annual accounts and directors' report, when the company is subject to statutory audit requirements.

Corporate governance

United Kingdom

Directors have a responsibility to prevent and detect fraud and other irregularities. In December 1994 guidance for directors of listed companies registered in the UK on 'Internal Control and Financial Reporting'. For all listed companies, the accounts must contain a statement on internal control. This would include:

- acknowledgement by the directors that they are responsible for the company's system of internal financial control;

- explanation that such a system can provide only reasonable and not absolute assurance against material misstatements or loss;

- description of the key procedures that the directors have established and which are designed to provide effective internal financial control;

- confirmation that the directors (or a board committee) have reviewed the effectiveness of the system of internal financial control.

Spain

Directors are liable to the company, the shareholders and the company's creditors for any damages or losses occasioned by illegal acts, or any infringements of the articles of the company or actions taken without due diligence on their part.

Audit requirements

United Kingdom

An audit is mandatory for all companies with a turnover greater than £350,000 per annum. For certain companies that are not members of a group and have a turnover between £90,000 and £350,000 per annum only an accountant's report is required. Dormant companies and certain non-group companies with turnover less than £90,000 do not require an audit.

Spain

An audit is mandatory for:

- companies which meet any two of the following three conditions at two consecutive balance sheet dates:
  - total assets under 300 million pesetas;
  - net annual sales under 600 million pesetas;
  - average number of employees under 50.

- companies quoted on the stock exchange;
- companies which issue debentures and bonds to the public;
- financial entities;
- insurance companies;
- regulated industries such as utilities;
- companies not obliged to be audited, when 5 per cent of shareholders request one;
- companies receiving state grants or subsidies, carrying out public works, rendering services or supplying goods to the state or public utilities within the limits established by the government by Royal Decree.

Appointment of auditors

United Kingdom

Auditors are normally appointed and reappointed at the AGM. Shareholders may, however, agree to dispense with this requirement and appoint auditors on a continuing basis. There is no minimum or maximum period for which auditors are appointed.

Spain

Companies must appoint auditors for a minimum period of three years. Upon the conclusion of this initial period of appointment, the auditors' term of office may be extended indefinitely on an annual basis.

SIGNIFICANT DIFFERENCES IN ACCOUNTING PRINCIPLES

Intangible assets

United Kingdom   **Spain**

Preliminary expenses and cost of issuing shares

These can be charged directly to the share premium account (where one exists) so avoiding a charge to distributable profits.

May be capitalised and written off over five years.

Start-up and business expansion expenses

Capitalisation is not permitted.

May be capitalised and written off over five years.

Self-generated intangible assets (research and development)

There is an option to capitalise development costs in certain situations and write them off over their useful economic life.

As a general rule they should be recorded at current cost in the profit and loss account. However, both research and development costs may be capitalised if they have future worth, relate to a specific project and the costs allocated to the project are clearly separated and identifiable.

Research costs must be written off as incurred.

If capitalised they must be amortised over a period of no more than five years.

Goodwill

Only purchased goodwill may be capitalised.

Both direct elimination on acquisition against reserves and capitalisation with amortisation over the estimated useful economic life through the profit and loss account are allowed, although the first treatment is preferred.

Negative goodwill is shown as a reserve.

Only purchased goodwill may be capitalised.

Goodwill is capitalised and amortised up to five years. It is also permitted to amortise goodwill over a period of up to ten years. However, the reasons for this must be explained in the notes to the accounts.

When negative goodwill arises, the cause should be analysed and a provision (deferred income) set up if necessary. Alternatively it should be applied in reducing the value of the purchased asset, for example, in the event of a demonstrable decline in value thereof. If the negative goodwill is treated as deferred income, it should be applied to the profit and loss account when the future losses are in the acquired subsidiary or when the subsidiary is subsequently disposed of.

Tangible fixed assets

United Kingdom

Spain

Valuation

Stated at cost or at revalued amount less depreciation. There are certain circumstances under which buildings are not depreciated.

Revaluation is common for land and buildings. Any revaluation surplus is treated as unrealised and taken to a separate revalua-

Stated at cost less depreciation. Assets can only be revalued in accordance with tax law, the last such law was in 1983.

tion reserve. When a revalued asset is sold the profit or loss on sale is calculated by reference to the carrying value of asset. (See definition of 'note of historical cost profit and loss' in contents of financial statements.

Investment properties

These are included at open market value and not depreciated, although this requires a true and fair override over the provisions of the Companies Act in accordance with SSAP 19.

These are included at cost and depreciated.

Depreciation and grants

The treatment of depreciation and grants does not significantly differ between the UK and Spain.

Leasing

There are three types of lease:

- hire purchase contract: the hirer may acquire legal title by exercising an option to purchase the asset upon fulfilment of certain conditions;
- finance leases: the lessee has substantially all the risks and rewards associated with the ownership of the asset, other than the legal title.

For both of these:

- the asset is capitalised in the lessee's accounts;
- the asset is depreciated over the period of contract or the asset's useful life, whichever is less;
- interest is taken to the profit and loss account.

Assets held under leases are recorded as *intangibles* if there is no doubt that the option to purchase is going to be exercised.

This is deemed to be the case when:

- the option to purchase is lower than the estimated residual value;
- the option to purchase is minimal compared with net book amount of the contract.

When the option to purchase has been exercised the total value is transferred from intangible assets to *tangible assets*.

The value of the asset is the fair value at the start of the lease. It is depreciated over the useful eco-

- operating leases: the lessee pays a rental for the hire of an asset for a period of time which is normally substantially less than its useful economic life. The lessor retains most of the risks and rewards of ownership of the asset. The payments are debited to the lessee's profit and loss account.

nomic life of the asset.

The total interest payable is also recorded as a deferred liability and taken to the profit and loss account under a financing criterion during the contract life.

Investment valuation

United Kingdom

Under the historical cost accounting rules, investments are stated at cost or realisable value if there has been a permanent diminution in value which is charged to the profit and loss account. Any provision for diminution in value which is no longer required must be written back.

Under the alternative accounting rules, revaluation to market value is allowed. Any revaluation surpluses and temporary deficits are taken to a revaluation reserve.

Spain

The treatment is identical to the UK, but valuation above cost is not allowed.

Stocks

Valuation

United Kingdom

Stock is valued at the lower of historical cost and net realisable value. Only under the alternative accounting rules may stock be stated at the lower of current replacement cost and net realisable value.

Spain

Stocks are valued at the lower of cost or market value.

Cost is defined as:
- cost of purchase: comprising purchase price including import duties, transport and handling

Purchase cost is as defined in Spanish GAAP.

Other acceptable methods of valuing stock are 'first in, first out' (FIFO) and weighted average.

costs and any other directly attributable costs;

● cost of conversion: comprising cost which is attributable to units of production (direct labour, direct expenses and sub-contracted work) and production overheads.

Market value is defined as:

● raw materials: net realisable value or replacement cost, whichever is less;
● goods for resale and finished goods: realisable value net of selling costs;
● work in progress: net realisable value of the same finished goods less pending production costs and selling costs.

Where individual valuation is not appropriate the use of FIFO, LIFO or weighted average are permitted. FIFO is the most common. LIFO is not accepted for tax purposes.

Debtors

There are no major differences except for 'notes receivable'.

Notes receivable

United Kingdom

Letters of credit and bills of exchange work on the same basis but are much less common.

Spain

It is common business practice in Spain that a substantial part of the company's sales are collected by means of notes drawn against Spanish customers and remittances and letters of credit granted by financial institutions in the case of foreign customers.

When funds are needed in the

course of business, companies discount the notes with full recourse at the bank and receive a credit in the company's bank account on behalf of the company's client; in return the company has to pay interest and a charge.

When notes are discounted with the bank, the company's balance sheet must show:

- an assets account called 'discounted notes pending maturity', which is included under trade debtors;
- a liability account called 'discounted notes', which is included under short term loans.

When the notes mature; the client pays the amount shown in the notes to the bank and the various balances on these accounts are written off. If not, the bank reclaims the money due from the company's bank account.

Advance corporation tax

United Kingdom

Under UK tax law, when a company pays a dividend to its shareholders it must also pay a part of its corporation tax liability for the year in which the dividend is actually paid (not declared). This is known as Advance Corporation Tax (ACT).

Spain

There is no Spanish equivalent but companies are required to pay amounts on account of the corporation tax charge for the year. These payments on account are based on the prior year's tax charge and are made during the year, on the basis of a timetable established by the tax authorities.

Any ACT paid during a year is deducted from the corporation tax liability for that year. If a dividend is declared but not paid by the year end, then a liability is set up for the ACT payable. As that ACT will be deducted from the following year's corporation tax liability, an equal and opposite debtor, ACT recoverable, will also be set up.

The only effect on the profit and loss account arises when a company pays a dividend but has no likely future tax liability (current or deferred). In this situation the ACT may be irrecoverable and would be written off as part of the tax charge.

Capital instruments

United Kingdom

Direct issue costs are deducted from the proceeds of the issues. Other issue costs should be written off as incurred.

Spain

Share issue costs may be capitalised and written off over five years. Bond issue costs may be capitalised as deferred costs and written off over the period of the bond issue.

Business combinations (FRS 6)

United Kingdom

Strict criteria set out when merger and acquisition accounting may be adopted. Merger accounting is compulsory in a share for share exchange where at least 90 per cent of the nominal value of the shares in the undertaking are owned by the parent company. In addition the following criteria must be met:

Spain

A *fusión* is the Spanish legal term for the merger of companies. Such a merger occurs when one of the companies transfers its assets and liabilities to another, and legally ceases to exist.

There are two types of *fusión*:

(i) when a company already incorporated absorbs another company's assets and liabilities; and

- no party is portrayed as acquirer or acquired;
- all parties to the combination participate in establishing the ongoing management structure;
- the relative sizes of the parties are not so disparate that one dominates the other by virtue of size;
- the consideration is mainly equity shares;
- no equity shareholders retain any material interest in the future performance of only part of the combined entity.

The FRS gives companies a choice of whether to adopt merger or acquisition accounting only in the case of a group reconstruction where the ultimate shareholder remains the same and the use of merger accounting is not prohibited by law.

All other business combinations must be accounted for as acquisitions.

Acquisition accounting must be carried out at fair value. The fair value of an asset is defined as the amount at which it could be exchanged in an arm's length transaction between informed and willing parties, other than in a forced or liquidation sale. No future plans or strategies may be taken into account when determining fair value. This means that it is not allowable to include provisions for post acquisition restructuring plans or future operating losses in the fair value exercise. These will be accounted for as expenses in the periods in which they are incurred.

(ii) when a new company as part of the incorporation and share capital payment process absorbs another company's assets and liabilities.

Mergers are accounted for in the following ways:

- merger of interests (*fusión de intereses*)

When there is no clear dominance by one company in the merger and the total assets and liabilities of each company are similar, the merger is recorded as an aggregate of the original book values of the assets and liabilities.

- acquisition merger (*fusión de adquisición*)

When one of the merged companies (A) has net shareholders' equity of more than twice that of the other company (B) it is assumed that company A has acquired company B.

In this case the assets and liabilities of company B are booked at fair market value.

- merger between related parties

In the case of mergers between group companies the final equity on merger is the same as the net equity recorded in the consolidated accounts of the group.

The Spanish treatment of post acquisition costs is similar to that of the UK, although it has not been specifically dealt with in the accounting literature.

The mechanics of acquisition accounting are largely similar to the UK except that goodwill is capitalised as discussed in intangible assets above.

RESERVES

United Kingdom	Spain

Statutory reserve–legal reserve

No comparable reserve in UK accounts.

Companies are obliged to transfer 10 per cent of the profits for the year to a legal reserve until such reserve reaches an amount at least equal to 20 per cent of the share capital. This reserve is not distributable to shareholders and may only be used to offset losses if no other reserves are available. Under certain conditions it may be used to increase share capital by applying the part exceeding 10 per cent of the capital already increased.

Dividends must not be distributed until the legal reserve reaches 10 per cent of the share capital.

Share premium account

The share premium account represents the consideration received for shares in excess of their nominal value but net of any share issue expenses. In certain cases, where shares are issued in exchange for acquiring at least 90 per cent of the equity share in another company, merger relief under the Companies Act 1985 applies and no share premium account will arise.

The share premium, arising from capital increases is subject to the same restrictions and may be used for the same purposes as the voluntary, ie distributable, reserves of the company, including conversion into share capital.

All intangible assets must be written down and any accumulated losses taken into account before the share premium or voluntary reserves are distributed.

This reserve is not distributable but may be used to write off preliminary expenses and premiums payable on redemption of debentures.

With the permission of the courts, an amount of the share premium may be redesignated as a special reserve and used to write off goodwill.

Revaluation reserve

The revaluation reserve represents the amounts capitalised in excess of historical cost when fixed assets are revalued. This reserve which is not distributable. If the asset is depreciated, the additional depreciation charge is transferred to the profit and loss reserves. A similar reserve movement occurs when the revalued asset is sold.

As discussed in the tangible fixed asset section, revaluations are only allowed under a specific law, which may be national (the last one was in 1983) or regional.

ACCRUALS AND PROVISIONS

United Kingdom

In the UK, financial statements reflect the financial impact of activities of the period and not only cash outgoings. As such, accruals are made for expenses where an invoice has not yet been received and provisions are made for pensions, deferred taxes and other items of a less quantifiable nature.

Spain

Accruals and provisions are the same as in the UK.

DEFERRED TAXATION

United Kingdom

Under SSAP 15, deferred tax is accounted for on a partial provision basis. The ASB is reviewing SSAP 15 and giving careful consideration to the full provision basis. A defer-

Spain

Deferred tax is accounted under the liability method.

A deferred tax liability should always be provided.

red tax liability should be provided only to the extent that it is probable that the liability will crystallise.

A deferred tax asset may be carried on the balance sheet when it is expected to be recoverable within the foreseeable future without replacement by equivalent debt balances. In practice these are rare.

A deferred tax asset may be included only when it is expected to be recoverable within the foreseeable future. That is expected when the following circumstances apply:

- the foreseeable future is shorter than ten years;
- the company does not usually make losses.

EXCEPTIONAL AND EXTRAORDINARY ITEMS

United Kingdom

Exceptional items

Exceptional items are defined as material items which derive from events or transactions that fall within the ordinary activities of the company and which individually or, if of a similar type, in aggregate, need to be disclosed by virtue of their size or incidence if the financial statements are to give a true and fair view.

As far as disclosure is concerned, there are two groups of exceptional items.

First, those exceptional items which must be disclosed separately on the face of the profit and loss account in all cases and be allocated to the appropriate heading of continuing or discontinued operations. These are:

- profit or losses on the sale or termination of an operation;

Spain

The term 'exceptional items' is not used in the Spanish legislation. It is common practice to disclose material exceptional items in the notes.

- costs of a fundamental reorganisation or restructuring;
- profit or losses on the disposal of fixed assets.

Second, other exceptional items which are debited or credited to the statutory format heading to which they relate, analysed between continuing or discontinued operations as appropriate. The amount of each exceptional item, either individually or as an aggregate of items of a similar type, should be disclosed separately by way of a note, or on the face of the profit and loss account in that a degree of prominence is required in order to give a true and fair view.

Extraordinary items

These are material items possessing a high degree of abnormality which arise from events or transactions that fall outside the ordinary activities of the company and which are not expected to recur. They do not include exceptional items nor do they include normal recurring adjustments or connections of accounting estimates made in prior periods. The ASB considers them to be so rare that no examples are given in FRS 3.

The permissible items for inclusion are much wider than in the UK. To be considered as an extraordinary item an event or transaction must:

- fall outside of the ordinary activity of the company;
- have a high degree of abnormality.

Prior year adjustments

Modification to prior year figures is permitted if:

- they contain a fundamental error;
- an accounting policy is changed.

Prior year adjustments are accounted under extraordinary items. No modification to prior year figures is permitted.

FOREIGN CURRENCY TREATMENT

United Kingdom

There are different accounting treatments for differences in exchange rates, depending on whether they are applied to short-term, long-term (projects over one year) or group investment.

For **short-term** balances, exchange rate differences, both realised and unrealised, are taken into the profit and loss account.

For **long-term** balances unrealised exchange gains are taken to reserves and reported in the statement of total recognised gains and losses.

Group investments in businesses conducted in foreign currencies are consolidated by applying the closing exchange rate to the balance sheet and either the closing or average exchange rate to the profit and loss account. Differences between opening and closing or average and closing rates are taken directly to reserves.

Finally, SSAP20 permits a net investment approach which allows group investments in a foreign currency to be hedged by a currency loan such that the net foreign exchange difference can be taken direct to reserves.

Spain

The treatment is very similar to the UK except that only realised gains (short- or long-term) are credited to the profit and loss account. Unrealised differences are recorded as a liability and are transferred to the profit and loss account when realised.

Specific accounting treatments exist for certain companies providing services at prices regulated by the state (eg electricity generating companies, motorway concessionary companies etc).

The treatment is as per the UK. In both countries, where the activities of an investment are closely related to those of the investor in such a manner that they may be considered as an extension of the activity of the latter, the conversion is carried out using the temporal method. This means that non cash amounts are converted at historical rates and exchange differences are taken to profit and loss.

This is not specifically considered by Spanish accounting standards.

PENSIONS

United Kingdom

Pension schemes are normally established by way of a legally separate fund, which is not shown on the balance sheet. Benefits are covered by the pension funds, therefore no provision is normally required apart from payments due to the pension fund. There are two categories of pension schemes:

- defined contribution schemes where the benefits are defined by reference to the contributions made and where the employer merely has to pay a pre-defined level of contribution;
- defined benefit schemes where the employee is guaranteed a benefit usually by reference to the final salary and the length of employment. Payments made by the employer to the scheme are dictated by actuarial assessment of the funding required to meet the cost of the benefits to be paid.

A benefit or surplus within the fund will accrue in the sponsoring company's accounts as the charge required by SSAP 24 is based on the long term cost (which may be different from the current funding requirement).

Spain

Provisions were not made obligatory until 1990 with the implementation of the revised 'General Accounting Plan' in that year. At present pension costs charged in any year are those relating to the year plus, transitionally until the year 2005 for past service costs for active employees, and 1997 for retired employees (see Chapter 9.1), a minimum of 1/15th of unprovided past service cost in respect of active employees and 1/7th for retired employees.

Part 5

Financial System and Banking

INTRODUCTION

During the 1980s and early 1990s the Spanish financial sector experienced a dramatic process of deregulation and emancipation to the free flow of capital investments. Monetary and administrative controls have been removed and a large number of more or less subtle barriers to financial investment in and out of Spain have been abolished. As a consequence of this, foreign investment in Spanish securities has grown to reach in some cases 40 per cent of the value traded, and the position taken by foreign institutional investors determines the daily behaviour of Spanish markets.

In less than a decade Spain has also witnessed an enormous development in the sector of financial services, with a large number of firms offering a wide variety of modern international services. The reader will find a detailed description of these developments in Chapter 5.1 and an introduction to the whole financial framework.

Banks have traditionally played a major role in the Spanish economy, due not only to their size but also to the underlying culture which has linked them with large industrial conglomerates. Banks tend to get involved in the development of emerging markets, like telecommunications for example, but they also maintain important stakes in all kind of more traditional industries.

The late 1980s and early 1990s have been years characterised by an intensive process of concentration in the banking sector. Whether this process will continue in the near future and which institutions could be involved has prompted rumours in the financial markets. Chapter 5.2 offers an interesting picture of the Spanish banking sector and its major players which will help the reader to assess their importance, while Chapter 5.3 studies in detail the services available from Spanish banks and considers possible developments in this area in the next few years.

5.1

The Spanish Financial System

Gaceta de los Negocios

The Spanish financial system is organised around two large markets, namely the government securities market and the stock market. There are also other less-developed markets, such as the private fixed-interest market and the recently established derivatives market. In this chapter reference will also be made to mutual funds, a form of collective investment that is on the increase in Spain. In general, the following three characteristics are common to the Spanish markets:

- high efficiency, despite the short time they have been established and the recent nature of the current regulations;
- high concentration. A large proportion of trading is centred on the government securities market, whereas the equity market records more moderate levels. Business on the Spanish stock exchanges is dominated, in any case, by a small number of blue-chip stocks;
- increasing presence of foreign investment. Active portfolio management of non-residents has been one of the most important driving forces behind the development of the Spanish markets.

The most important financial market in Spain in terms of size is the government securities market, with a mean daily trading volume of 350,000 million pesetas (1994 figures). This is a relatively recent market, which was institutionalised in 1987 with the introduction of the book entry system and rationalisation of the number of instruments traded. It leads the most developed markets, since it permits efficient price-setting and its interest rates serve as reference for all the capital markets and for the banking system. If 1987 was a decisive year for the Spanish government securities market, its second 'Big Bang' was in 1991 with the introduction of internationalisation. This has made the market more operative and the inflow of capital from non-residents, particularly from institutions with active portfolio management, has led to rapid development of the market, especially in trading of medium- and long-term securities.

The government securities market arose as a consequence of the increasing weight of government debt in the economy and is designed to meet the financing requirements of the public sector, both at national and regional (Autonomous Community) level, with the lowest possible cost/risk ratio. Nevertheless, government debt policy also has other aims, such as contribution to improved operation of the markets or encouragement of private saving. This market took off when the state began to develop financing policy distant from the privileges granted up to 1984 by the Bank of Spain; a process that culminated in prohibition by the central bank of acquisition of government securities directly from the Treasury, in accordance with the Maastricht Treaty, and in particular in the 1994 Bank of Spain Independence Act.

Since the book entry system was introduced in April 1987, the instruments traded on the government securities market have been basically reduced to two types: short-term financing (Treasury Bills) and long-term financing (government bonds and debentures).

Treasury Bills are the most important debt instrument issued by the Treasury. They are issued at a discount, with a par value per unit of 1 million pesetas and with maturities of three, six and 12 months. They are directed towards domestic savers interested in short-term investment. **Government bonds and debentures** are identical to Treasury Bills save in that they have longer maturities: from two to five years in the case of bonds and more than five years in the case of debentures. These instruments are directed towards institutional investors and the demand includes a high proportion of non-resident investors, due to the fact that yields on government stock are exempt from taxation in Spain and, in consequence, the withholding tax on the coupon is immediately reimbursed.

The government securities market is organised around the Book Entry Register of the Bank of Spain, which is the governing body. It acts as a central register and, together with the management entities, makes up the book entry system. Any individual or corporate person may open an account in the central register for subscription of government securities directly from the Bank of Spain. At a secondary level are the market members: account-holding entities with their own accounts and management entities. The account-holding entities are required to have a minimum capital of 200 million pesetas and may only operate on the market on their own behalf, whereas the management entities have either full or restricted powers according to the kind of intermediation they undertake. Those with full powers may operate on their own behalf and may also perform any authorised operation with their clients. Capital of 750 million pesetas is required, as well as a minimum client balance of 20,000 million pesetas. This group includes the market makers, another more select group of entities with a special commitment and whose purpose is to contribute sufficient liquidity to the market, listing purchase and sale prices for certain issues and with a minimum trading volume.

With regard to the form of operation, distinction may be made between two markets, namely the primary and the secondary markets. The primary market refers to issue of securities by the state and operates in Spain by means of competitive auction, with maximum limits and means of award. All bids for securities are received by the Treasury and are arranged in decreasing order according to the price offered. Once the volume to be issued has been established, the minimum price accepted, or the marginal price, is determined. All bids made offering prices equal to or higher than the marginal price are then awarded or distributed on a pro rata basis and the Treasury establishes a public issue schedule to coincide with the redemption dates of the assets. On the secondary market, different forms of trading coexist. The general system is for account-holders to perform operations between themselves, by telephone, either directly or through an intermediary or broker. There is also a wholesale trading system, known as the 'blind market', on which the parties do not know their counterparties, the listings are firm and the transactions may be made either electronically or by telephone. This latter system is almost exclusively reserved to the market makers. A third trading area comprises the management entities and their third parties. This is the most usual form of trading of government securities, in which the abovementioned entities acquire securities on the primary market for subsequent sale to non-residents, mutual funds, pension funds, insurance companies, non-financial companies or individuals.

The development of the government securities market runs parallel to non-resident interest in Spanish securities. This has permitted the generation of an active sub-market between non-resident third parties, with its activity based on Euroclear and Cedel, the international settlement and clearing systems on the Eurobond market.

STOCK EXCHANGES

The Spanish stock market is organised as a dual system in which the four traditional stock exchanges (Madrid, Barcelona, Bilbao and Valencia) coexist with a national stock market based on the Stock Exchange Interconnection System (SIB). The SIB is managed by the stock exchange company in which each of the four companies governing the traditional exchanges has a holding. In turn, these governing companies are responsible for management and administration of the respective stock exchanges. With the stock market reform of 1988, the figure of the stockbroker was replaced by new corporate intermediaries that may be divided into two categories: stock market companies and stock market agencies. The principal difference between these two groups lies in the fact that the agencies may only perform simple inter- mediation functions and may not trade on their own behalf, nor offer credit nor underwrite issues. The minimum capital required of stock market agencies is 150 million pesetas, whereas a minimum of 750 mil- lion pesetas is required of stock market companies. Both the companies and the agencies are subject to supervision, inspection and control by the National Stock Market Commission (CNMV) (see also Chapter 5.2).

Trading on the Spanish stock exchange operates by means of an auto- mated trading order-driven system, with immediate circulation of data on operations performed in order to give greater transparency to the price-formation process. The automated trading system is based on the Spanish Stock Exchange Interconnection System (SIBE) which, on 2 November 1995, replaced the Computer-Assisted Trading System (CATS) and works by matching purchase and sale prices. The market operates continuously from 11.00 to 17.00 hours, with a pre-session from 10.00 to 11.00 hours. The electronic system channels 95 per cent of the trading volume, although the traditional floor system still exists in Spain, limited to small companies listed on one or several of the four exchanges. Floor trading is conducted in successive periods of ten min- utes, for different groups of shares, between 10.00 and 12.00 hours. The maximum price fluctuation allowed is 10 per cent in the first period and 20 per cent in the second. Since 1992, settlement and clearing of oper- ations is made through the book entry system, with creation of the Stock Settlement and Clearing Service (SCLV) in which all the differ- ent stock exchanges and attached companies (stock market companies and agencies and brokers) participate. The SCLV handles clearing of stocks and cash resulting from stock market trading and keeps the accounting register of stocks represented by means of book entries and admitted for trading on the stock exchanges. The settlement period for transactions is five business days as from the date of the operation.

Each stock exchange has its own index, although the most important index, by virtue of its higher circulation and use, is the General Index of the Madrid Stock Exchange. This is due to the fact that the Madrid Exchange records the highest trading volume, accounting for more than 75 per cent of the total. However, the automated trading system also has a selective index, the IBEX-35, which consists of the 35 leading stocks and represents the most liquid shares traded in the system. The IBEX-35 is reviewed twice a year, at the beginning of each calendar half-year. The index is adjusted when any of the companies included make a capital increase or are affected by a merger or absorption; it is not adjusted as a result of payment of dividends.

The Spanish stock market is characterised by a high degree of concentration. Despite the large number of companies listed on the market (763 at the end of 1993), only a small proportion of these may be considered significant, in terms of both market capitalisation and trading. Furthermore, the trading volume is concentrated on very specific sectors, with banking, energy and telecommunications accounting for almost 70 per cent. Broking activity is also highly concentrated, since more than 60 per cent of the market share corresponds to the ten most active members. The Spanish automated trading market reflects a high level of correlation with the foreign markets, due to the process of internationalisation seen in recent years. Operations by non-residents have grown significantly and currently account for 40 per cent of the market. The average P/E ratio (ratio between price and earnings per share) on the Spanish automated trading market is one of the lowest.

PRIVATE FIXED-INTEREST

This is a market, not well developed in Spain, on which all securities with pre-established yields issued by private or public companies, autonomous bodies and credit entities are traded, with a view to obtaining financing directly from the final investor. A large number of securities of very different kinds are traded on this market: some are issued at a discount, others operate by means of regular coupons, and the securities may be short-, medium- or long-term. In addition, all kinds of international innovations, such as warrants, zero coupons, prepayment options, indexed floating rates, etc are traded on this market. Despite the diverse nature of all these operations, the market may be divided into two segments: notes, and bonds and debentures. The private fixed-interest sector has a long history in Spain, although it has only been developed in the last three decades, and is important in issue of securities by public sector companies, electricity companies and some companies in the communications sector. The issue requirements have been established in highly detailed legislation by the National Stock Market Commission (CNMV), in an endeavour to protect the interests of the small investor, and the issuers must receive the approval of the CNMV. The issuing company is obliged to inform this latter of all the characteristics of the issue (the persons to whom it is addressed, the rights and obligations of the holders, the legal and financial nature of the securities, the issuer) and of the company's economic situation, by means of the audit reports of the annual financial statements of the last two years prior to the issue. All this information will be contained in the Issue Particulars, which must be deposited with the CNMV and made available, free of charge, to the possible subscribers and the general public.

The financial instruments present on the private fixed-interest market may be divided between short-term securities (with maturity of less than 18 months), particularly notes and mortgage bonds, and long-term securities which include the bonds and debentures issued by institutions other than the state.

Notes are issued by both public and private bodies and offer implicit returns. They are most common in the form of commercial paper issued by private, financial or non-financial, companies. The issues are generally made by means of a programme with a maximum issue balance and are directed to small investors and mutual funds. They are awarded by competitive auction, at which the securities are acquired by intermediaries for subsequent placement with final investors. In some cases issues are made 'to measure', with specific paper designed by the issuer for a specific investor and with agreement on the terms and characteristics of the issue between the issuer and the final investor. The Spanish national railways, RENFE, was the first company in Spain to issue commercial paper on a regular and large-scale basis and has developed its own system based on book entries centralised within a small number of collaborating financial institutions.

Bonds and debentures are medium- and long-term securities normally issued by large public companies, financial entities and electricity companies. The issuers have a tradition and presence on the market and are sufficiently well-known to the investors (companies such as Telefonica, for example). The most usual form of issue on the Spanish market has been the unsecured bond, with explicit coupon and single repayment, although a number of variations have also been developed. An important phenomenon on the Spanish fixed-interest market is the increasing presence of foreign issuers that have opted to issue part of their debt in pesetas, thus creating the **matador bonds**. Since 1992 these bonds have been fully liberalised and are generally issued unsecured, with maturities of between three and ten years. The most usual method of issue is syndicated underwriting through financial entities that undertake to place the bonds among their customers.

Private fixed-interest securities are traded on two kinds of secondary markets, one directed to small investors and the other with a more institutional nature. The first is represented by the stock exchanges (up to 1987 the only secondary market organised in Spain), and the second by the AIAF market, or wholesale segment of the market.

The AIAF was created by an Order of 1991 as the sole authorised non-official market trading bonds and debentures, commercial paper and mortgage securities in the fixed-interest segment. Long-term securities in pesetas issued by non-residents are traded in the matador bond segment. The AIAF is the market's governing body and is organised around the member financial entities that operate on their own behalf and on behalf of others, with no restrictions whatsoever. Furthermore, before an instrument is traded, ESPACLEAR, a company that acts as register, settlement and clearing house of the securities traded on the AIAF market, must be informed.

Credit rating was unusual in Spain up to the beginning of the 1990s when the demand first appeared, leading to large-scale expansion that has granted the private fixed-interest market greater transparency. Since 1992 there are three rating agencies in Spain: Moody's Investor Service, SA, IBCA Rating España, SA and Iberating, SA, in which Standard & Poors has a holding. The Kingdom of Spain holds the maximum rating (Aa2 AA), together with a number of Autonomous Communities (Spanish regional governments), large public companies and financial entities. The minimum rating issued for a parent company in the long-term is A (Iberating) and A3 (Moody's) and, in consequence, only highly solvent issuers are classified, all with the 'degree of investment' or 'prime 1'.

DERIVATIVES

The development of derivatives in Spain is a recent phenomenon since, although they had been traded since 1989, it was in 1992, with the birth of MEFF Holding, that they began to take off. MEFF Sociedad Holding is the governing company of the derivatives market, together with MEFF Renta Fija and MEFF Renta Variable, companies entrusted with management of derived products on the fixed-interest and equity markets, respectively. This structure has given the Spanish derivatives market a greater degree of importance, and has rationalised the number of products on offer. One of the novel features introduced by MEFF in Spain is the roll-over contract which permits transfer of a position in one contract to the next contract. This makes it an effective instrument for hedging operations and also for investors who are looking for more risky or more speculative positions. This market has high growth potential, particularly if it is compared with its European counterparts or with the derivatives market in the United States.

In the fixed-interest segment, particular mention should be made of the importance of **notional 10-year bond futures**, launched by MEFF in 1992, since these are the fixed-interest futures with the highest rate of development. Futures are also traded on 3- and 5-year bonds, in order to make the market more operational, but the trading volumes are very low. **Interest rate futures** have also been developed in Spain, on MIBOR (the Madrid interbank market) and 90 and 360 days. In the case of the equity market, MEFF Renta Variable has developed **futures and options contracts** on the IBEX-35, the selective index of the Spanish automated trading market. The high degree of liquidity, representation and transparency of this index means that it meets all the conditions for derivatives trading. In addition to these contracts, options on shares are also traded, although they are limited to certain stocks. These options currently exist in Spain over shares of ENDESA, TELEFONICA, BANCO BILBAO VIZCAYA and REPSOL.

The MEFF futures and options markets are governed by the 1991 Regulations which establish the composition, operation, transactions and rules of operation of these markets. Derivatives trading systems differ between fixed-interest and equity. In the case of fixed-interest, there are 73 market members, of whom 50 are settlement and custodian members, 15 are settlement members and eight are traders. The shareholders and members of MEFF Renta Fija (fixed-interest) include a broad representation of the Spanish financial institutions. Any client may have access to the market once they have opened a trading account with any of the members of the Chamber. There is also a more restricted group, the market makers, whose function is to make trading liquid. Daily positions are taken by means of a real-time electronic system, with cover established through the General Guarantees System which restricts the number of positions that may be covered on a person's own behalf during one session. In the case of equity, trading on MEFF Renta Variable corresponds to the principle of unit of price and the operations have public nature. The MEFF S/MART electronic system means that information on the positions taken and the amounts to be settled is continuously updated.

INSTITUTIONAL INVESTMENT

Collective investment institutions (IICs) are considered to be those market financial instruments that grant to their individual participants the results obtained from the collective assets contributed by these latter, independently of the legal structure of the collective assets. These institutions may or may not be financial in nature. Financial collective investment institutions include fixed-capital investment trusts or floating-capital investment trusts (SIMs or SIMCAVs), mutual funds (FIMs) and money market mutual funds (FIAMMs). Non-financial collective investment institutions are made up of property investment funds, property investment trusts and other funds (works of art, philately, etc). Authorisation from the Ministry of Economy is required for creation of a collective investment institution, together with registry with the National Stock Market Commission (CNMV).

Mutual funds are the most popular collective investment system in Spain. They represent professional portfolio management with diversification of risk and restricted costs per operation. However the most important aspect of these funds, and that which has led to their great popularity, is their fiscal treatment. If held for more than a year, mutual funds are taxed as irregular, rather than regular, income, and they are exempt from taxation, by law, if held for more than 15 years and a day. They pay 1 per cent under corporate income tax. In individual income tax, any capital gains generated by mutual funds have a correcting coefficient of 7.14 per cent per annum as from the second year, with total exemption as from the 15th year if the fund is maintained.

The regulations governing the collective investment instruments date from 1984, although these regulations were not implemented and the funds did not begin to grow in Spain until 1990.

Mutual funds consist of assets contributed by a group of investors. Their investment policy is directed by a management company and their assets are held by a deposit entity under the control of the National Stock Market Commission (CNMV) and the Directorate General of the Treasury. The realisable value of a fund is the ratio between the net assets and the number of units and is the price at which units may be bought or sold. According to the manner in which investors receive their returns, a distinction may be made between **income funds**, which periodically distribute profits, and **capitalization funds**, which reinvest any income into the fund. A further distinction may be made according to the maturity of the financial instruments in which the funds invest, since whereas ordinary mutual funds (FIMs) have no restrictions on the maturity of the stocks held in their portfolios, money market mutual funds (FIAMMs) make 90 per cent of their investments in instruments with maturity of less than 18 months. These funds have grown at a tremendous pace in Spain in recent years, with an increasing number of investors preferring the short term. The policy of the FIMs, however, is directed to the long term, with a minimum capital requirement of 500 million pesetas. FIMs are obliged to invest at least 80 per cent of their assets in fixed-interest securities, or in equities listed on a stock exchange or on other organised markets. Units must be repaid within a maximum of 72 hours. On the contrary, FIAMMs invest in short-term money market instruments such as Treasury Bills, repos and commercial paper, with average maturity of less than 18 months. The minimum assets amount to 1,500 million pesetas and at least 90 per cent of assets must be invested in fixed-interest securities traded on an official market or in other short-term stocks or assets with high liquidity.

The *Fondtesoros* (literally, Treasury funds) constitute a special group of funds, 95 per cent of whose assets are invested in government securities. These funds may be either FIMs or FIAMMs, according to the maturity of the securities held. They have grown significantly in Spain, with total assets as of 31 December 1995 of a record figure of more than 12 trillion pesetas.

Investment trusts (SIMs) are on the decline in Spain, as a consequence of the rise in mutual funds. There are several differences between mutual funds and investment trusts:

- investment trusts are companies with shares, whose object is to invest on the stock exchange, whereas investors in mutual funds acquire units whose value varies over time;
- in mutual funds, the daily realisable value coincides with the stock market value, whereas in investment trusts this is not the case, since they are generally listed with a sharp discount on their realisable value;
- in investment trusts the price depends on supply and demand; in mutual funds the price is determined by the realisable value;
- there is no guarantee of liquidity in investment trusts, whereas it is guaranteed by law in mutual funds.

Fixed-capital investment trusts have become less important in the Spanish financial system due to the low liquidity of their shares with which to attract investors. **Floating-capital investment trusts**

(SIMCAVs) were introduced to counteract this effect, since their capital may be increased or reduced, in accordance with their by-laws, by sale or acquisition of their own shares without the necessary agreement of the General Meeting of Shareholders. In reality, however, nor do they play an important part on the market.

Pension funds constitute another form of collective investment. The corresponding regulations establish that 90 per cent of the assets of pension plans and funds must be invested in financial assets traded on officially recognised organised markets with regular operations, in credits backed by mortgage guarantees and in property. Within this percentage, investment in bank deposits may not exceed 15 per cent of the fund. As a liquidity coefficient, 1 per cent of pension funds' assets must be held in demand deposits or money market assets with maturity of no more than three months. The fiscal advantage of these funds over other forms of saving is that the contributions are classed as deductible expenses in Individual Income Tax (IRPF), although with a limit of 15 per cent of total employment income and with a maximum contribution of 750,000 pesetas per annum. This figure has recently been raised to 1 million pesetas by the Ministry of Economy. Moreover, these are the only funds in which a change in the management entity entails no fiscal penalisation. The principal disadvantage of the pension funds, however, is that the sums contributed are only available upon retirement, invalidity or death.

Insurance companies form an important part of the collective investment institutions since they channel a large proportion of the savings of individuals. The sector is divided between many small companies, although its weight on the markets has increased in recent years as the insurance companies have gradually abandoned the property investments that were very common up to the early 1990s.

TRENDS ON THE SPANISH MARKETS

1996 began with the Bank of Spain's decision to cut interest rates by 25 basis points on 12 January. The reference rate now stands at 8.75 per cent. It will be an atypical year, marked by an electoral process that will have a direct effect on investment. Nonetheless, the expectations regarding the general election have not prevented foreign money from returning in force to the Spanish stock markets. Following a certain crisis in investor confidence, the government securities market has benefited from this inflow of capital which has served to take yields down to minimum levels, below 10 per cent in the longer maturities. And more significantly, the peseta has become the strongest currency in the European Monetary System, boosted by the entry of foreign capital into the country.

The performance of the Spanish markets in 1996 will depend on a variety of factors. The international context will be determinant, especially if the prospects of a slow rate of growth in all the developed economies are confirmed. The forecasts of international bodies and experts estimate economic growth for Spain below 3 per cent. Interest rates will also affect the Spanish markets, since although the general trend is for maintenance, the majority of analysts believe there is still room for a cut in long-term rates, due to moderation in prices and containment of the public deficit. This could lead to a flat interest rate curve. The peseta could post moderate appreciation against the German currency, due to the gradual decrease in the political risk premium.

The prospects for the Spanish stock market are positive. Corporate balance sheets are sound and corporate profits are expected to increase significantly during the year. This, together with a reduction in the political risk factor following the general election in March and falling interest rates, leads us to contemplate returns, for the Stock Market as a whole, in the order of 20 per cent in 1996.

The experts forecast that 1996 will be a good year in fixed-interest, especially in the medium- and long-term, although lower returns are expected than in 1995. In the case of equity, the estimates are more positive, thanks to corporate recovery and a more favourable economic climate.

5.2

The Spanish Banking System in 1995

Fernando Cortiñas, Instituto de Empresa

Spain, like most of the countries in continental Europe, has a financial system based on the 'universal banking' concept. This means that, unlike those existing in Anglo-Saxon countries, any financial institution in Spain could engage in different activities within the industry, eg investment, corporate or personal banking. For this reason, many Spanish financial institutions were in the past very active in 'industrial banking', holding huge stakes in non-financial companies, mainly utilities and manufacturing concerns. Although these stakes are still significant today, financial institutions in Spain are following a trend to divest their non-financial activities, concentrating their efforts and resources in banking.

THE STRUCTURE OF THE BANKING SYSTEM

In Spain in mid-1995, there were more than 300 financial institutions, but only 217 of them held total assets of more than 1,500 million pesetas each (US$12 million). Together, these 217 institutions represented total assets well above 112 trillion pesetas, about US$925 billion, comprising deposits of 62 trillion pesetas and outstanding loans of 48 trillion pesetas.

The Spanish banking system is made up of three different types of institution:

- *bancos*;
- *cajas de ahorro*;
- *cooperativas de crédito*.

Bancos are financial institutions, state or privately owned, equivalent to what in the English-speaking world can be defined as banks in its widest concept, from investment to retailer banks. According to official data provided by the Spanish Association of Banking (*Asociación Española de Banca Privada* – AEB), at the beginning of 1995 there were 165 banks, 110 of Spanish origin and 55 of foreign origin, 23 from EU countries and 32 from non-EU countries (mainly Switzerland and the US). In mid-1995, *bancos* concentrated almost two thirds of the total assets in the system; national banks represented about 53 per cent, and the remaining 13 per cent was under the control of foreign banks or Spanish subsidiaries of foreign banks.

At the beginning of 1995, banks employed more than 150,000 people in almost 17,500 branches, as follows:

Bank origin	Spanish	Foreign (EU)	Foreign (Non-EU)	Foreign (Total)	Total Spain
No of banks	110	23	32	55	165
Employees	147,135	2,343	1,146	3,489	150,624
Branches	17,373	96	37	133	17,469

Source: *AEB, Informe Anual 1994*

Cajas de ahorro, in English known as savings banks, are state-owned, non-profit financial institutions whose main purpose is to promote credit with social aims. They generally depend on governments at provincial level (*cajas provinciales*) or even at town hall level (*cajas municipales*) and, as non-profit institutions, their earnings are reinvested in order to increase their capital base.

Beyond their specific legal form, another feature that in the past distinguished the *cajas de ahorro* was that they operated under certain constraints regarding their geographical expansion. They could only act within the limits of the region to which they belonged, and if they wanted to go beyond these boundaries they needed special authorisation. However, this constraint disappeared a few years ago, resulting in a very intense merging and acquisition activity. According to the 1994 annual report of the Spanish Confederation of Savings Banks (*Confederación Española de Cajas de Ahorro* – CECA) at the beginning of 1995 there were 54 *cajas de ahorro* in Spain.

Together the *cajas* handled about one third of the total assets in Spain's financial system, and two of them – *La Caixa de Estalvis i Pensións de Barcelona* (known as *La Caixa*) and *Cajamadrid* – ranked among the top ten Spanish financial institutions.

The third branch of the Spanish financial system is composed of the *cooperativas de crédito*, privately-owned credit cooperatives or mutual banks. There are two different types of cooperatives: the *cooperativas de crédito profesionales y populares* – professional associations related to urban areas, and the *cajas rurales* – those formed by farmers, which represent the bulk of the *cooperativas*.

Cooperativas are important from a social point of view, insofar as they provide credit to small businesses and entrepreneurs who otherwise would have difficulty obtaining finance from banks; they are also important in terms of geographic coverage: in mid-1995, the *cooperativas* had 3,541 branches, mainly in rural areas, with about 11,200 employees.

However, when considered from the perspective of their relative share of the total assets in the financial system, they are negligible. Although there are more than 100 *cooperativas* they account for less than 3 per cent of total assets, and only four of them rank among the top 100 Spanish institutions; the biggest, *Caja Laboral Popular*, with about 600 billion pesetas in total assets, occupies only the 38th place in the Spanish ranking of financial institutions.

A HIGHLY-CONCENTRATED SYSTEM

Since the late 1980s, the financial sector in Spain has experienced strong consolidation, and it seems that this trend will continue in the future. As a result of this, the Spanish banking system has become very concentrated.

In mid-1995, the first seven financial groups held almost 67 trillion pesetas, representing about 60 per cent of the total assets in the system as follows:

Position	Group	Total assets (trillion pesetas)
1	Banco de Santander-Banesto	14,3
2	BBV (Banco Bilbao-Vizcaya)	13,4
3	Argentaria	12,1
4	BCH (Banco Central Hispanoamericano)	10,3
5	La Caixa (caja de ahorro)	8,5
6	Cajamadrid (caja de ahorro)	4,7
7	Banco Popular	3,3
Total		66,6

Source: *Cinco Dias*, 21 July 1995

This concentration was fuelled by the deregulation process which started in the late 1970s. Until then the Spanish financial industry was a closed, exclusive club, an oligopoly reluctant to compete. In was in the mid-1970s when the regulators – the *Banco de España* – decided to open the financial system, forcing the institutions into competition.

Barriers to geographic expansion and the opening of new branches were removed, foreign banks were allowed to operate in Spain under the same conditions as those awarded to national institutions, rules regarding prices and introduction of new products and services became more flexible, and new accounting rules aimed at increasing information transparency were introduced. This new competition forced the established players to become more efficient or lose out completely. Slowly, deregulation began to bear fruits, beginning in the second half of the 1980s, when it fuelled a strong merging and acquisition activity that led to a higher concentration in the system.

Competition proved to be healthy both for the financial institutions as well as for their customers. After the consolidation process, *bancos* and *cajas de ahorro* have a stronger competitive position. They are bigger and leaner, providing better products and services, and have reduced very heavy cost structures.

PRESENT CHALLENGES

In spite of all the progress made, there is still plenty of room for improvement. The financial industry in Spain is still over-large: too many institutions, too many branches, and excessive overheads indicate that there is a need for further efficiency. The products and services offered in different banks and savings banks are more or less the same. New products and services are quickly and widely copied, so product differentiation is not a key factor in attracting or keeping clients. Price has become a very important issue, and increased competition has meant a decrease in margins. In turn, squeezed margins are forcing financial institutions to rethink strategies to reduce costs. One of the most controversial aspects is the role of traditional branches, which are simultaneously an asset and a liability. 'Distance/vicinity to the branch' are still the main criteria by which Spaniards choose their banks and is the reason why Spain has such an extensive branch network. If banks want to extend market share, a wide network is required. But branches are very expensive to maintain, and experts, consultants and analysts disagree about what the future role of the traditional branch should be. Some are in favour of a reduction in the number of conventional branches, eliminating those less profitable, and developing new distribution channels. Others favour a change in branch functions, emphasising the more added-value 'front-desk' activities – as points of sale of products and services – and minimising the 'back-office' activities. This second opinion is winning ground, and in the foreseeable future the conventional branch will not be at risk of extinction. However, in the fight for profitability, new channels are being developed, more to complement the traditional branches rather than to replace them.

NEW CHANNELS

Telephone banking

In telephone banking, Spain has made significant inroads. The first Spanish telephone bank – *Argentaria's Banco Directo* – was established in 1991. Since then, about a dozen institutions have launched telephone banks: *Bankinter's BKTEL* was the second, followed by *Banco Pastor, Banco de Sabadell, BBK, BBV, Barclays, Deutsche Bank, La Caixa, Caja de Tarragona, Cajamadrid* and *Banco de Santander's Openbank*.

Although the market penetration of telephone banking is very low – 2 per cent of the total client base, compared with an 8 per cent penetration in other European markets such as Sweden, Belgium, Finland or France – growth expectations are high, and experts agree that during 1995–96 the number of clients will be doubled.

ATMs

In their efforts to redefine the role of conventional branches, institutions have strongly developed the automatic teller machine (ATM) network. The rationale is to encourage customers to use ATMs to perform routine transactions – information enquiries, deposits, cash withdrawals – cutting down on the need for bank employees to perform these tasks.

In 1995, Spanish banks had two ATM networks, *4B* and *Servired*, with almost 7,900 ATMs. At the same time, the *cajas* had their own exclusive ATM system, *Tarjeta 2000*. Efforts are now being made to integrate the three systems. The situation with ATMs resembles that of telephone banking: even though the improvement in ATM usage has been impressive, there is still plenty of room for growth. In terms of monthly transactions per ATM, Spain, with about 2,300 transactions in 1994, ranked well below the European average of 3,500 transactions, and well below countries such as Sweden, which boasted almost 10,000 transactions.

The same argument can be used when we consider the use of ATMs in terms of transactions per capita. During 1994, according to data provided by Retail Banking Research Ltd, Spaniards made 17 transactions per capita, compared with the 37 made by the Finns or the 30 made by the Swedes.

Other alternatives of remote or electronic banking, for example computer banking, are in their early stages, and their operations volume is negligible.

RISK MANAGEMENT AND SERVICE, TWO WAYS TO IMPROVE PROFITABILITY

Beyond the redefinition of the role to be played by the branches network, other challenges that Spanish banking institutions will have to face are risk management and service. Improving the quality of the loans portfolio will reduce non-performing loans, helping to increase profitability. And improving the quality of service will be one of the most effective tools in helping the banking institutions to differentiate the good ones from the bad ones. Given that products are the same and price competition cannot be sustained in the long run, the best way to attract and keep customers will be offering them good service. Unfortunately, by European standards, Spanish banks are lacking in this area.

Weaknesses

In spite of the consolidation process, the average Spanish institution is still smaller than those of other European countries; another weakness is that the transformation costs of the Spanish institutions are still high, especially among the smaller ones. Another weakness is a relative lack of international experience, compared to its European neighbours.

Trends and perspectives

For the reasons described above – smaller relative size, squeezed margins, high transformation costs, relative backwardness in service quality – we believe that during the next few years the consolidation of the Spanish financial system will continue. In the process, many smaller and weaker institutions will disappear, by mergers or absorption. Among the more likely candidates to be swallowed by bigger institutions there is a handful of relatively profitable and healthy medium-sized banks. A recent example of this was *Banco Herrero*, absorbed by *La Caixa*.

Beyond their financial health, they also offer interesting branches networks. There were some talks among them in order to create a bigger 'federated' bank. As isolated entities, they are weak medium-sized banks, too small to survive on their own but big enough to attract larger, ambitious and more aggressive banks looking for expansion. The talks failed and now, running the risk of being swallowed by bigger institutions, their future may be similar to the situation suffered by *Banco Herrero*.

The consolidation process will be even deeper in the *cajas de ahorro* side, and it can be expected that during the five years following the publication of this book, the number of savings banks will be halved. The bigger *cajas* may target the smaller ones or even smaller banks, as has been the case with *La Caixa* and *Banco Herrero*.

Despite the unsettled times ahead for the Spanish banking system in the short term, we think it is solid and competitive enough to overcome difficulties successfully. These difficulties, after all, will be good training for Spanish institutions, if they want to survive and succeed in a more competitive, unified European financial market, the real challenge for the future.

THE CHANGING FINANCIAL SYSTEM

The Spanish financial system is the cornerstone of the country's economy. The total assets of the five big Spanish banks alone represent almost 80 per cent of GDP whereas in countries such as the United States the banking system accounts for only 20 per cent of savings.

Nevertheless, the financial system is immersed in a period of profound change as a result of the introduction of the Single Market in financial systems. Spain's entry into the European Community represented a great upheaval for the financial system whose consequences, still latent, will be analysed below. First, however, distinction should be made between the three principal areas that make up the financial system: credit, stocks and insurance. These areas may be differentiated, not only by the nature of their activities, but also by the bodies entrusted with their supervision and control.

Act 3/1994, of 14 April 1994, defined credit entities as companies whose habitual activity consists in receiving deposit funds and other repayable funds and in granting loans on their own behalf. The supervisory body is the Bank of Spain. The Act distinguishes between the following entities:

- the Official Credit Institute (ICO) – the state's financial agency;
- banks;
- savings banks – includes the Spanish Confederation of Savings Banks (CECA).
- credit cooperatives.

The second group of credit entities is made up of companies that operate on the different stock markets. The control body in this case is the National Stock Market Commission (CNMV). These entities may be distinguished as follows:

- stock market companies and agencies. The difference between the two is that only the companies, and not the agencies, may trade on their own behalf;
- collective investment institutions. Financial entities that openly obtain and manage funds, assets and rights of the general public.

The third main group of the financial system (although with much less weight and less well developed) consists of insurance companies, supervised by the Directorate General for Insurance. Two basic types may be distinguished:

- insurance companies, which assume their clients' risks in exchange for payment of premiums;
- pension funds, created exclusively to comply with pension plans.

As indicated above, financial entities may be differentiated, fundamentally by the nature of their operations, but also by their different supervision and control bodies: the Bank of Spain, in the case of credit entities, and the National Stock Market Commission, in the case of companies and agencies operating on the stock markets.

The basic functions of both these bodies are to safeguard the solvency of the entities operating on the different markets, on the one hand, to guarantee the stability of the financial system, and on the other, to protect the customers of these financial services.

The process of European and Monetary Union (EMU) has been the principal cause of the transformation of the Spanish financial system; the Treaty of the European Union has required changes to be made in Spanish legislation. The Bank of Spain Independence Act, 13/1994, of 1 June 1994, granted the central bank the power to formulate and instrument Spanish monetary policy, in addition to exercising supervisory functions over both credit and other financial entities.

The Bank of Spain

Current Spanish legislation defines the Bank of Spain as a public corporation, with individual legal status and full private and public capacity, acting with full autonomy in respect of the State Administration for compliance with its objectives. The Bank of Spain has six basic functions:

1. Monetary policy and issue of currency:
    - formulation, instrumentation and management of implementation;
    - issue of legal tender peseta bank notes;
    - quantification and circulation of coin.
2. Instrument exchange rate policy. The Bank of Spain may hold and manage reserves of foreign currency and precious metals.
3. Guarantee correct operation and stability of the financial and payment systems.
4. Perform treasury services and act as financial agent of the national debt.
5. Supervise credit entities and financial markets.
6. Other functions, such as advising the government, preparation of studies and reports on economic cycle, etc.

The Bank of Spain is headed by a Governor, appointed by the King at the proposal of the Prime Minister and chosen from among persons of recognised economic and financial prestige. The Governor has a non-renewable six-year mandate and may not act in a professional capacity with either credit entities or stock markets during the first two years following the end of the term of office. The Governor must be a Spanish national.

The Governor of the Bank of Spain proposes the name of the Deputy Governor, who is appointed by the government. The Council of Government of the Bank of Spain is made up of the principal persons responsible for economic and monetary policy and is the supreme decision-making body. The Executive Committee is made up of the Governor, the Deputy Governor and two Directors and is concerned with more operative and routine matters.

The National Stock Market Commission (CNMV)

The CNMV is entrusted with supervision, inspection and control of the stock markets and of the activities of both the entities and individuals operating on these markets. It was created by the Stock Market Act, 24/1988. Similarly to the Bank of Spain, the CNMV is a public corporation with individual legal status and full private and public capacity.

In addition to supervision and inspection of the stock markets and of the entities and persons operating on these markets, the CNMV is responsible for ensuring correct data circulation, market transparency and correct price formation. It also has an advisory role to the government and proposes measures for development of the markets.

In terms of organisation, the CNMV is dependent on the Ministry of Economy. It is governed by a Chairman, who is appointed by the government, and by a Vice-Chairman and a Board of seven members (the Chairman and Vice-Chairman of the CNMV, three Directors, the Director General of the Treasury and Financial Policy and the Deputy Governor of the Bank of Spain).

5.3

Banking Services in Spain

Dr Víctor Urcelay Yarza amd Fernando Moroy Hueto, ESTE

> Those who arrive and occupy the battlefield first will have time to rest and await the enemy. Those who arrive late will have to go into action when they are still exhausted.
>
> Wu Su Zi (Commander of the Chinese army – 490 BC)

For some time now, most financial institutions, even those which work to a universal banking model, have been vigorously promoting commercial banking due to the considerable importance of the retail business in the overall balance sheet of the entity.

Besides the quantitative importance, what is most relevant is that the results of retail business are clearly stable in contrast with the more volatile results of other areas of business, such as the money and financial markets, where a period of substantial returns can be followed by one of heavy losses, in line with the instability of the markets where they operate.

Commercial banking is developing with decreasing margins. However, these margins are still appreciably high in comparison with those of our European neighbours (see Table 5.1) and this means that, in Spain, it is a strategic development business for the country's main finance groups, despite the strong competition. In this respect, we should bear in mind the dynamic projects by entities such as BBV, Argentaria – Caja Postal, La Caixa, Caja Madrid, etc, to open new offices, which would seem to validate the model of Spanish banking distribution, based on an extensive, dense network of 'small' banking offices, in contrast with other European distribution models. Commercial banking strategy is based on two areas: control and monitoring of credit risk, and management of the other retail banking businesses.

Table 5.2.1 *Commercial banking: margins (1993)*

	Margin of intermediation (*)	Operating costs (*)	Company resources (*)
France	0.93	1.38	3.02
Italy	3.17	2.75	8.89
United Kingdom	2.45	2.77	3.95
Germany	2.18	1.95	5.38
USA	3.87	3.88	8.23
Japan	1.25	0.96	3.72
Spain	3.16	2.57	9.96

* % of total mean assets
Source: Asociación Española de Banca (AEB)

PRESENT AND FUTURE LINES AND STRATEGIC BUSINESSES OF COMMERCIAL BANKING

To perform a more detailed analysis, we will divide these businesses into resources and services, and business investment. (See Figures 5.2.1 and 5.2.2.) Analysis of these strategies will be based on the two fundamental objective segments of retail banking: individuals and small enterprises, and large businesses.

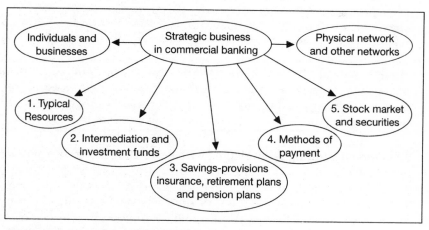

Figure 5.2.1 *Resources and services*

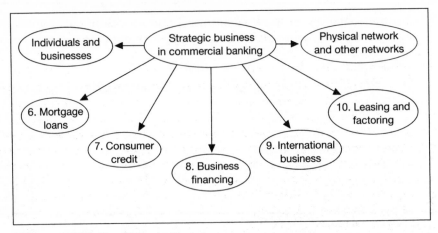

Figure 5.2.2 *Credit investment*

The following should be considered in the areas of deposit gathering and banking services:

Typical resources

This basically includes management of the customer's transactional liquidity and channelling of traditional fixed-term savings through fixed-term deposits. Now that the era of the 'superaccount' (a high-return deposit account, which most banks were offering by the early 1990s) is over, we do not foresee any special war on this business variable, which will basically include the customer's operative or transactional account (where payroll, direct debits, etc are dealt with).

We do not think that marketing will be aimed at price in the individuals section, especially if the current tendency of falling interest rates grows. It will probably involve more formal developments in the account which increase its added value, such as a comprehensive statement of account showing all the customer's balances, a monthly itemised breakdown of deposits and debits, like a sort of home accounting system, etc.

A development we think is overdue in commercial banking and which seems to have far-reaching strategic implications is the launching of a suitable transactional account for senior citizens. The design of a transactional account for this sector of society should combine economic remuneration of the account with other elements highly valued by senior citizens (special travel offers, culture, information on pensions, wills, etc).

The same will occur with the youth sector, although in this case it would seem to be a more difficult sector to manage, especially to retain and consolidate. The profitability of this sector is also unreliable.

In the large businesses sector, the availability of services in the transactional account which allow the company optimum management of collections and payments is fundamental. This is currently one of the areas where greater technological resources are being contributed to commercial banking so that businesses can modernise their collection and payment systems.

1. Typical Resources

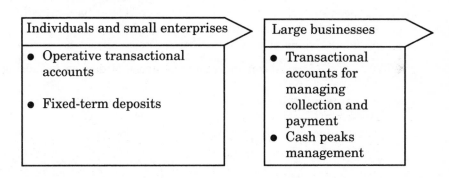

Individuals and small enterprises	Large businesses
• Operative transactional accounts • Fixed-term deposits	• Transactional accounts for managing collection and payment • Cash peaks management

In the large businesses sector, the nature of the relationship between businesses and financial institutions is changing rapidly. For the company, the financial institution is a supplier/customer of goods, in this case, money – and therefore falls into the supplier/customer relationship.

Another result of the severe competition to gain a market share in this sector is that we have entered into a relationship where there is too much negotiating. Almost every item that can be negotiated (loans, business portfolio, foreign business, etc) is negotiated on a monthly, weekly and almost daily basis.

It would appear that the trend, which will become clearer as it grows, is for the company to move to a higher general relationship of trust, avoiding the time lost in excessive negotiations with the money supplier/customer. This process of company-bank friendly integration (partner bank) is especially evident in large companies and multinationals.

Nevertheless, the strong points of the service a financial institution offers the business sector in general should be as a provider of services with two clear objectives:

- to contribute added value to the company;
- to help the company reduce its costs.

Today, granting a loan to or discounting a bill of exchange from a company has become a commodity. These activities alone are insufficient for the fundamental goal of the relationship between a company and a financial institution, ie, the organisation and design of the collection and payment cycle which allow the company to reduce costs by simplifying their administration.

To do this, it is necessary to carry out intense data processing development via the service internally referred to as electronic banking, which we will deal with later. The basic functions of electronic banking fulfil the fundamental objective of automating the administration of the company's collection and payment system. These basic functions include the following:

- accounts information, in accordance with Rule 43 of the Higher Banking Council (Consejo Superior Bancario – CSB);
- payment orders, in accordance with Rule 34 of the CSB (issue of cheques and transfers);
- direct debit of receipts, in accordance with Rule 19 of the CSB;
- transfer of bills, in accordance with Rule 32 of the CSB;
- loan advances, in accordance with Rule 58 of the CSB;
- real-time consultation of bank account balances and transactions.

Resource management in the large-business sector involves another service which is developing at an exceptional rate, especially for companies of a certain size that want to optimise their cash peaks. This is the service through which companies can contract manage their excess liquidity, acquiring specific financial assets. It is a very competitive business with small margins, but it is absolutely necessary to serve a specific part of the business sector and can give rise to different kinds of spin-off business through the transactional support account.

Returning to the private sector, fixed-term deposits fall within the strategy for gathering investable deposits. One of the reasons for this strong growth, contrary to previous forecasts predicting a decline, is to be found in the transfer of large balances from investment funds, as a result of the low returns obtained by investors during 1994 which encouraged them to seek returns which are guaranteed and established beforehand, characteristic of fixed-term deposits.

At any rate, we think that this is a mature product without potential for growth, especially if we take into account the fact that the consumer's desire for previously established guaranteed returns can be currently satisfied via alternatives such as mixed life insurance policies and guaranteed investment funds which offer very good tax advantages as well as providing an attractive guaranteed return.

Intermediation and investment funds

In this area, following the negative expectations for returns on funds in 1994 and early 1995 which gave rise to wholesale transfer to typical bank deposits, and from funds invested in medium- and long-term fixed-return and variable-returns schemes to those invested in the money markets, the situation has stabilised. As a result of this transfer to typical bank deposits, the ratio of investment funds to deposits has dropped appreciably in banks and to a lesser extent in savings banks, as shown in Figure 5.2.3, and stood at 16.3 per cent at the end of March of 1995.

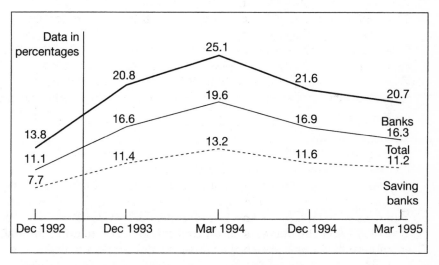

Figure 5.2.3 *Ratio of investment funds to deposits*

For the future, the improvement of returns in 1996 will help to increase the volume of funds, although not necessarily at the same rate as in 1992 and 1993.

The emergence of guaranteed funds will once again attract investors expecting a certain surge in the product with the development of these new 'second-generation' funds which, by guaranteeing a specific return, fulfil the objective qualities of the product that the most conservative investors missed in 1994, characterised by instability in the markets.

Throughout the last four months of 1995, many institutions launched new guaranteed funds onto the market, anticipating a considerable balance increase, together with the issues made in June and July, as shown in Table 5.2.3.

Table 5.2.3 *Net worth of guaranteed funds launched in June and July 1995*

Fund	Minimum contribution (In PTA)	Term (years)	Annual return (APR)	Volume gathered (millions of PTA)
Santander Doble Asegurado	100,000	7 years and 6 months	9.68	66,000
BBV Bono 98	100,000	3	9.25	17,000
BBV Bono 2000	100,000	5	9.50	11,000
BBV 2005	100,000	10	8.50	2,100
FT Bankinter Fondiesoro	50,000	7	10.41	15,000
Centrofondo 4 (BCH)	100,000	7 years and 3 months	10.03	7,500
Fondirecto (Argentaria)	100,000	1	9	19,000
				137,600

We believe that the development of this type of guaranteed fund could be very important in that it combines two basic variables demanded by savers-investors: attractive guaranteed returns and tax advantages.

With regard to liquidity, it is worth mentioning that the policy with this type of product is to maintain the investment until the end of the indicated period, because, as we have mentioned, the guaranteed return is only obtained if the investor keeps the investment in the fund without interruption for the established period. Also, to avoid speculating, these types of funds usually have considerable reimbursement commissions for relatively long periods from the time they are first marketed.

The combination of this type of product with life insurance could give rise to new development in this important line of business, which we believe will provide an increasingly large contribution to the balance sheets of the institutions under the heading of Services Income.

Savings-provisions: insurance, retirement plans and pension plans

Considerable developments are expected in this line of business, both in risk insurance (especially life insurance), financial insurance (popularly known as retirement plans) and pension plans.

Savings insurance or retirement plans guarantee a specific return and provide excellent tax advantages insofar as the returns generated by capitalising the premiums paid are not taxable until they are made available in the form of capital or income once the period of the contract has expired.

Besides the attractive tax advantages described, these savings insurance policies or retirement funds have a second considerable objective for the saver: liquidity. This is a considerable difference as compared to pension plans, another instrument of savings-provision, which provide reasonable initial tax advantages by reducing the saver's taxable income.

The strong development expected in savings insurance and pension plans is conditioned by the current serious concern regarding the inevitable reduction in pensions paid out by the social security in Spain (see Chapter 9.1).

Methods of payment

We expect strong growth in this area and special attention and strategic dedication from the institutions due to the considerable contribution this implies for the balance sheet from services income.

In Spain, credit cards made a rapid appearance on the market as a method of payment and grew at a considerable rate. Unlike other European countries, Spain made the transition directly from cash to credit cards as a method of payment. Spain skipped the normal process of cash to cheque and subsequently to credit card.

This gave rise to extraordinarily rapid growth in the use of credit cards by the customers of financial institutions. At the same time, however, Spanish banks and savings banks were developing Europe's most extensive network of automatic tellers (in 1994, Spain had the highest number of automatic tellers in Europe, with 21,200 machines). Spain thus has a tremendous amount of credit cards and automatic tellers.

Figure 5.2.4 and Table 5.2.4 show data from December 1993 showing the number of credit cards, automatic tellers and point-of-sale terminals (POST), according to the three payment method organisations in Spain (4B System, SEMP and CECA).

Table 5.2.4 *Credit cards in Spain*

	Card	4B System	SEMP	CECA
Credit	Visa	2,733,655	2,803,116	2,513,723
	Mastercard	113,019	189,966	
	Eurocard			
Debit	Visa	5,474,564		
	6000			12,600,000
	Servired		5,964,766	
Private cards	El Corte Inglés		3,000,000	
	Galerias			
	Preciados		1,800,000	
	Pryca		1,200,000	
	Continente		1,000,000	
	Solred		125,000	
	Others:			
	H24			
	Zara			
	Milano			
	Jumbo			
	Cortefiel			
	etc		875,000	
T&E	Amex		270,000	
	Diners		100,000	
Cash cards		4,835	2,872	13,143
TVPs		102,327	300,000	62,901

These institutions have made a significant effort to reclassify the card, which was used as a means of withdrawing cash from automatic tellers, to a debit card which can also be used in shops. This differentiation of debit cards and credit cards is understood by the consumer and resulted in strong growth in this sector, especially with regard to debit cards associated with products; consumers found it easier to understand that these cards are charged to their current account.

From a marketing point of view, the growth in the number of cards and in the amount of activity seems complicated unless it occurs through products and services with a strong tendency to promote credit cards.

It would seem that the following will be two important axes of development within the intensive and extensive strategy concerning debit and credit cards:

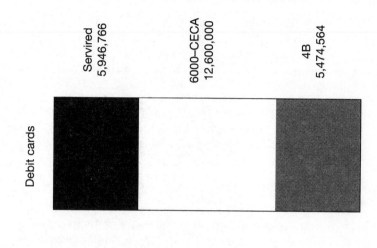

Debit cards

Servired
5,946,766

6000–CECA
12,600,000

4B
5,474,564

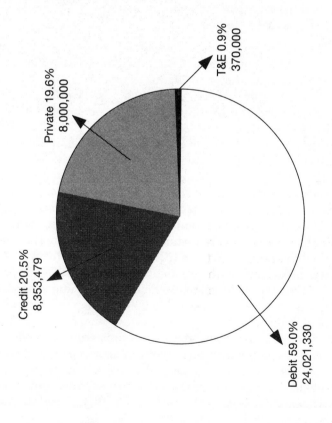

T&E 0.9%
370,000

Private 19.6%
8,000,000

Credit 20.5%
8,353,479

Debit 59.0%
24,021,330

Total cards issued in Spain: 40,744,809

Figure 5.2.4 *The Spanish plastic money market (December 1993)*

- the use of original and aggressive promotional activities;
- the gradual development of affinity cards.

Approving a mortgage or consumer credit, or depositing a pay cheque provide a privileged situation for marketing these cards and this is a relatively mature business which requires original and aggressive promotion. Future trends in the strategic areas of commercial banking are as follows:

(a) the development of affinity cards and private cards in Spain;
(b) the definitive position of cards in terms of payment methods and consumer needs: the appearance of smart cards;
(c) the future: virtual money?

We will now mention a few of the strategic aspects of these future trends.

Development of affinity cards and private cards in Spain

We feel that affinity cards will develop gradually, but not as spectacularly as in the United States, the United Kingdom and, to a lesser degree, in other European countries. A bank's interest in launching an affinity card is motivated by:

1. The need to stand out and gain a market share in this relatively mature business: there are approximately 10 million families in Spain and, as shown in Figure 5.2.3 and Table 5.2.4, at the end of 1993, there were 8,050,494 Visa cards in circulation (Mastercard and Eurocard statistics are not significant) issued by savings banks grouped together in the CECA (Confederación Española de Cajas de Ahorros – Spanish Confederation of Savings Banks), by banks and associated entities grouped in the 4B System and the other financial institutions linked to Visa España through the SEMP (Sociedad Española de Medios de Pago – Spanish Association of Payment Methods). It appeared that with this saturation in the issue of credit cards, the only way of growing in the business was to seize a market share from the competition and an adequate vehicle for this would be affinity cards.

    At individual level, Banco Popular is the undisputed leader. It has issued the most cards (55,000) which provide it with billing of 25 billion pesetas.

    Throughout Spain there are approximately 140,000 Visa affinity cards which represent a total turnover of nearly 38 billion pesetas. This market is divided as follows: approximately 100,000 Visa cards correspond to institutions included in 4B Systems (especially Banco Popular, BCH, Banesto and Banco Sabadell) with billing of 33.5 billion and the rest, with about

40,000 cards, correspond to institutions which issue Visa cards (Classic and Gold cards) through a licensing agreement with Visa España.

2. The financial institutions' need to meet the demands of the promotional institutions by providing them with good service while producing a certain 'social dividend' through charity organisations with a high degree of social support and a good public image (this last point is more relevant for banking institutions than for savings banks which achieve their 'social dividend' more clearly through charity work).

   There are also affinity cards which are not linked to charities. For example, the one with the greatest acceptance on the market is the Visa Iberia of Banco Popular which is related to Iberia Plus' frequent flyer programme where users earn points which can be used toward flights with each purchase made with that card.

   There are also affinity card programmes with financial institutions which are linked to certain football clubs: the Visa Real Madrid of Banco Directo, the Caixa Card with the Español and Valencia Football Clubs, and the BBV through its affiliate Banca Catalana which has issued nearly 17,000 Visa-Barça cards. The Visa-Barça card has an estimated turnover of 1.5 billion pesetas. Banco Sabadell (which began exploring this market in 1990) has the Visa RACE-Banco Sabadell affinity card with the Catalonia Royal Automobile Club for which 10,000 cards have been issued with annual sales of nearly 3.5 billion pesetas.

3. Increasing the level of turnover and average consumption per card. It appears that there is greater loyalty involved in the use of these affinity cards on behalf of holders in their regular payments. This would explain the fact that average consumption or billing per card is higher for affinity cards than for normal credit cards (some financial institutions confirm that spending on affinity cards is at least 15 per cent higher than normal cards). It also seems that affinity card programmes tend to have a lower level of late payments because the group is clearly defined in advance and usually keeps up to date on payments so it can receive the real or social benefits offered by these cards. This occurs in general in the rest of European and American financial systems, even though repayment through the affinity card can be potentially more complex in that it may be paid by direct debit through another bank which is not the issuing bank.

   Another final point to be analysed is the strategic reach of private cards and their relation to affinity cards. We also feel that private cards will undergo progressive development in the future (we can see in Figure 5.2.3 and Table 5.2.4 that at the end of 1993 there were about 8 million private cards in Spain led by the Corte Inglés[1] card).

The advantages of private cards:

- they allow the issuing establishments to gain a great deal of information about their customers;
- they provide a marketing tool which distinguishes establishments by creating a link between the establishment and the customer involved as a key part of their value;
- private card programmes are generally less expensive than affinity card programmes in terms of the cost of becoming a member of the card (in private programmes it is usually free) and the results of subsequent dealings (eg, if the establishment provides credit through the private card);
- private cards are linked to a particular establishment. Thus, establishments can provide advantages to those customers who buy at their shops, that a service affinity card could not offer;
- private cards allow businesses to offer their customers a wide range of payment methods at the point of sale. The most traditional method is to allow card holders to pay at 90 days with no extra charge on the purchase of certain articles. This flexibility is not usually possible with affinity cards.

We expect progressive development of affinity card programmes with the understanding that progress will be gradual and highly selective on behalf of the financial institutions, which are not completely sure about the extension of these cards through which they would obtain a doubly negative effect: on the one hand, the cards would reduce their services income in the part they would have to give to the associated organisation and, on the other, the differentiating and somewhat 'exclusive' nature of the affinity cards would be eliminated.

Position of cards in relation to payment methods

The launching of the smart card. This is without a doubt one of the marketing and technological advances with the furthest strategic potential in the history of payment methods in Spain.

Before going into the definition and objectives of the smart card or electronic wallet, we should analyse each type of card (smart card, debit card, credit card) in terms of their ranking and the frequency and volume of transactions. As shown in Figure 5.2.5, the smart card is aimed at activity sectors with low-value transactions, which have not been traditionally dealt with by current payment systems.

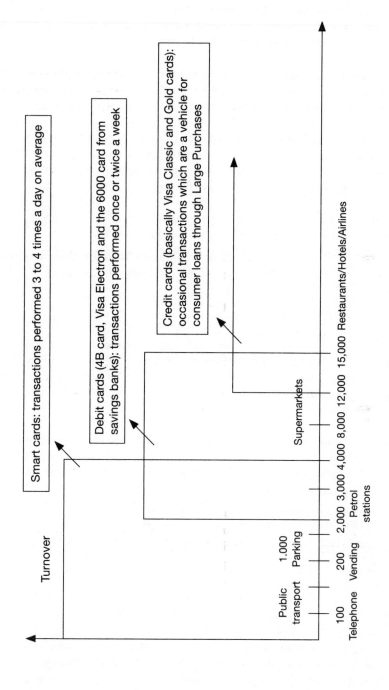

Figure 5.2.5 *Smart cards: breakdown by market / amount*

We refer to the group of daily transactions such as cigarette vending machines, drink and snack vending machines, telephone boxes, public transport, car parks, taxis, newsstands, lottery offices, etc and all daily transactions for a value of less than 4,000 pesetas which could be channelled through the smart card to be discussed below.

Debit cards could cover amounts between 2,000 and 15,000 pesetas (4B cards, Visa Electron and the 6000 card from savings banks). It would correspond to transactions performed once or twice a week.

Finally, for amounts above 15,000 pesetas, we have credit cards (in Spain, mainly Visa Classic and Gold cards). They correspond to occasional transactions and those for specific sectors with a frequency of once or twice a month.

The use of credit cards to buy a certain product or service starting at 15,000 pesetas and theoretically with no upper limit make this a privileged credit vehicle for consumption, at least to a certain amount.

This is an important strategic development which financial institutions have experienced in relation to credit cards and their use as credit vehicles for consumption to a certain amount. In the 1980s, especially in the last half when there was a strong consumer surge in Spain, consumers who went to an establishment to buy a car or an appliance, etc had not settled or arranged financing terms beforehand, meaning that the promotor or seller was successful in marketing a certain consumer loan as opposed to the services of other institutions.

In the 1990s, particularly 1993–95, the situation has changed considerably: there is a great deal of late payment and a marked reduction in consumption, creating growth difficulties for institutions within this profitable section of business.

Given this situation, it would appear natural to think that for those quality customers who are going to purchase something, financing should be handled by the institution of which they are customers. To this end, the ideal vehicle is the credit card, which becomes the natural instrument of consumer loans.

Customers can carry out their purchases or consumer actions by charging the normal limit on their credit card or by charging this new pre-authorised credit limit for large purchases by calling a specific telephone number and specifying that this purchase should be charged to that limit. This large purchase method provides for financing from three months to three years at an interest rate which is usually one percentage point higher than the standard rate for consumer loans.

This pre-authorised or pre-agreed limit for consumer loans built into the credit card depends on each customer by virtue of scoring methods to evaluate the overall relationship with the customer. The maximum authorised amount is usually 1 million pesetas.

We believe that in this line, the strategic development of the credit card as a vehicle of consumer loans up to a certain amount and for a specific time period will continue because of the considerable advantages for customers who know that they can count on a certain level of financing to make a purchase or perform a consumer action without having to go to the bank first (without papers or guarantees) through this system, which is referred to in payment methods jargon as Large Purchase.

As with other business areas we have discussed, this one calls for a certain level of technology to set up the system and particularly the internal scoring system of credit cards which allows for automatic assignment to each customer of a specific pre-agreed or authorised credit limit. This level of technology is not possible for all financial institutions and is what makes the difference between 'how' it is done as opposed to 'what' is done and will lead to a successful or unsuccessful action (BBV estimates that the Tarjetón should not produce a late payment percentage of more than 4 per cent).

Thus, the future of payment methods for private individuals is broken down according to Figure 5.2.6.

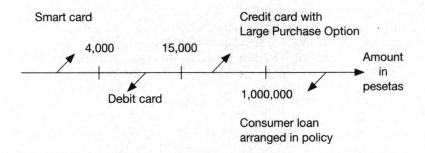

Figure 5.2.6 *Payment methods for individuals*

For the business sector, the company credit card (business card) generally has three highly valued advantages for companies:

- the card's information by-product: extensive statistical reports through which company expenses can be monitored (expenses per employee, by department and item, monthly and yearly summaries, etc), thus expediting administrative and control tasks;
- employee infidelity insurance;
- accident insurance and travel assistance insurance.

Offering a company credit for the accounts of executives who use it often provides a considerable source of business when evaluating the overall relationship with the company.

The smart card

As we have seen, the smart card or electronic wallet is perfectly placed when analysed by sectors and amounts spent, ie, it is a card which will not cannibalise the markets of current credit and debit cards.

Moreover, it seems to have an important market niche: a study done by Price Waterhouse indicates that the total small payment market could represent the considerable amount of 10 trillion pesetas and estimates that 85 per cent of these payments could be channelled through smart cards.

The smart card is a card with a smart chip which is read on contact (because the chip is visible). It is an advanced intelligent card. At present, development of the smart card has technological and operative aspects:

- in terms of technology, the adopting of a suitable standard both for the smart card itself and the terminal where it will be used;
- in terms of operation, to be used in current automatic teller machines and the availability of new smart terminals at points of sale or wherever the smart card is used.

The good news in terms of technology is that the three leading institutions in payment methods in Spain, the 4B System, CECA and SEMP will constitute a permanent organisation which will allow for progressive coordination of payment systems in Spain. This would particularly aid the development of smart cards, which each of these institutions had announced separately, and would thus make it possible to use a single standard. Visa has announced the launching of its smart card and some 4B banks have done smart card tests in the city of Valladolid.

Recently, CECA announced it would have a smart card ready for mass marketing (to be called Dinero 6000) at the end of 1996. It is one of CECA's basic strategic lines for 1996, together with the development of telephone banking and electronic banking.

THE FUTURE: VIRTUAL MONEY?

It is difficult to predict the future but it would appear that the current level of development in telecommunications, information highways, the Internet, etc, will create a type of electronic trade where the consumer is given multimedia access to a huge catalogue or shelf of products.

The supplier/consumer relationship will clearly be completely remote and even with a link which does not belong to the consumer or the supplier. The key to all this is how payment will be made using this network: with credit cards or with what some are calling virtual money?

After this brief review of the five main business areas related to resources and services which form part of the business of commercial banking, and to advance some conclusions on the other five which are related to credit investment, we can state the following:

- determining the proper strategic course of the growing business areas of commercial banking calls for profound, overall knowledge of these businesses and the theoretical and practical mechanisms of strategic marketing;
- once the course has been set, the strategy is validated by the balance sheet. Financial institutions will have to develop a technological and management capacity which is not within the reach of all of them;
- we must not forget that in business the most important thing is to 'do things well', ie, 'how' is more important than 'what'. However, today, 'how' is changing very quickly.
  From the single, outdated tactic of 'how' based on 'pumping up the network', to the modern tactics of 'how': capacity for technological development, adequate management information, planning and sales management, training and network motivation, technology to sell more at a higher profit (electronic catalogue of products, customer profitability simulations, support systems for proactive sales, etc);
- it is particularly important that the entire organisation is deeply integrated in a common project: permanent customer satisfaction.

The purpose of any business resides in something beyond it: creating and satisfying the customer. Structure must follow strategy and management must be management with goals and self-control. (Peter Drucker)

NOTES

1 El Corte Inglés is the largest chain of department stores in Spain.

Part 6

Distribution in Spain

INTRODUCTION

The way a distribution system is set up requires a major strategic decision which will depend on factors like your position in the market, the size of your company, your type of product, the existing channels of distribution, etc.

There is also the legal side to keep in mind. Spanish law makes a clear distinction between agents and distributors. Since the contractual system in labour relations could be markedly protective for one of the parties, the type of relationship you wish to enter should be doubled-checked. Article 6.2 goes into detail on the legal aspects to be considered.

Distribution is a very dynamic sector in Spain, which is evolving at a quick pace. High street traditional trade is being seriously threatened by growth in the number of large stores. It is a well-known development in the UK and in the rest of Europe. As in all these countries, there is also a passionate debate about the convenience of removing limits to opening hours which is supposed to benefit large areas and shopping centres (two phenomena which go side by side) and the importance of preserving the high street environment, applying some restrictions which would limit the competition of the big players. Although intended to offer a compromise solution, the recently passed Trade Law is thought to work on the side of traditional smaller shopkeepers.

The higher urban density of Spain brings new factors into play. Large distribution companies are opening outlets inside the cities with very low labour requirements. It is the case of some chains of discount stores or highly specialised convenience shops which equally threaten the future of the traditional trade. In Chapter 6.3, prepared by the *Mercado* magazine, the reader will find a study of the situation of this sector in Spain which will help to understand the changes that are currently operating.

6.1

Trading with Spain

Leslie Stern, DTI Export Promoter for Spain

Trading with Spain is no more complicated than trading with any-where else, and a lot easier than with many countries, a fact often over-looked by many would-be exporters. It is worth recalling that of the 200 plus markets that the United Kingdom trades with each year, any member of the European Union (EU) offers particular advantages over other markets. Relatively close at hand, and well-served by frequent flights, it is quick, easy and relatively cheap to get there. The infra-structure is good – and improving – and it is easy to move around the country at low cost. This impacts directly on operating costs, and thereby minimises sales costs.

Like any member state of the EU, Spain is a well-documented market. Thus, real practical information on the size, value and structure of the market can readily be obtained from good commercial libraries, the DTI's Export Market Information Centre in London, or possibly the Business Studies Department library of local universities.

Potential trading partners can also be identified from **Spanish trade exhibitions' Catalogues**, and appropriate trade magazines. Even if you do not speak Spanish, you will recognise an advertisement as such in a trade magazine – cross check the nature of that advertiser's busi-ness in a trade directory. The UK trade association to which you belong may be able to make contact with the corresponding Spanish trade association – and even obtain a list of members.

The simplified procedures of the EU, both for moving goods and for get-ting paid, apply to trade between the UK and Spain. Spain is the UK's eighth most important trading partner. This means that hundreds of Spanish companies are already accustomed to doing business with

British firms. British exports of goods and services amount to some £5.2 billion each year, ordered, delivered and paid for in full: do not, therefore, be put off by second-hand horror stories about payment. In the context of getting paid, remember that every High Street bank in the UK operates in Spain, directly or indirectly, and you should therefore always involve the bank in making arrangements to get paid: your bank manager, unlike you, has colleagues in Spain who can help.

All too often British companies overlook the fact that Spain is a major trading nation in its own right, and the Spanish economy is bigger than all of Benelux put together, and bigger than all of Scandinavia put together – think, for example, of the trading links with Latin America for obvious linguistic and historical reasons. While distribution arrangements may be more fragmented in Spain than in the UK, for geographic as well as historic and political reasons, Spain is nonetheless a mature market with well-established channels of marketing, sales and distribution. Because of potentially fragmented distribution, the newcomer to the market, particularly the smaller company, would do well to think of tackling penetration of the Spanish market on a regional basis, as many distributors really do only operate in their own region, and then 'leap-frog' from one region to the next as market penetration grows.

The benefits of the single market make it significantly easier to trade between member states. At the same time, you should also recognise that if it is easier for you to sell to your Spanish customer, this also applies to your competitors within the community. This in turn imposes strict disciplines of commitment to the highest levels of customer service – just as high as you give in the domestic market. Be aware also that your Spanish customer is able to buy more easily, and can change suppliers at short notice, if dissatisfied with your service.

All the conventional options for distribution are available in Spain to the would-be exporter, just as in any mature market, from selling direct, via agents or distributors, through to the more sophisticated joint venture or acquisition. However, most newcomers to the Spanish market are likely to opt for direct selling, via a distributor or an agent. The right type of distribution for your product is in reality achieving a suitable balance between the needs and practices of the market-place for your product – how do your competitors distribute? – and the resources you have to put into development and management of the Spanish market.

The use of the commission agent has long been a traditional way for British companies to go to market. While still appropriate in some sectors, agents are disliked by many major players because of the uplifted prices required to cover the payment of commission. As communications between the UK and Spain are so good, major players often prefer to communicate directly with their UK trading partners. Remember too that, although the commission agent does not set out to introduce you to customers who don't pay, the management of the credit control and payment collection falls on the UK principal, which can result in a heavy administrative burden as your client base grows. Remember that the payment of agents in Spain is in accordance with the EU directive on agency agreements (just as in the UK), which rightly protects agents from unfair dismissal, and can result in compensation being paid for early termination. A reasonable performance target, mutually agreed on start-up and written in to any agreement, can be useful for monitoring progress: achievement of the target confirms the validity of the agent, whereas failure to achieve agreed targets facilitates termination.

The alternative is the distributor, whether stocking or non-stocking. In the latter case, your distributor sells on his own account and invoices his customer, but goods are dispatched directly to the distributor's customer from the UK principal. While a distributor reduces the administration work that the UK principal must carry (you are only dealing with one account) the addition of the distributor's margin may make your price high. Additionally, you may need to build in some incentive to persuade your distributor to promote your products more strongly than other lines he may be carrying.

The most effective distribution is undoubtedly market-driven: the end customer, or end user, is usually the best-placed to tell you the best option. Major players, in particular, are likely to be inundated with product offers, so your first task is to interest that end customer in your product: after all, if the end customer is not interested, even the best distributor won't be able to sell your product. Once you have generated an interest in the product, ask the open question about how distribution should be handled – direct, via an agent or via a distributor? If the end customer prefers to deal direct, you have protected your margin – and saved a margin! If the response is either an agent or a distributor, ask for a referral or introduction. You can be sure that the end customer will not send you to someone he does not want to do business with. Your approach to that third party is then quite different as you are no longer just another UK company looking for an agency agreement or a distribution arrangement. Rather, you are coming to see that third party because their major customer has asked you to.

Where are the opportunities in the Spanish market? The answer is that they are everywhere. Young Spaniards – 53 per cent of the 40 million population is under 35 – like to do the same as youngsters elsewhere in Europe. They eat at McDonald's or Burger King, drink Coke or Pepsi, wear Levis or other branded jeans and Nike trainers, and use Sony headsets. Spanish business people use Amex and Diners Club cards, and have mobile or car 'phones: simply put, the brand affiliations are the same as in the rest of Europe.

For consumer goods, there are a number of different market opportunities: you must go for at least one, but it is possible to go for more than one. The domestic market of 40 million consumers; the tourist market of more than 60 million annual visitors; while a third possibility is the expatriate communities, not just the British, living in little enclaves all around the Spanish coast. Although the latter is not easy to reach, it can be a very lucrative market.

Do not overlook the Canary Islands, counted as a separate market in British statistical terms and, although correctly two provinces of Spain, needing to be serviced as a separate market in terms of marketing, sales and distribution. A domestic population of 1.6 million with some eight million tourists visiting annually, this market is almost totally serviced by imports.

In the capital goods area, Spain is the recipient of huge amounts of funding from the so-called 'Structural' and 'Cohesion' funds of the European Union, allocated to major improvements in transport infrastructure – roads, railways and airports. Funding is also being spent on what might be called the 'environmental' sectors – waste management and water treatment, as well as the 'high-tech' areas of telecommunications and information technology. Access to this funding will require commitment to, and involvement in, Spain: it is not about selling to Spain, it's about being there, working with your trading partner.

Make it easy for your targeted customer to buy – make the first approach in Spanish. The penetration of the English language is growing and many buyers, particularly in major companies, speak English, or have bi-lingual secretaries if they don't. Common courtesy, however, demands the first approach is in their language. Do not let language difficulties get in the way: in the short term, you can use interpreters, and the written word can be translated both ways. Learn at least the courtesies, if only to be able to apologise for not speaking Spanish. In the longer term, why not learn the language? An easy language to learn, your efforts will be greatly rewarded in enhanced customer relations.

With regard to product labelling and instructions in Spanish, the use of professionally translated versions for inclusion with your product is a minor inconvenience at low cost. Do not, however, double stock differently labelled products – add the appropriate labels and instructions as the order is prepared for dispatch.

Facilitate the buying process by helping your potential customer to understand your product offer – and your price. You can perfectly well trade in pounds sterling ex works, but to help the buying decision, if your price is £1 ex works, why not say 'that is *about* (and this covers you for currency exchange fluctuations) 190 pesetas ex works, which is *about* 210 pesetas delivered to your warehouse in Zaragoza – if you buy 5,000 of them.' Your potential customer can then add to the 'landed cost' his cost of sales, and his margin, and quickly calculate his selling price. Your potential customer does not know our market, but knows the Spanish market and can thus react, either nodding, that is, agreeing to buy at that price, or with a sharp intake of breath! In the latter case, recognise that you are no longer dealing with an enquiry – you are now negotiating, and most importantly, you are helping your customer to make the right buying decision.

6.2

Legal Agreements Relating to Opportunities and Representatives

Juan I González and Gabriel Núñez, Uría & Menéndez, London Office

INTRODUCTION

The completion of a European Union (EU) internal market requires the adoption of harmonisation measures to facilitate the development of businesses across Europe in a more effective way. Yet the differences in the legal regimes of EU member states are so important that before doing business in an EU country it is necessary to be familiar with its legal system. Companies or individuals aiming at conducting business in Spain have different choices when deciding strategies to enter the Spanish market. Here we describe briefly how these different strategies can be summarised.

A foreign company may only require an individual in Spain who, in addition to other marketing abilities, has the right contacts and language skills to market the products or services which are manufactured and marketed by the foreign company in its country. Depending on whether the Spanish link will be acting as a partner or co-investor, as an independent economic operator or as a mere middle man, the possible legal structures offered by Spanish law can vary. It should be noted that the Spanish law on contracts is very flexible. In fact, the parties to a contract may agree whatever pacts, clauses, terms and conditions they deem convenient, as long as these are not contrary to the 'law, the moral or public policy'. As a result, under Spanish law the parties have considerable discretion for establishing the rights and obligations corresponding to a supplier, an agent, a distributor, a franchisee, etc.

It is worth bearing in mind that EU rules, either those rules of harmonisation such as the EU Directive on Commercial Agents or the EU Antitrust rules, may apply to all these kinds of agreements in addition to the (strictly speaking) Spanish rules.

COMMERCIAL AGENTS AND SIMILAR SPANISH LEGAL STRUCTURES

It is common knowledge that to do business in another country with the assistance of certain types of sales representatives, independent agents or brokers, or through a distributor, has substantial advantages for a company willing to enter into a new foreign market. In the case of Spain, if the foreign company is well advised, the advantages are not only financial (the investment to be made is minimal) but also may avoid important liabilities, such as those liabilities arising from Spanish Labour Law, the application of which would represent a substantial burden on the supplier, who would be treated as an employer in a country where the protection afforded to employees by law is recognised to be more intense than in other EU member states.

As a guideline, the following types of legal relationships for the promotion and sale of goods of a foreign manufacturer may be distinguished:

1. *Employees*. Persons responsible for the promotion or execution of commercial transactions within the premises of their principal subject to the working hours imposed by their principal. The general rules established by the Spanish Statute of Workers (*Estatuto de los Trabajadores*) would be applicable. These rules imply a high degree of protection for the employee, since dismissal by the employer is limited to the causes set out in the law and minimum compensations are mandatory in most cases of termination.
2. *Sales representatives*. Although held to be employees, sales representatives who act for one or several principals, not assuming any risks which may arise from the commercial transactions in which they are involved, are subject to special labour conditions. The relationship between the principal and the sales representative is subject to special rules regarding the form of their contract, its duration, holidays, working hours, remuneration, customers, termination, compensation for termination, etc.

3. *Commercial agents.* As explained above, commercial agents are persons devoted to the promotion or execution of commercial transactions on a continuous basis for the account of one or more principals, but who have their own autonomous economic structure, ie their own facilities and staff. The key element is that the commercial agent should have the ability to organise its professional activities and the time devoted thereto according to its own views. If these persons follow instructions given by the principal in areas such as working hours, itineraries, prices, ways of ordering supplies and executing contracts, the existence of a labour relationship (probably, a sales representative relationship) will be presumed.

In addition, under Spanish law there are other ways of representing someone else's business interests. This is the case of commissioned agents (*comisionistas*), persons who are engaged to execute a specific assignment and to enter into contractual agreements following the instructions of the principal. Furthermore, the Spanish Civil Code permits the existence of representatives in general and not necessarily for commercial matters. Moreover, a supplier may enter into a consignment agreement (*contrato estimatorio*) in which the supplier consigns his goods to be sold to a retailer who does not receive title to the goods but assumes the obligations of a custodian.

A quite recent Spanish law on Agency Contracts, Law 12/1992, of 27 May 1992 – the Agency Law (*Ley de Contrato de Agencia*) – implemented Directive 86/653 EEC, of 18 December 1986, on Commercial Agents. According to the Agency Law, commercial agents are defined as those physical or legal persons who are bound to another, the principal, on a continuous or permanent basis and who in exchange for a remuneration may promote commercial transactions on behalf of the principal and, if authorised to do so, may even execute those transactions on behalf of the principal, acting in all cases as a self-employed intermediary.

As a general rule, the commercial agent should be acting independently from the principal in order to ensure that no labour relationship exists regarding the principal. Nevertheless, Spanish Courts have tried to enlarge the scope of the legal protection provided to workers in Spain. In these circumstances, legal advice not only on the drafting of the contract but also regarding its performance by the parties should be carefully sought in advance in order to ensure that the relationship with a commercial agent is not taken by Spanish labour authorities as a relationship which would imply further obligations to the principal as employer.

As far as commercial agents are concerned, it is advisable to include clauses in the contract regarding financing and method of payment for customers, the agent's obligations, its remuneration (either a lump sum, or a percentage on sales or a combination of both), the duration (either a fixed duration or indefinite). It should be noted that the application of the Spanish Agency Law is mandatory and, accordingly, the mandatory jurisdiction is the court where the agent is domiciled.

Finally, it should be noted that agents who specialise in specific sectors of the market may be subjected to the particular rules of the sector. For instance, this is the case of credit entities' agents that have been recently regulated under Royal Decree of 14 July 1995 and, among other requirements, must be reported by the principal to the Bank of Spain.

EXCLUSIVE DISTRIBUTION AND AGENCY AGREEMENTS

Distinction between agency and distribution

An agent acts on behalf of his principal whether in his own name or in the name of the latter, under commission and therefore generally not assuming the inherent risk of the transactions executed by him. Conversely, a distributor acts on his own behalf and in his own name, generally obtaining a profit upon resale and thus assuming all the risks that the transactions of purchase and resale may bring.

Notwithstanding the particular features of agency and distribution contracts, both exclusivity and indefinite duration pose similar problems in connection with the termination of these contracts.

As opposed to agency contracts, distribution agreements are not specifically contemplated or regulated by Spanish law as such. However, exclusive distribution agreements are regulated under Spanish Antitrust Law. Exclusive distribution agreements are permitted where only two companies participate and where they affect solely the Spanish domestic market and satisfy the following conditions:

(i)   one party undertakes with the other to sell solely to this party certain products for its resale on all or part of the Spanish market; and

(ii) the particular agreement falls within the scope of the EEC Regulation 1983/83 of the European Commission, of 22 June 1983, which defines the exclusive distribution agreements that are not deemed to be contrary to Article 85 of the Rome Treaty.

Distribution agreements are relatively common in Spain. Their existence and regulation from a competition law point of view are considered both by EEC Regulation 1983/83, for those agreements which affect trade between member states of the EC, and by Royal Decree 157/1992, for those agreements which affect only the Spanish domestic market. Moreover, substantial case law of the Spanish Supreme Court has discussed some of their features, which are explained below. Regarding antitrust rules, no restriction on the supplier can be imposed other than the obligation not to supply final customers directly within the territory allocated to an exclusive distributor. On the exclusive distributor, the supplier may impose, for example, the obligation of not dealing with goods competing with the contract goods, a restriction from seeking clients outside the contract territory, etc. However, no restrictions of competition other than those permitted by the applicable antitrust rules are permitted, eg to restrict the freedom of the distributor to fix prices.

Termination and compensation

As mentioned above, there are no express legal provisions under Spanish Commercial Law governing termination of exclusive distribution agreements as such, as opposed to some other European legal systems. On the contrary, the Agency Law provides for detailed rules in this regard. Although the Spanish Supreme Court of Justice has held in certain cases that the legal principles applicable to agency and distribution agreements are very similar and often the same, it would appear that applying the agency rules on indemnities upon termination cannot be accepted for all distribution agreements.

In a distribution agreement, both parties act independently and each of them assumes the risks involved in the transactions they execute. Thus, it appears that it may not be completely accurate to apply by analogy all rules on agency contracts to distribution agreements.

Nevertheless, principals should be aware that the analogical application of rules on agency contracts to distribution agreements is not a strange approach, and appears to be quite a widespread trend in Europe. A basis for such extension may be found in the Agency Law, which states that in the absence of specific laws, the Agency Law applies to all the different kinds of agency contracts whatever the denomination is.

Spanish courts clearly recognise today the right of the agent – and sometimes even a distributor – to be indemnified. Such right may arise from two situations of a different nature, which do not necessarily exclude each other, but which constitute independent causes giving rise to a right for compensation. On the one hand, the mere fact of termination may give rise to the obligation to indemnify the agent or distributor, whenever an element of abuse of right or bad faith is found and proven to have determined termination by the principal or supplier. On the other hand, a right for compensation may arise based on the notion of 'unfair enrichment' resulting from termination, because of the appropriation at no cost to the supplier of the customer's network generated by the agent or distributor, ie, taking advantage of the latter's goodwill created by his previous commercial efforts.

However, should the grantor of the exclusivity have a just cause (*justa causa*) to terminate, there will be no right to indemnity or damages, neither for the mere fact of termination, nor for the loss by the agent or distributor of its client network.

In accordance with the foregoing, in those cases where the contractual relationship is unilaterally terminated without abuse or bad faith, the agent or distributor will only have the right to be indemnified for the loss of his previously acquired clientele. Unfortunately, no clearly established rules are found in this regard in the Spanish courts case law.

However, as a guideline for calculating such an indemnity, two circumstances may need special consideration:

(a) the foreseeable reorientation of the distributor's business to adapt it to the newly created situation; and

(b) the advantageous situation for the supplier derived from its situation of owner of the brand name with which the products became known. A situation which, when it prevails at the termination of the agreement, would allow the supplier to benefit from the clientele created by the promotion activity of the distributor and by the prestige added to its product derived from the confidence inspired by the distributor.

Under the Agency Law, the maximum compensation a commercial agent may be entitled to, that cannot be increased or otherwise reduced by the parties, is the average annual amount received as remuneration in the last five years or during the period in which the agency agreement was in force. As explained above, the aforementioned rule could also apply to a distribution contract, making it more worrying for a foreign supplier.

FRANCHISING AGREEMENTS

Franchising agreements understood as agreements on which the franchiser authorises the franchisee to use certain trade marks or signs and know-how in the context of the resale of goods or the provision of services are not regulated as such by Spanish law.

However, Spanish and EU antitrust rules contemplate these agreements. Clauses regarding quality controls, best endeavours, etc, are permitted. Conversely, clauses imposing restrictions on price fixing, market sharing, etc, are not permitted. Not much case law of the Spanish Supreme Court of Justice exists on franchising. However, the Court for the Defense of Competition has become active with regard to franchises and its resolutions are helpful in analysing what the position is in Spain regarding certain features of franchising.

Part 7

Marketing in Spain

INTRODUCTION

The commercial value of a given market will be directly related to your ability to design an appropriate marketing strategy and employ within it the correct promotional tools. It is important to understand your market and hence to transform vague concepts like population size, income per capita or market size into an effective marketing plan. When putting this plan into practice, advertising is a vital concern. Media play a key role here, via their ability to reach your target customers as accurately as possible.

When entering a new market, you will need to find sources of market information and decide on your media plan. Part Seven addresses these problems, shedding light on where to find relevant information. Chapter 7.1 offers the reader a complete picture of the media sector in Spain with detailed description of the size of each medium in terms of its cost as well as consumer type.

The second chapter is a comprehensive compilation of sources of market information and their respective uses. Readers will also find contact details in the section of useful addresses.

Finally, Javier Suso, a qualified expert in the area of marketing, will give you tips on how to take advantage of the means available to create your marketing and media plan.

The Media in Spain

José Antonio Llaneza, Optimum Media España

To get a picture of the media sector in Spain, we can begin by making an estimate of the market based on information available for 1994. It should be emphasised that this sector has grown at a rate of more than 20 per cent per annum during the 1980s. This rate slowed during the 1990s and in 1993 it became negative, a situation we should see reversed this year.

The publicity market in conventional media in Spain, according to the Infoadex[1] report, increased in 1994 to 567,161 million pesetas, an increase of 1.2 per cent on the previous year, in prices of the day. The breakdown is shown in Table 7.1.1.

Table 7.1.1 *The publicity market in conventional media in Spain*

	Million pesetas	% Market share
Television	210,817	37.2
Newspapers	180,952	31.9
Magazines	76,651	13.5
Radio	53,025	9.3
Outdoors	25,748	4.5
Sunday supplements	15,318	2.7
Cinema	4,650	0.8

Regarding market concentration, the Infoadex report indicates that of the 980 advertisers, 14.2 per cent spend 92.7 per cent of the total. The 642 advertisers with an annual expenditure of more than 100 million pesetas make up 88 per cent of the total amount for this year. In this context and among the 20 top advertisers in Spain there are nine automobile firms and five consumer food companies. In the first place again is *El Corte Inglés*,[2] the same as in 1993. Table 7.1.2 shows the top 20 advertisers in Spain in 1994:

Table 7.1.2 *The top 20 advertisers in Spain in 1994*

	Investment (millions pesetas)
El Corte Inglés	10,468,8
Procter & Gamble España	8,134,2
Fasa Renault	7,882,7
Citroen Hispania	7,521,8
Seat	5,765,2
Ford España	5,689,5
Henkel Iberica	5,653,3
ONLAE (Lotteries)	5,569,1
Nestle España	5,529,0
Peugeot Talbot España	5,374,7
Volkswagen-Audi España	4,800,1
Fiat Auto España	4,782,2
Leche Pascual	4,730,8
Nutrexpa	4,340,1
Opel España	3,771,3
Ente Publico RTVE	3,427,8
CIA Coca Cola de España	3,023,9
Telefonica de España	2,796,7
Danone	2,793,5
Teleshop Vital	2,558,3

Following the report we can look at the principal media in a bit more detail. **Television** was dominated by the national channels, reaching the following levels of advertising investment shown in Table 7.1.3.

Table 7.1.3 *Advertising levels in television advertising*

Channels	Investment (millions pesetas)
Antena 3	63,057
TVE-1	51,403
Tele 5	41,412
LA 2	13,580
Canal	1,996
CCRR	10,218
Regional	29,151
Total	210,817

The **newspaper** market, being the second largest, had the highest growth in 1994, reaching a volume of 180,952 million pesetas, of which the ten main newspapers in order of expenditure had a market share of 45 per cent of the total as shown in Table 7.1.4. The first three newspapers by volume of investment reached 25 per cent of the market between them.

Table 7.1.4 *Top ten newspapers in order of advertising expenditure*

	Investment (million pesetas)	% market share
El País	13,679	8.6
ABC	13,345	8.4
La Vanguardia	12,620	7.9
El Mundo	8,100	5.1
El Periódico	6,200	3.9
Diario 16	5,710	3.6
El Correo Español	3,428	2.1
La Voz De Galicia	3,362	2.1
El Diario Vasco	3,025	1.9
El Día De Tenerife	2,777	1.7

The **magazine** market, third most important by investment volume, had the highest decline with respect to 1994, as much as a result of the economy as due to the fierce competition from other media, especially from television. In this sector where the concentration of the market is lower due to the high number of players, the principal magazines are shown in Table 7.1.5.

Table 7.1.5 *Principal magazines*

	Investment (million pesetas)	% Market share
Hola	3,725	6.2
Tiempo	2,459	4.6
Nuevo Estilo	1,648	3.1
Elle	1,486	2.8
Diez Minutos	1,466	2.7

MEDIA AUDIENCE

Once we have made an economic quantification of the market we can move towards analysing the different media from the audience point of view. For this analysis we shall use the data from the General Media Study – *Estudio General de Medios* (EGM)[3] accumulated totals for 1994, as well as the data from the audience meter – *Audimetria de Sofres* (AM), this time based on 1995 data. According to EGM's data (individuals over 14 years of age), the importance of the different media is shown in Table 7.1.6.

Table 7.1.6 *Importance of various media*

	million readers
Television	29,229
Radio	17,918
Magazines	17,460
Newspapers	11,908
Sunday supplements	11,662
Cinema	2,518
Video	1,628
Total	32,332

From the same source, the population coverage for the total of individuals and housewives varied from 90 per cent for television, with the highest importance of any medium, to the lowest, the video, scarcely reaching 4 per cent of housewives. Figure 7.1.1 shows the importance of each medium. The audience structure, by social class and age, can be seen in Figures 7.1.2 and 7.1.3.

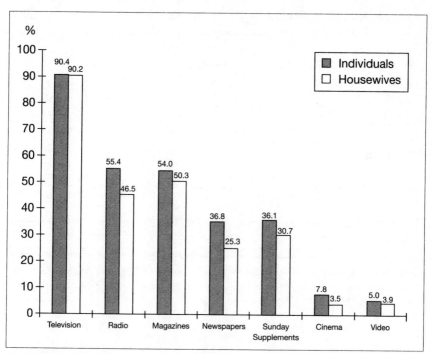

Figure 7.1.1 *Importance by medium*

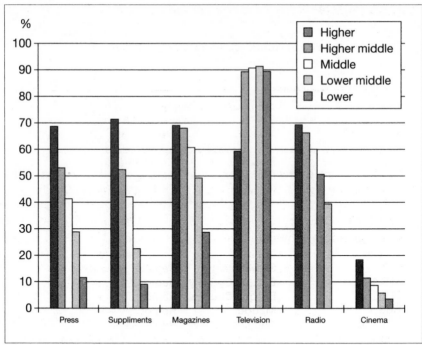

Figure 7.1.2 *Audience by social class*

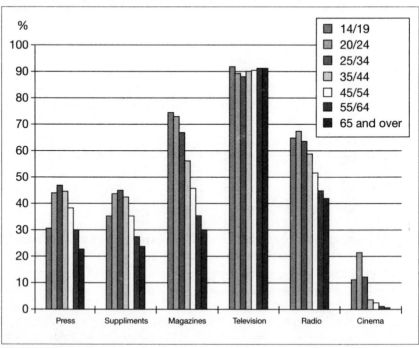

Figure 7.1.3 *Audience by age*

TELEVISION

The 13 networks in Spain are shown in Table 7.1.7.

Table 7.1.7 *Spain's 13 television networks*

Network	Scope	Ownership
National		
TVE 1	National	Government
TVE 2	National	Government
Antena 3	National	Private: Group Z
Tele 5	National	Private Berlusconi/Kirsch
Canal Plus	National	Private: Canal Plus: France & Prisa
Autonomous Communities		
TV 3	Catalonia	Regional government
C33	Catalonia	Regional government
ETB 1	Basque Country	Regional government
ETB 2	Basque Country	Regional government
TM3	Madrid	Regional government
Canal Sur	Andalucía	Regional government
Canal 9	Valencia	Regional government
TVG	Galicia	Regional government

In addition to the networks already mentioned there are a large number of privately-owned local television stations with hardly any audience. As for cable television, it is estimated there are about 200,000 homes with cable, and a rapid development expected in the coming years. As for satellite television, according to EGM (May 1995), its penetration has reached 450,000 homes (3.8 per cent of Spanish households). This represents 0.6 per cent of Spain's potential viewers. In total, these channels reach 90.4 per cent of individuals, with a household coverage of 99.3 per cent (colour television accounts for 97.4 per cent of households).

The medium of television has seen an explosion of private television channels during recent years, and an increase in consumption according to *Sofres AM* (in minutes per day) as shown in Figure 7.1.4.

The viewing habits of the Spanish are different from other countries, in terms of the peak audience being after dinner and the shift of 'prime time', as is shown in Figure 7.1.5. Consumption by hourly periods is shown in Figure 7.1.6.

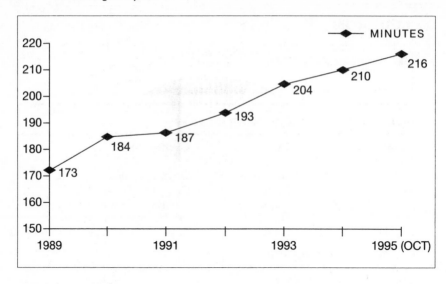

Figure 7.1.4 *Television consumption*

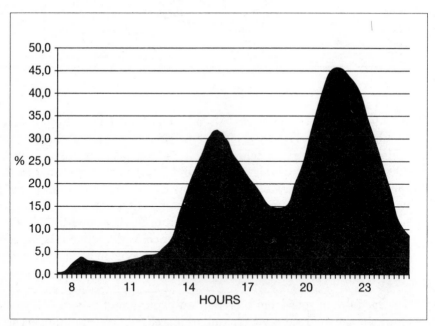

Figure 7.1.5 *Distribution of television audience*

With regard to the market share between the different channels, one can see a clear growth in the private channels since they started their transmission, reaching 48 per cent of the total audience in October 1995. (See Figure 7.1.7)

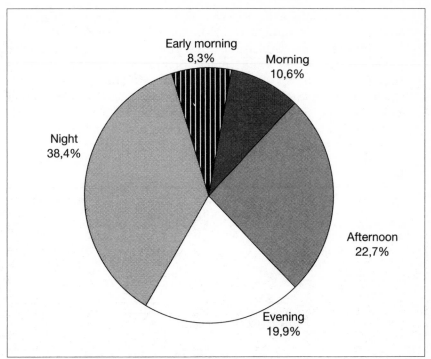

Figure 7.1.6 *Consumption by parts of the day*

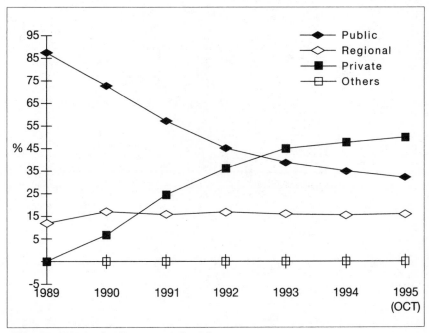

Figure 7.1.7 *Audience market share*

At the moment the split between the different channels is showing a tendency towards stabilisation, although the entry of local television and above all cable television will certainly produce greater market fragmentation. In any event, competition continues and is shown in the programming war established between the different channels and the aggressive commercial policy which has generated saturation publicity campaigns. (See Figure 7.1.8.) From the economic standpoint there is no parallel between the audience market share and commercial figures, for the year 1994. (See Table 7.1.8.)

Table 7.1.8 *Audience market share*

	Audience market share	Sales %	Pesetas (millions)
TVE 1(*)	28.1	30.3	59.591
Antena 3	25.6	32.1	63.057
Tele 5	18.4	21.1	41.412
Autonomous regions	15.7	14.8	29.151
La 2	9.3	6.9	13.580
Canal +(**)	2.1	1.0	1.996
Others	0.8	–	N/A

(*) Including local TV but not Canary Islands
(**) Only including advertising when not encoded

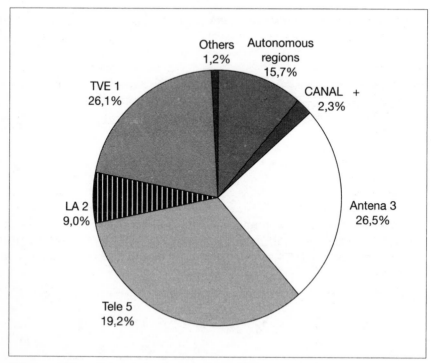

Figure 7.1.8 *Market share by channel (1)*

These theoretical deviations, among other things, are a consequence of different commercial policies, resulting from the different type and coverage of the channels. (See Figure 7.1.9.)

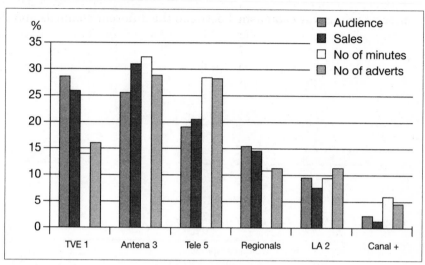

Figure 7.1.9 *Market share by channel (2)*

With respect to advertising saturation and from a base of the legal maximum permitted to advertising of 12 minutes per hour, the daily advertising share of the national channels in September 1995 according to *Sofres'* data is shown in Figure 7.1.10. Nevertheless, these data which refer to midday, according to *Optimum Media* are broken down during the day as shown in Figure 7.1.11. In summary, we find a highly competitive market in expansion phase.

THE PRESS

There are 144 newspapers in Spain, of which practically all are dailies. According to the Official Circulation Office – *Oficina de Justificación de la Difusión* (OJD), the number of copies in circulation during the last three years is shown in Table 7.1.9 (see also Chapter 7.2). Of the total corresponding to 1994, the first ten daily newspapers make up 57.5 per cent of the total. (See Table 7.1.10.)

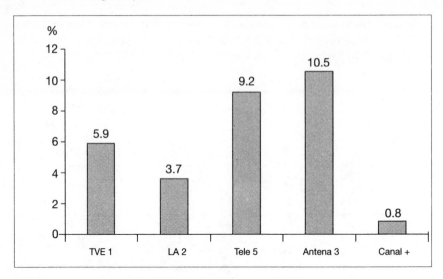

Figure 7.1.10 *Percentage of advertising (daily total)*

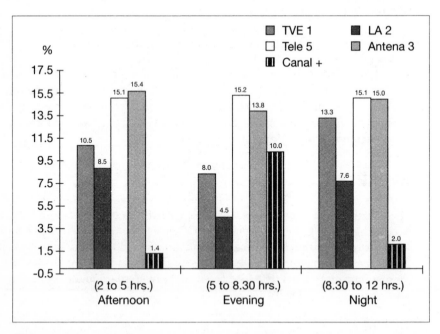

Figure 7.1.11 *Percentage of advertising (daily total by parts of day)*

Table 7.1.9 *Copies of newspapers in circulation*

	Copies	**%**
1992	3,681,352	–
1993	3,780,676	2.7
1994	3,986,340	5.4

Table 7.1.10 *The top ten daily newspapers*

		Locality	**Circulation**		**%**
			1993	**1994**	
1	Marca	Madrid	333,396	421,294	26.4
2	El Pais	Madrid	401,258	408,267	1.7
3	ABC	Madrid	334,317	321,571	(3.8)
4	El Mundo	Madrid	209,992	268,748	27.9
5	La Vanguardia	Barcelona	208,029	207,112	(0.4)
6	El Periodico	Barcelona	185,517	193,576	4.3
7	El Correo Español	Bilbao	133,954	137,647	2.7
8	As	Madrid	140,213	121,793	(13.1)
9	La Voz De Galicia	La Coruña	107,446	113,086	5.3
10	Sport	Barcelona	88,972	100,405	12.8

Among these are three daily sports newspapers (numbers 1, 8 and 10). Newspaper audience has experienced sustained growth in recent years until 1993, as reflected in Figure 7.1.12. Comparing the data for the leading ten newspapers, one can see little connection between the circulation, the audience, and the sales turnover. (See Figure 7.1.13.)

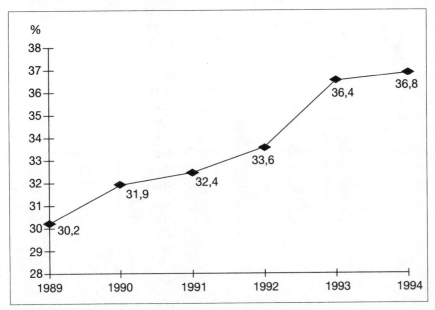

Figure 7.1.12 *Percentage of advertising (daily total)*

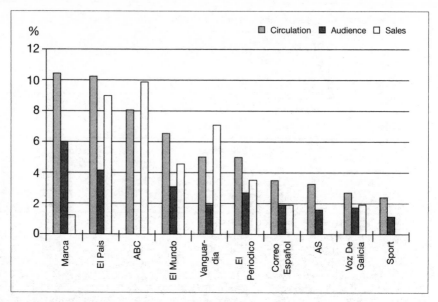

Figure 7.1.13 *Newspaper market share*

As well as the newspapers we should consider the Sunday supplements, despite their audience being connected to the newspapers. Their circulation is significant, although lately they have suffered a decline in their sales of advertising space. (See Figure 7.1.14.)

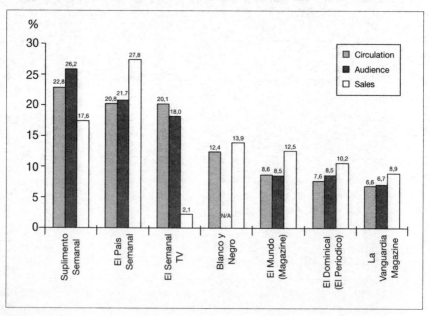

Figure 7.1.14 *Market share of Sunday supplements*

In the newspaper sector in recent years there has been an important process of concentration, in some cases over and above that seen in the other media. The main newspaper groups are shown in Table 7.1.11.

Table 7.1.11 *The main newspaper groups*

Group	Total circulation	Newspapers
Prisa	429,278	El Pais
		Cinco Días
Grupo Z	348,131	El Periódico
		El Mediterráneo
		La Voz de Asturias
		Sport
Recoletos	460,341	Expansión
		Marca
Prensa Ibérica	444,523	Faro de Vigo
		La Nueva España
		Levante
		Diario de Ibiza
		Diario de Mallorca
		Información
		La Opinión de Murcia
		La Provincia
		Diario de las Palmas
Grupo Correo	504,270	El Correo Español
		El Diario Vasco
		El Diario Montañés
		El Norte de Castilla
		El Comercio
		La Verdad
		Ideal de Granada
		Hoy
		Sur
		La Rioja

The total circulation of these groups reached 2,186,543 in 1994, 54.8 per cent of the national total. Some of these groups are present in other media, for example, the *Prisa Group* controls the radio stations *Ser* and *Dial* as well as *Canal Plus* where it owns 25 per cent of the capital. *Group Z* controls *Antena 3 TV* and a large number of magazines (*Tiempo, Interviu,* etc.). Also participating in various magazines is the *Group Recoletos* (*Telva, Actualidad Económica*). *Group Correo*, in addition to an interchange of directors with *Prensa Española* (*Abc* and *Blanco y Negro*), their 31 per cent interest in *Taller de Editores* (*Suplemento Semanal* and *Semanal TV*), and 8 per cent in *Group Recoletos*, are also negotiating their entry in *Tele 5*.

In the economic sector, there are three newspapers; the 1994 data are shown in Table 7.1.12. This is a modest sector with a strong concentration of sales in Madrid (43.5 per cent).

Table 7.1.12 *Main economic newspapers*

Newspaper	Circulation	Audience	Advertising revenue (million pesetas)
Expansión	39,047	99,000	1,142
Gaceta de los Negocios	17,554	Not controlled	1,098
Cinco Días	21,011	Not controlled	1,033

MAGAZINES

In this, the medium most affected by the economic crisis as well as increased competition from television, the market share has reduced in total. As we have already seen, the market has decreased by 11 per cent in 1994 in comparison to 1993 and, in parallel, the leading magazines have suffered the biggest declines in their circulations, particularly in case of the television magazines. The ten leading magazines by circulation in 1994 are shown in Table 7.1.13.

Table 7.1.13 *The top ten leading magazines in 1994*

	Sector	Circulation	% Increase (decrease) 1993
Pronto	Women	697,541	(7.3)
Hola	Women	659,270	0.4
Supertele	Television	592,164	(13.5)
Teleprograma	Television	407,096	(41.7)
Teleindiscreta	Television	398,437	(38.2)
Lecturas	Women	336,121	3.3
Semana	Women	322,085	(10.4)
Clara	Women	309,347	2.6
Diez Minutos	Women	306,926	(13.3)
Muy Interesante	Sensational	288,590	(2.0)

It is important to note the absolute domination of the women's magazines, the huge loss of circulation we have mentioned in the TV magazines, as well as the lack of general information magazines.

Market shares of the 15 magazines with the highest circulation are analysed, and the percentages are based on the leading 50 titles in each classification in 1994. To indicate the importance of these 15 magazines, we note that the total market share within the leading 50 in each classification was 62.1 per cent of the audience, 56.1 per cent of the circulation and 40.8 per cent of the investment. (See Figure 7.1.15.) To finish, the circulation leader in each segment is shown in Table 7.1.14.

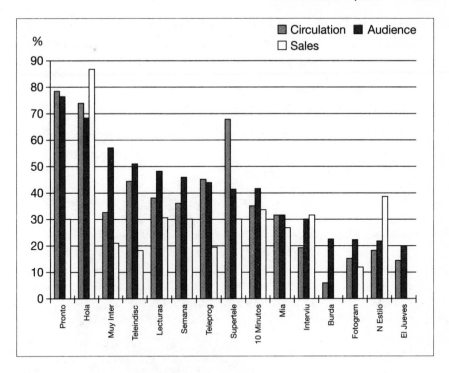

Figure 7.1.15 *Magazine market share*

Table 7.1.14 *Magazine market share*

Segment	Magazíne	Frequency	Circulation
General information	Intervin	Weekly	167,191
Womens	Pronto	Weekly	697,541
Television	Supertele	Weekly	592,164
Automotive	Automóvil	Monthly	54,084
Economy	Act. Económica	Weekly	28,915
Sensational	Muy Interesante	Weekly	288,590
IT	Hobby Consolas	Monthly	142,031
Male	Man	Monthly	55,403
Fashion and beauty	Clara	Monthly	309,342

RADIO

The consumption of radio in Spain in 1994, according to the EGM, is 102.5 minutes per day per inhabitant. This consumption is highest from Monday to Friday, where it reaches 112.7 minutes, and lowest during the weekends at 82.8 and 71.3 minutes for Saturday and Sunday respectively.

In the distribution of consumption, the morning, with 40 per cent of the total, is the most popular time, the rest of the day being divided up almost equally. (See Figure 7.1.16.) In Figure 7.1.17 we can see the audience distribution during the day, where in addition to the total it shows details of formula radio and conventional radio.[4]

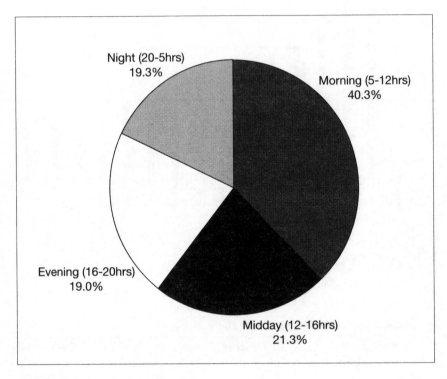

Figure 7.1.16 *Radio consumption*

The total number of stations in Spain is 1,458, although the majority of the audience is concentrated in the main networks grouped according to Table 7.1.15. Not included in the list are the transmitters of the *Radio Nacional de España* (RNE), the public network, as it does not allow advertising.

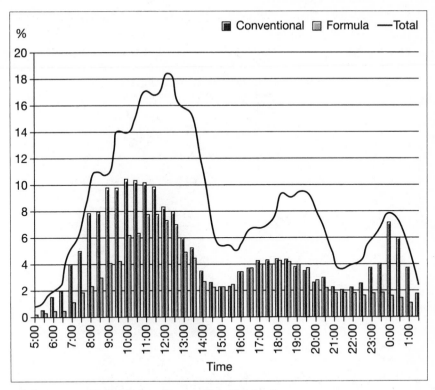

Figure 7.1.17 *Radio audience distribution*

Table 7.1.15 *Main radio networks*

Network	Type	No of transmitters
Ser	Conventional	172
	Formula (40 principal)	66
Onda Cero	Conventional	124
	Formula	39
Cope	Conventional	101
	Formula (Network 100)	47
Dial	Formula	77
M-80	Formula	35
Ibérica	Conventional	23
Radiolé	Formula	6
The rest		769

The audience market share is shown in Figure 7.1.18 and Figure 7.1.19, separating conventional transmitters from the formula transmitters. When it comes to comparing the audience market share according to sales turnover, the networks are grouped on function of their ownership: *Group Prisa* (*Ser, Dial, M-80* and *Radiolé*), *Onda Cero* and *Cope*. (See Figure 7.1.20.)

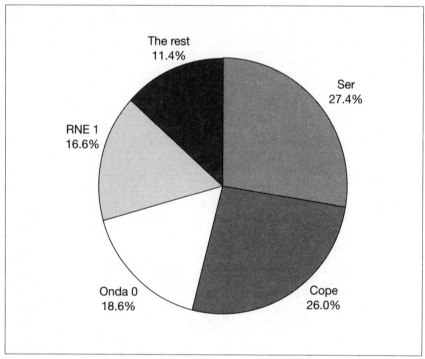

Figure 7.1.18 *Network market share (conventional)*

THE OUTDOORS

Dominating the outdoors advertising sector are four main groups: hoardings, telephone cabins, canopies, and others (stadia, buses, etc). The approximate number of locations and turnover is shown in Table 7.1.16.

Table 7.1.16 *Main outdoors advertising media*

Type	Number	1994 (million pesetas)	1993 %	Market share %
Hoardings	43,900	11,536	–	44.8
Telephone cabins	33,600	1,776	12	6.9
Canopies	21,300	7,415	20	28.8
Others	n/a	5,032	4	19.5

In the hoardings group, more than three quarters of the market is controlled by seven companies of which the most important, *Avenir*, controls about 25 per cent of the locations. The telephone cabins are controlled by just one company, a subsidiary of the Spanish publicly-

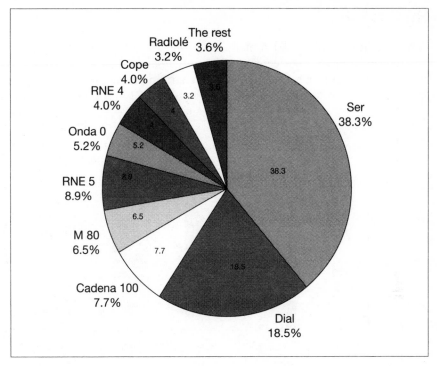

Figure 7.1.19 *Network market share (formula)*

owned telephone company. Regarding the canopies, three companies control most of the sector, and one of these, *Camusa*, manages half of it.

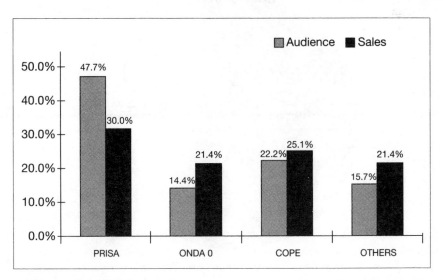

Figure 7.1.20 *Market share*

THE CINEMA

This medium, which had a clear reduction in audience in the 1980s, decreased from 13.5 per cent in 1982 to 6.3 per cent in 1991. From the beginning of the 1990s, there has been a slight improvement, reaching 7.8 per cent of the audience in 1994. (See Figure 7.1.21 and Figure 7.1.22.)

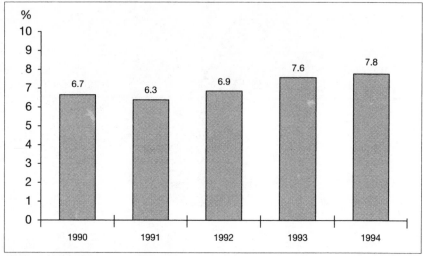

Figure 7.1.21 *Cinema audience*

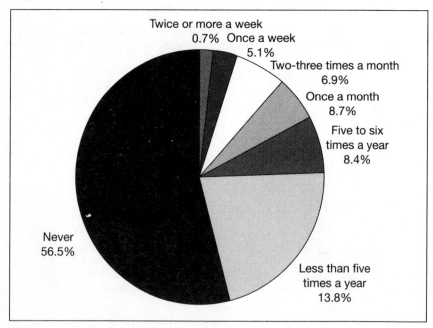

Figure 7.1.22 *Cinema-going habit*

NOTES

1 Infoadex is a company dedicated to measurement of advertising audiences. It was created as a joint venture of AC Nielsen and Duplo.

2 The holding of companies headed by *ECI* is the largest private non-financial organisation. Its turnover is in the region of two per cent of GNP.

3 EGM is published by the Spanish Association of Media (Asociación Española de Medios de Comunicación – AIMC).

4 'Formula radio' and 'conventional radio' are Spanish terms. Formula radio refers to stations which focus upon a single subject: music, education, or sport for example. Conventional radio stations transmit a succession of programmes on different subjects.

Sources of Information for Media Planners

Francisco Javier Suso

CIRCULATION VERIFICATION OFFICE – OJD (OFICINA DE JUSTIFICACION DE LA DIFUSION)

This organisation has been set up by advertisers, advertising agencies, newspapers and magazines for the sole purpose of monitoring the circulation, recording the distribution and readership of newspapers and magazines which provide this information on a voluntary basis. The data are collected by means of an audit which lasts one year. A report is produced at the end of each year, showing average monthly circulation figures for national and provincial distribution in Spain, and abroad. Factors which may have a positive or negative effect on these figures are noted: price variations, sales promotions, advertising campaigns, group subscriptions and so on. Any publicity media which are not registered with the OJD may not publish or declare circulation or distribution figures unless such information is supported by a notarised certificate.

Main categories defined

Effective circulation – this is the total number of copies of a single issue of a title which comes off the press in saleable condition. Torn or imperfect copies are not included.

Regular subscriptions – these are copies sent periodically and regularly to a known recipient, during the audit period at the agreed price.

Group subscriptions – these are subscriptions taken out *en bloc* by a person or entity other than the publishing company, for subsequent delivery to known recipients.

Single copy sales – these are copies sold to the public through press distribution channels and the individual issues sold by the publication on their own premises. Block sales for subsequent sale to known recipients are also audited under this heading.

Regular services – these are copies sent regularly to certain organisations or individuals. For example, advertiser copies, complimentary copies, non-profit organisations, copies required by law for verification, etc.

Distribution – this is the figure obtained by adding together total copy sales, subscriptions and regular services.

SOFRES AM – TELEVISION VIEWER PANEL

This panel is made up of a fixed sample of 2,500 households, representing 7,951 individuals over the age of four in Peninsular Spain and the Balearic Islands.

Sample type: aproportional – the sample has been extended to ensure improved representation for autonomous regions which have their own regional television channels – Madrid, Galicia, Euzkadi, Cataluña, Valencia and Andalucía. In these areas therefore the sampling error is lower than in the rest of the regions, partly compensating for the greater population variance in the television viewer phenomenon. Households are selected using Random Route and quota methods.

Audience measurement

Once the household has been contracted for a period of three years, the audimeter is connected to the main and secondary television equipment on the premises, the video and the telephone. If the household selected does not have a telephone, one is installed at the cost of Sofres AM.

All members of the household are then instructed how to work the equipment, and how to personally log on, pressing the button when in front of the television and how to log off when leaving the room where the television screen is located.

From then on, a record is kept of every time any equipment is turned on or off, the channel tuned in each one, all changes of channel showing the new channels and the people in front of the television screens in the household.

The audimeter has a sound signal to remind the panel member to register his or her presence when switching on the television and log off when leaving the room in which the television is situated. Of course, when the equipment is switched off, all the audience for this is logged off.

The audimeter can identify up to 250 different channels from any type of signal: land, cable or satellite.

Data collection for central processing

The Sofres AM central computer is connected automatically by telephone to all panel homes and collects the information stored in the audimeters in order to:

- validate the responses and the sample;
- weight the sample to balance it;
- calculate the results.

At the same time, using data from other sources as a basis, other information is loaded into the central computer:

- breakdown of broadcasts with spots, promos for channels, programmes, subprogrammes and all kinds of items.

The system monitors the following:

- *Audimeter*

- Correct functioning of the equipment.

- *Sample*

- Atypical or extreme audience;
- households and individuals with no audience;
- other controls (annual telephone survey);
- correct use of remote control;
- periodic sample census.

Results

Every day at 9 o'clock viewer data are obtained on a minute-by-minute basis, from a simple advertising spot to the longest programme. The audience can be broken down by sociodemographic variables and by household ownership of certain equipment such as: type of television, colour or black and white, second set, remote control or video recorder.

This enables us to obtain detailed information about the viewers, their development, sociodemographic composition, time spent in front of the television and monitor the quality and quantity of variations. It also enables us to study:

- *migration* – viewers moving from one programme to one on another channel and returning to the original programme;
- *loyalty* to a programme, average audience during a broadcast. Maximum audience. Minimum audience. Total Audience;
- *duplications* between programmes.

In addition to standard audience measurements, the information from panel viewers can be cross-referenced with data from other sources. Sources such as INFOADEX provide information regarding the content of programmes.

For example, by crossing the viewing audience with advertising spots appearing on television channels, we can calculate the real audience for the spots and real coverage for campaigns broadcast. Crossing audience and content for different types of programmes enables us to study the maximum, minimum and average audience for films, comedies, films for television, crime series, religious, comedies; and within these, Spanish, French, etc. For example, taking films shown on the leading Spanish television channel at peak Saturday viewing times we can identify the audience for westerns, comedies, thrillers, adventure films and identify the socio-demographic variables, identifying the audience for each type.

These surveys provide information which is extremely useful to television channels, for programme scheduling. It is also useful for media planners, although the socio-demographic variables information often turns out to be insufficient for media planning. The information regarding programme content and audiences forms the basis of information for audience prediction programmes such as MARS.

GENERAL MEDIA SURVEY (ESTUDIO GENERAL DE MEDIOS – EGM)

This survey is carried out by the Association for Research in Communication Media (AIMC). The survey title is the name of the former company, Estudio General de Medios, founded in 1969. The Board of this non-profit company is made up of three partners representing advertising agencies, communication media and advertisers and is chaired by a representative of the advertising agencies.

Characteristics of the General Media Survey

Television

- National television;
- regional television (*televisión autonómica*);
- satellite television.

Radio

- National networks
- regional networks (*cadenas autonómicas*);
- individual stations;
- independent stations.

Magazines and Sunday supplements, Daily press and Cinema as a general medium.

The General Media Survey is a media/product survey, that is to say, in addition to obtaining information on the media audience it includes questions regarding consumer products, ownership of household goods and services used by the audiences and population surveyed. The information on media and products is fleshed out with data on leisure activities, pastimes, cultural activities and centres of interest for all the population studied, thus making the study very useful for the marketing of communication media and marketing in general.

In addition, the General Media Survey includes a wide range of socio-demographic variables: sex, age, social class, civil status, family role, family size, presence of children in household, dwelling, province, region, cultural and socio-work level, work status.

Technical characteristics

Sample: 40,000 annual interviews with individuals over the age of 14. It operates in three phases with approximately 13,333 valid interviews per phase (February–March) (May–June) and (October–November). In each phase, or periods, the field work lasts eight weeks.

- the sample is divided into seven subsamples for each day of the week;
- *sample design:* multistage and stratified (by province/dwelling) and distribution of interviews in proportion to the population for each day of the week;
- *selection:* using Random Route methods;
- *selection:* random selection of individuals, in households;
- *interviews:* face-to-face. Media consumption is studied asking for 'day-after' or 'last period' recall.

Audience consumption habits are also collected and data on audience composition.

This multimedia/product survey is the oldest of its kind in Spain, having been set up in 1969. It is continually adjusted to guarantee stability of data. It is a professional association survey, funded by advertisers, advertising agencies and communication media. The reliability and cleanliness of data are guaranteed by the Technical Committee which ensures that there is no bias in favour of any one of the three blocks of agency, media or advertiser contributors.

The survey is designed for individual or multimedia publicity planning. It enables audience data to be crossed with ownership of household goods, consumption of products, purchase of household products over the last 30 days (housewives), use of services, centres of interest and lifestyles.

MARKETING AND MEDIA INFORMATION SYSTEM (SISTEMA DE INFORMACION DE MARKETING MEDIOS – SIMM)

This database – in principle a bi-annual product – monitors certain types of attitudinal and psychological variables according to product consumption, use of services, leisure and advertising media audiences. The first survey carried out in 1992 was owned by INTERDECO and implemented by:

● Dympanel: design and recruitment of sample, design of questionnaire and field work;
● ODEC: recording, processing, analysis, tabulation and preparation of data for users;
● The General Media Survey provided the data for the second phase in 1992.

The data are compared against and balanced with the General Media Survey and results are produced by ODEC. The geographical scope of the study is Peninsular Spain and the Balearics, it covers individuals over the age of 14, and its sample size and structure is 7,500 individuals.

Group	Sample	Sampling error
Housewives	2,753	± 1.9%
Women: not housewives	863	± 4.0
Men: head of family	2,915	± 2.1
Men: not head of family	954	± 4.0
For a confidence interval of 95.5%		

This data source is designed to study the behaviour of adults over the age of 14, according to their use of advertising media, consumption of products and brands, use of services – with a brand name. Another part of the SIMM survey covers the use of leisure time, lifestyles and certain attitudinal and psychographic variables and gathers opinions on the religious, political and social family context. This survey is carried out in the majority of European countries, so comparisons can be made between various European countries.

This study is also designed to complement the General Media Survey (AIMC) since the publicity media audience results, classification and socio-democraphic variables have been adapted to match those of this survey.

It is used to obtain the following information:

For publicity purposes:

- Brand market and positioning;
- definition of target markets;
- analysis of consumption of generic products and specific trade names;
- exposure to communication media;
- application of socio-styles to creative strategies.

For marketing applications:

- Market analysis;
- analysis and positioning of competition;
- repositioning analysis;
- target group analysis;
- consumer analysis, consumption frequency;
- surveys of decision-makers and specifiers;
- points of sale;
- products, services, brands.

LIFESTYLES

The 'mentalities' and 'lifestyles' are groupings of individuals in the market according to psycho-sociological criteria regarding:

- current behaviour;
- attitudes;
- motivations and aspirations;
- impulses and feelings;
- socio-demographic characteristics.

The 'mentalities' and 'lifestyles' have been designed according to criteria of the Advanced Communication Centre of Paris – with its six types of 'mentalities' and 16 'European lifestyles' which are defined below:

- six mentalities (homogeneous population groupings);
- 16 lifestyles. Each 'mentality' is subdivided into groupings of individuals having similar characteristics as regards the focus of their 'centres of interest' and their declared attitudes on current topics and personal, family, international, social and religious dynamics (see Table 7.2.1).

Table 7.2.1 *The different mentalities and lifestyles*

Mentalities	Lifestyles
Ambitious	Dandy, business
Anti-establishment	Pioneers, protesters
Militants	Scouts, citizens
Dreamers	Romantics
Worthies	Moralists, gentry, disciplinarians
Retired	Prudent, defensive, vigilant, forgotten

In the 1992 INTERDECO SIMM survey consumption and brands were analysed in 25 market sectors, which can be broken down and segmented by socio-style, mentalities and consumption of various forms of media, enabling a wide range of consumer segmentation for each market. An infinite number of relationships and matches can be established between a wide range of marketing variables, enabling the market to be defined for products and media within each sector.

Features of the SIMM survey

The sample base is 7,500 interviews. The survey universe covers the Peninsula and the Balearic Islands. It does not cover the Canary Islands. It studies: the five national television channels and the regional networks; the Sunday supplements; the main daily national and provincial newspapers; the radio networks and large independent stations. Consumer characteristics: buyer, consumer, consumption intensity, purchase location, usual brand and 'other brands' consumed across 25 sectors: 341 categories of products and services with a total of 4,720 brands.

GENERAL AUDIENCE SURVEY – EGA (ESTUDIO GENERAL DE AUDIENCIAS)

This survey is sponsored by the Fundación General de la Universidad Complutense de Madrid, which funds its operation to the tune of 200 million pesetas each year. The EGA survey has experienced various problems in recent years, first appearing in 1993 and not published again until 1995.

At present, it consists of three discrete media surveys:

1. EGA press circulation;
2. EGA radio audiences;
3. EGA press readership.

The fieldwork for all three surveys is carried out by SIGMA 2.

A different director manages each survey and it has been agreed that there should be a User Committee which all survey subscribers may join. This will be responsible for supervising the report production process and any changes in methodology or techniques employed.

EGA press circulation – survey of press and magazine circulation

Frequency: three phases each year/four reports per phase. The survey focuses on buyers of newspapers and magazines at news-stands. It studies press buyers and the audience for newspapers or magazines purchased by respondents, to enable more precise calculation of the number of readers per copy bought at the news-stands.

It analyses:

- total sales;
- socio-economic variables for buyers and readers;
- readers per copy;
- buying habits and buying intentions;
- specialist information (editorials, finance, automotive, politics, etc).

The fieldwork is carried out by surveying press buyers at the news-stand from a national sample.

EGA radio

A radio survey which uses the Mediametric measuring methodology of the French organisation which has carried out a similar survey in France for a number of years. Frequency: quarterly; using day-after recall with the CATI system (Computer Assisted Telephone Interview). The survey universe is individuals over the age of 14 living in single family households throughout Spain (including the Canaries). The sampling procedure is multistage and stratified. Individuals are selected by the quota method according to population distribution.

Telephone numbers are selected by a random procedure using the CODITEL database (subsidiary of TELEFONICA). Sample: in the current model, the total number of interviews each year is 53,000. The information includes listener habits and socio-demographic data. The audience is collected every quarter of an hour, by station, channel and programme.

SOFEMASA DIRECTORS

Press readership survey of directors and managers

This survey provides an analysis of reading habits of daily papers and magazines and centres of interest of Spanish directors and managers. It covers their personal purchases and decision-making authority for the goods and services of their company. The survey has been operating since 1990.

Methodology – personal face-to-face interview at workplace, and structured questionnaire.

Sample – 2,200 working managers; 1,400 directors of companies with 10 to 500 employees; 200 professionals; 100 legal professionals; 100 technical professionals; 200 teachers; 200 civil servants.

Types of information

- Goods and services for the company;
- major management themes; finance, marketing, foreign trade, management, etc;
- personal consumption;
- hobbies;
- media consulted: magazines, main newspapers.

PLEX

This is a special programme for planning and evaluating outdoor advertising campaigns. It is sponsored by the Spanish Association for Outdoor Advertising and the AIMC. It is distributed free of charge.

PLEX is based on the established Copland formula model, which studies the routes taken by individuals in cities to identify how many per person exposures occur in specific time periods. The object of the study is to establish the audience for outdoor advertising measured as:

- coverage;
- showings for specified periods of time, size of city and number of

sites. The survey measures the results in terms of coverage, showings or exposure opportunities among individuals over the age of 14 living in households in the city studied and number of sites in the city, during the following periods:
- week
- fortnight
- month

Size of city: population of 40,000 to 3,900,000 in the tables. The standard evaluations may be applied to four types of target groups:
- individuals
- men
- women
- housewives

The field work is carried out in three cities:
- Madrid
- Valencia
- Oviedo.

These are representatives of a large, medium and small city. The results are extrapolated using the B Copland formula for any city up to 3,900,000 inhabitants. The results are presented in the form of tables and graphs showing periods of 7–14 or 28 days; coverage: size of population and number of sites; showings: target: individuals, men, women, housewives.

CIES

This study surveys a range of media: television, radio, daily papers and magazines. Areas surveyed include: Vizcaya, Guipúzcoa, Alava, Rioja and Navarra. The methodology is similar to the General Media Survey; frequency: three phases per annum with four monthly reports; owned by the Autonomous Governments of Euzkadi, Rioja and Navarra. Sample: País Vasco: 1,100 interviews/phase; Navarra: 900 interviews/phase; Rioja: 900 interviews/phase.

INFOADEX (information on advertising expenditure)

This organisation was formed by the merger of AC Nielsen Co (Repress Division) and Duplo-Triplo, two companies previously monitoring total advertising expenditure and broadcast advertisements in Spain. It surveys brand advertising expenditure in the media.

OTHER DATABASES AVAILABLE

Organisation	Content
A C Nielsen	Database operating since 1964, based on a retail panel including outlets selling food, photographic, perfumery, haberdashery, dairy, white goods and brown goods; chemists, tobacconists, delicatessens, pharmacies, bars and hotels
Dympanel	Consumer panel (3,000) for food, drinks, toiletries, textiles, perfumery, cosmetics and hygiene.
Areas of research	Statistics regarding vehicle registration, saloons, vans, trucks on the Spanish market.
IMS	Survey of pharmaceutical products: ethical, semi-ethical and OTC.

7.3

Buying Media Space

Francisco Javier Suso

The purchase of space on television is somewhat complex, in both administration and operation.

First, the advertiser must present an advertiser 'accreditation' to the television company and to the contracting agency which then handles the administrative procedures required to make a firm purchase of space. In most cases, this is processed through another, centralised media purchasing agency (Central de Compras or Agencia de Distribución de Medios) using official standard forms.

Once these preliminary procedures have been completed for each of the stations on which the client wishes to advertise, an application for space is then submitted on standard order forms. These orders must be endorsed by a bank or payment made when the space is actually allocated to the advertiser.

There are various payment options: under the advance payment method, the advertiser receives a discount for prompt payment; under the 30 days method, there is no additional charge on the invoice; under deferred payment an additional charge is made when payment is delayed beyond this period.

The orders are processed and spaces allocated. If the required space is not available, applications are rejected or a counteroffer is made for other spaces with a similar audience and value to the initial space, on adjacent dates. If the counteroffer space is suitable for the campaign, this is accepted. If it is not considered suitable, the negotiation starts again with a second counteroffer. This whole process can be handled over the phone or by personal visit to the advertising department of the individual television company, where space availability is processed by computer.

If all goes well and space is available as requested, the advertisement is allocated.

SALE OF SPACE ON TELEVISION NETWORKS

Every day there is an increasing range of space available on television, which is categorised as follows:

- *Ordinary advertisements* For spaces of 20 seconds and above, grouped in blocks of a maximum of 12 spots, for which the total duration shall not exceed an average of 280 seconds.
- *Extraordinary advertisements* To be placed in spaces in blocks similar to those of the ordinary category and of variable duration, sometimes longer than 15 minutes, for insertion in retransmissions which do not fall into a regular category of broadcast for the network eg retransmissions of football, Olympic Games, national and international football championships, Holy Week processions, bullfights, motorsports, horse jumping, international cycling events, OTI festival, end of year advertisements, etc.
- *Special advertisements* This section includes all advertising not described in the previous two categories: free write-ups, programme sponsorship, gifts, brand mentions, product and brand appearances in programmes, prize draws, mentions, packaging and overprinting.

Ordinary advertisement space may be bought in various ways:

- *Direct purchase or 'contratación libre'* Space is bought on an individual basis at the basic tariff rate, with guaranteed positioning and broadcast time. Some networks offer significant discounts for spaces at specific times.
- *Packages* Purchase of a block of spaces to be used within a specified period.
- *Customised packages or modules* These packages are designed for broadcast at fixed times, and to reach different target groups, such as: housewives, men, young people, children or individuals in general.

In some cases, the minimum gross rating point (GRP) for the purchase is guaranteed. If the agreed GRP is not achieved, the network gives the advertiser additional spaces until the agreed GRP level is reached. Planned spaces may be broadcast by the network at any time within predetermined 'bands' or schedules.

It is advisable to negotiate advertising schedules in advance with the Publicity Department of the television company, since an exchange of 'bands' may be possible. For example, a campaign aimed at mothers and young children may be improved by exchanging morning weekday spots, when the child viewer audience is virtually zero, for space at the same time on Saturdays or Sundays or in children's programmes in the afternoon of the working days.

There is rather more freedom in planning these 'packages' since we are only obliged to contract for a minimum percentage of the total investment in some of the time bands.

- *'Strips or bands'* By this method, space is bought at the same time for seven consecutive days, and the advertiser receives one free exposure, or a significant discount on the basic rate, the *precio de salida,* for another week, limited to a specified time band.

On some networks, such as Televisión Española and Antena 3, it is possible to buy space for certain regional areas and by module or band. An individual agreement must be made for each special or extraordinary advertisement.

NEGOTIATING PURCHASE DISCOUNTS

If space is contracted through advertising agencies, two types of discount are available: First Agency Commission Discount, usually 10 per cent. Once this discount has been deducted, a second discount is applied to the net invoice figure. This discount or *rappel* increases as a function of the net invoice volume of the agency making the contract with the television company. This second discount is applied at the end of the year.

Depending on the general supply and demand, television companies offer special discounts for campaigns, for first-time advertisers, for first advertisements for a product on the network, or simply because they need to invoice more to meet their budget. At other times, a small additional discount may be offered for an exclusive campaign, the season when the planning takes place, type of schedule selected, etc.

Large buying groups commit to purchase large volumes of rating points from the television companies at previously agreed prices, which means that they can offer advertisers space with very advantageous conditions. When using this method of buying space advertisers need to be alert to the quality of space purchased.

Our recommendations

How to know whether your creative style is working in Spain
Test your advertising with the help of a qualitative research organisation which has a good reputation or is known to you.

- If you do not know what advertising to place or which agency to use and you have little time in which to decide, invite offers. Ask for assistance, for example from the Spanish Advertisers Association (Asociación Española de Anunciantes) or the Association of Advertising Professionals – ATP (Asociación de Titulados en Publicidad) who can provide you with suitable names.

In this case, it is advisable to invite agencies to pitch for the creative aspects of your campaign, providing you already have a clear idea of your publicity argument. If you have the slightest doubt you should not make a decision. Consult a qualitative marketing research organisation or a publicity adviser (*asesor publicitario*) who will design a brief for the competition and take responsibility for testing the creative ideas presented by the invited agencies. Seek a good mix between international agencies working in the country and local Spanish companies.

Remember, after USA and UK companies, Spanish agencies have won the greatest number of awards for creative merit in worldclass advertising competitions and you may well be pleasantly surprised.

- If you require a full service package including those provided by account executives, copywriters, media planners, qualitative researchers or specialists in sales promotion, graphic design, audiovisual presentation, you will certainly want to seek the services of a multinational: you will receive a full service if you are a large account.

  If you are a medium-sized account, ask to meet each member of the team personally, put faces to names. Ask them to provide you with a full CV of each member of the team, so that you know about their skills and experience. Do also ask about other clients for whom they are working, because you will be competing with these companies for the time the team spends on your account.
- If you have services and creative direction organised and you only need to plan and buy media, you have two options:
  1. Assign all administration functions to your advertising agency, although we would advise you to personally monitor your buying office, always through the advertising agency so that it does not lose its personality and professional pride.
  2. Assign the planning and purchase functions to two separate

companies, one to plan and the other to contract and buy media space for you. In this way you will buy only what you need and not everything and anything which can be bought for a given budget. Don't be taken in by the buyers of 'RP garbage'. Buy only what you need for your campaign and not a single rating point more.

Part 8

The Labour Market

INTRODUCTION

This section offers the reader a general picture of recent developments in the Spanish labour market, both from an economic and legislative point of view, in the light of the recent changes introduced in the Workers' Statute in 1994 (legislation governing the relationship between employers and employees). A remarkable feature of the Spanish labour market (15.5 million people) is its high level of unemployment (23 per cent), relative to other member states of the European Union. Observers have tended to blame this on the rigidities of the contractual system and the uncontrolled growth in salary rates. The disordered restructuring of Spanish industry and agriculture might also be partly responsible.

It should be noted however that Spanish unemployment data are recorded through a national Employment Survey (Encuesta de Población Activa), which yields figures that significantly exceed those for registered unemployment. Using registered unemployment, the figure for most European countries (including the UK) would place Spanish unemployment in the region of 15.5 per cent of the active working population.

No matter which way unemployment is recorded, the figure still seems to be very high. Regarding the policies proposed for its reduction, there has been general agreement on the necessity to introduce greater flexibility in the types of employment contracts and in the social protection they provide. This has been the aim of the changes introduced in the Statute of Workers in 1994, not much contested by the unions. Some other important reforms, like the introduction of temping agencies, also address the problem of rigidities in the labour market.

Political commentators have also drawn attention to the existence of a certain shift in the major unions (UGT, and CCOO), from direct confrontation on deregulation to a more collaborative relationship with employers, aimed at establishing common objectives and a trade-off of the efforts required to reach them.

The following chapter, written by Caroline Welch from IDS, will provide you with a picture of the Spanish labour market. The second chapter, by Fraser Yonson and Alex Valls from Baker & McKenzie, offers a deeper insight to labour law.

8.1

The Spanish Labour Market: An Overview of Developments and Trends

Caroline Welch, IDS Employment Europe

THE LABOUR MARKET IN SPAIN

In less than two decades the Spanish labour market has undergone rapid and profound change. Since 1980 the move off the land, the decline in traditional manufacturing industry, the rise in services and the influx of some 1.5 million people, largely women, onto the labour market have all reshaped the jobs scene.

Statute law provides the main underpinning for the structures of industrial relations, with statutory and constitutional guarantees of freedom of association and trade union rights, and statutory forms of employee representation at workplace level. Both trade unions and employers' organisations must meet statutory criteria of representativeness in order to engage in collective bargaining. Legislation governing employment contracts stems from the provisions of the 1978 constitution, the 1980 Workers' Statute, the 1980 Basic Employment law and the 1994 reform of the Workers' Statute. Under legislation governing the regional governments of Spain, the Ministry of Labour and Social Security is gradually transferring powers in several areas of employment to the regional governments.

Regional authority over labour matters

Central government organisations are represented in local offices (*Dirección Provincial de Trabajo y Seguridad Social*) in each of the 53 provinces. However, since 1981 the regional dimension has had increasing importance. The autonomous communities have their own elected governments, with limited but important powers, especially in the area of social policy. For example, they are increasingly important in job creation and training – and central government is gradually transferring to their control some aspects of labour policy, such as management of the Mediation, Arbitration and Conciliation Institute (IMAC). Substantial powers in labour matters have been devolved in specific cases: Catalonia, for example, has control over a wide range of measures relating to business start-ups, monitoring adherence to job classification and grading (see below), working time, industrial disputes etc.

Reform of the Workers' Statute (1994)

The important and controversial reforms of the Workers' Statute in 1994 imply a major overhaul of the whole structure of labour relations, forms of contract, individual and collective bargaining by deregulating aspects of a formerly highly-centralised and regulated system. The thrust of the reforms was to promote self-regulation between the social partners by individual or collective bargaining.

Prior to the reforms, functions, procedures, staffing, pay, promotion and many other features were shaped by the Francoist labour ordinances (*ordenanzas laborales*) through which employment conditions were regulated. Most employees still expected full-time employment with stable conditions. One of the rigidities of the labour market is a strict adherence to job classification systems imposed by the ordinances, allowing for little flexibility or transfer even within a company. Although collective bargaining has been free to evolve since 1977, few ordinances were formally abrogated and in any event many of the assumptions and concepts they contained were incorporated into the new collective agreements. One important element of the 1994 reforms was the government's decree that ordinances should be replaced by collectively agreed provisions by the end of 1995. The implications for collective and individual contractual arrangements are considerable.

Neither the national employees' organisation (CEOE) nor the major trade unions (UGT, CCOO) advocate decentralisation of bargaining to workplace level. The philosophy behind the reforms of the Workers' Statute was in large part to try and decentralise those relations but in the absence of a well-developed culture of local bargaining it may be difficult to achieve this for some time.

Female participation in the labour market

One of the major changes affecting the labour market was the dramatic rise in the participation of women: between 1984 and 1994 the size of the female workforce rose from 4 million to 5.7 million, whereas the male workforce remained largely stable (9.5 million). As the numbers of jobs available has remained relatively constant over the same decade, this has naturally pushed up the unemployment rate.

Subsidised fixed-term contracts became an instrument of government policy to combat unemployment. Subsidies encouraged employers to take on first-time job seekers, young people and the long-term unemployed, but trades unions in particular became increasingly disillusioned with the burgeoning numbers of people on fixed-term contracts without the full protection afforded to those on permanent contracts. In 1993, 48 per cent of all new hirings were fixed-term, with one third of employment contracts accounted for by fixed-term contracts. The high numbers of seasonal workers in agriculture, but more importantly the tourist sector, partly account for this. Part-time employment is a small but growing part of the labour market, with some 5 per cent of employees working part-time (c 1.6 per cent of men and 12.8 per cent of women – 1993 figures). Some 78 per cent of part-timers are women, and 50 per cent are aged between 20 and 30. Most part-time employment tends to be for unskilled work in sectors such as hotel and catering, or retail. Only 2 per cent of part-time work is for higher or technical functions.

Unemployment

In the fourth quarter of 1995, the unemployment rate, as measured by the monthly household survey, stood at 23.5 per cent, the highest in the European Union. Although the rate of those registered with the official placement agency INEM is somewhat lower at 15.8 per cent, the seriousness of the jobless problem is acknowledged universally. Unemployment is characterised also by:

- high youth unemployment: 41 per cent of jobless aged between 16 and 29;
- a higher rate among women (31 per cent) than men (18 per cent), partly explained by the increase in female participation;
- long-term unemployment: 38 per cent have been jobless for over two years, and a further 19 per cent for over one year.

Various national programmes have attempted to tackle the issue and a number of collective agreements contain limited jobs measures. Most often these involve early retirement options with replacement by young recruits. A number of company collective agreements signed in 1995 pledged to convert temporary or work experience contracts into permanent ones, with others seeking to reduce the use of overtime. State subsidies are available to recruit from 'at risk' groups (such as the over 45s, the long-term unemployed, ethnic minorities etc), but these have been taken up by relatively few companies. Apprenticeship contracts, also reformed in 1994, have on the other hand proved popular. Apprentices may be taken on at specified rates below the minimum wage for up to three years. Over 116,000 were signed in 1994, and many (59 per cent) were at or above the national minimum wage rates. The recently-legalised temping agencies have taken on 120,000 young people, with, according to the agencies, 35 per cent retained on permanent contracts by contracting firms. Evidence would indicate that graduates are using temping work to gain a foothold in the labour market.

Collective agreements and contracts of employment

The present pattern of collective bargaining has been shaped by a mixture of laws, national framework agreements and collective agreements. Contracts of employment must by law respect any collectively-agreed terms and conditions that apply. Collective agreements at undertaking level must in turn conform with the minimum conditions laid down at a higher level, such as provincial or national industry level. Companies in financial difficulties may negotiate exemption from pay clauses in collective agreements. They may be endorsed by a simple majority of each of the negotiating parties. It should be pointed out that although trade unions have low membership levels (c 12 per cent of the workforce), they have considerable statutory powers and rights. They have broader support at workplace level through statutory works councils and other employee representation (see also Chapter 8.2).

Coverage of the workforce by collective agreement varies significantly between sectors, ranging from 42 per cent in the service sector, to 95 per cent in industry. There is also considerable variation within sectors: whereas 89 per cent of workers in financial services are covered by collective agreements, this falls to 48 per cent in retailing and only 3 per cent in the repair and maintenance sector. There have been few strong discernible trends in pay negotiations in recent years, though the number of agreements concluded rose steadily in the 1980s. This was largely due to a rise in company-level agreements from 1,778 in 1982 to 3,286 in 1993, covering some 5 per cent of the workforce. Collectively-agreed settlements outstripped the cost of living by 1.5 per cent to 2 per cent in the late 1980s with a parallel reduction in agreed working hours from an average 1,877 per year in 1982 to 1,763 in 1993.

The 1994–95 pay round saw agreed increases of around 3.6 per cent (inflation was 4.4 per cent for the year), with some 70 per cent of workers also covered by an automatic revision clause. Employees outside the scope of collective bargaining are mostly executives and skilled or technical employees. In recent years there has been a tendency to include clauses banning overtime work (44 per cent of sectoral agreements), sustain manning levels (61 per cent), curb temporary employment contracts (41 per cent) and ensure continuing training (72 per cent). A small but significant number of collective agreements in 1994–95 traded job protection for pay cuts – a new feature.

Structure of pay and terms

Individual remuneration customarily consists of a large number of elements which can, in some cases, virtually double the agreed minima. The main components include the *plus convenio* (collective agreement ratification supplement) which can amount to more than basic pay, seniority payments, bonuses, incentive payments, a variety of allowances, profit-sharing systems and payments for overtime, shift or night work. It is standard practice to make a 13th and 14th month payment, and not uncommon for a 15th month to be paid.

A collective agreement will typically cover, besides remuneration, working time (most often expressed as annual hours), job classification, annual leave and other time off, promotion and relocation procedures and disciplinary procedures.

Dismissal practice

One of the criticisms levelled at the Spanish labour market is its inflexibility, particularly relating to employee mobility and dismissal procedures. Under the labour ordinances every employee was assigned to a tightly-defined job category, and many of these had remained unchanged since the 1960s. A number of changes were made in the 1994 reforms to loosen up these rigid classification criteria as well as amend dismissal procedures. In line with the EU Directive, the notion of collective dismissal was introduced. Prior to the changes, the most common procedure for reducing workforces was the non-renewal of fixed-term contracts, reflecting their massive use in the 1980s. Of new unemployment benefit claimants in 1994 some 80 per cent had not had their contracts renewed, just over 10 per cent proceeded to contest the dismissal, 3 per cent were subject to collective dismissal procedures, 1 per cent of cases went to a labour court and less than 1 per cent were effected through objective dismissal. The 1994 reforms introduced the option of dismissal 'for reasons of organisation or production' (see Table 8.1.2).

In cases of objective dismissal employees are entitled to compensation of 20 days' pay per year of service up to 12 months' pay (see Chapter

8.2). However, in many cases compensation actually paid is much higher: a recent survey showed that although average costs for a dismissal on objective grounds in Spain was 231 days' pay (as against 315 in the UK), maximum payments could be as much as 1,260 days' pay. This is partly explained by a long-held, but technically erroneous, interpretation of requirements for claiming unemployment benefit. Employees often understand that they will only receive benefits if the dismissal is officially 'sanctioned' by the labour authorities. The majority of employees have therefore had recourse to IMAC to agree a settlement above the minimum. In all, 87 per cent of cases entering the labour courts have come via IMAC, and typically it was thought that a dismissal would only be recognised as genuine if the employee produced evidence of a settlement of some 35 days per year of service. This is explained by the wording of the Unemployment Protection Act which requires a claimant to produce a conciliation agreement from the employer 'with agreed compensation of no less than 35 days' pay' – which has come to be interpreted as 35 days' per year of service.

Table 8.1.1 *Statistical overview: Spain and the UK*

	UK	**Spain**
Population	58.2 million (1992)	39.1 million (1993)
Labour force**	25,729,000 (excl unemployed)	15,564,000 (1995)
Economic growth	2.75% (1995)	3% (1995
(1995/96*)	3% (1996)	3.2% (1996)
PSBR/GDP	4% (1995)	6% (1995)
Per capita income	US$16,227	US$12,797
(GDP per head)	(1992 figures: prices using purchasing power parity)	
Price inflation	3.2% (1995)	4.4% (1995 EPA)***
	3% (1996)	3.5%–4% (1996)
Pay growth	3.5% (1995)	4.4% (1995)
	4% (1996)	3.5%–4% (1996)
Unemployment rate	8.1% (1995)	23% (1995)
	men: 10.9%; women: 4.4%	men: 18%; women: 31%
Youth jobless rate (16–25 yrs)	20%	41%
Female participation rate	52.8%	32%
Part-time work	25% work part-time	5% work part-time
	(of which 90% are women)	(of which 78% are women)
Rate of unionisation	37%	12%
Taxation rates	20/24/40%	20% to 56%
Social security	10.2% employer	31.6% employer
	10% employee	6.6% employee
National minimum wage	No minimum wage system	64,920 pesetas per month (paid 14 X per year)

*   Forecasts
**   The UK workforce in employment is defined as employees in employment, the self-employed, HM forces and participants in work-related government training programmes. The Spanish labour force figures include all persons aged 16 or over who are in employment, self-employed or available for work.
*** National Employment Survey.
     Main sources: *Boletín de Estadísticas Laborales*, IDS Report, IDS Employment Europe, IDS Pay and Conditions in Spain.

Table 8.1.2 *Main points of amendments to Workers' Statute (May 1994)*

Subject (Article)	New measures and changes
Pay (Arts 26, 29, 30, 32)	More scope for collective bargaining to determine pay structure. Pay need no longer be defined against annual hours. Seniority pay limits lifted. Statutory supplements for overtime (75%) and nightwork (25%) abolished, to be set by agreement.
Recruitment (Art 16)	INEM recruitment monopoly abolished. No need to register contracts with INEM or notify them of contract termination. Temping agencies to be permitted.
Contracts of employment (Arts 8, 15)	Forms of contracts streamlined, and no longer presumed to be permanent. Apprenticeship contracts, part-time contracts and work experience contracts regulated by new decree-law. Use of fixed-term contracts to be defined largely by collective agreement.
Probationary periods (Art 14)	Upper limits of 2 months for unqualified workers (3 in firms of less than 25); 6 months for qualified workers maintained.
Job classification and transfers (Arts 23, 24, 25, 39, 40, 41)	Employee classification and relocation procedures devolved to collective bargaining. Job description and grading system to be collectively agreed on basis of qualifications, professional role and job content, with non-discrimination clause inserted. Temporary and permanent grade transfers facilitated.
	Geographical transfer of staff no longer requires labour authorities' permission. Workforce consultation required for collective transfers. Employee has right to opt for dismissal with compensation.
	Changes to employment terms now to differentiate between individual and collective. Individuals to be given 30 days' notice; collective changes require 2 weeks workforce consultation period and 30 days' notice, plus authorisation.
Working time (Arts 34, 35, 36, 37, 38)	Working time limits made more flexible in line with EU Directive. Max 40 hour week may be averaged over 1 year, collective agreements may extend 9 hour working day. Break of 15 mins per 6 hours. Government powers to change working time limited. Hours restrictions introduced for under 18s.
	Nightworkers defined as those regularly working 3 hours between 22.00–06.00, and a third of annual time between these hours. Government may limit nightwork in certain sectors for certain workers. More stringent health and safety requirements including health checks, and right to change to daywork.
	Minimum weekly rest period of 1.5 days (2 days for under 18s) can be averaged over 14 days. Leave provisions may be collectively agreed, and employer no longer has right to refuse leave at peak periods.

Termination of contract (Arts 47, 49, 50, 51, 52, 53, 55, 56)	Termination 'for reasons of organisation or production' introduced. Collective dismissal redefined along lines of EU Directive, with separate procedures for individual and collective dismissals. Small firms no longer need to find alternative employment for workers dismissed on objective grounds.
	Disciplinary dismissal procedures may be extended by collective agreement, and employees awarded right to be represented by trade union. Where incorrect dismissal procedures followed, new procedures for second attempt.
Collective agreements (Arts 82, 85, 89)	Companies in financial difficulties may be exempt from the provisions of collective agreements. Social partners to define scope of applicability of collective agreements. Reference to collective agreements having the force of law removed. Agreements may include procedures for resolving disputes. Agreements can now be endorsed by simple majority rather than 60% approval by both sides.
Employment incentives (Art 11; December decree)	Apprenticeship contracts provided for, with pay below statutory minimum. Annually defined target groups to enjoy employment subsidies (1994: disabled, unemployed over 45 and long-term unemployed taken on by small firms).

Source: *Estatuto de los Trabajadores*, 1994. Reproduced from IDS Employment Europe 391 (July 1994)

PAY AND REMUNERATION TABLES

The tables below show the breakdown of company pay, as stipulated in the collective agreement of a large car manufacturing company. As the figures show, daily basic pay is more than doubled by the various incentives and bonuses paid out. Even for the higher technical/administrative grades, basic pay makes up only just over half of total pay. (The figures exclude overtime pay and shift allowances.)

Table 8.1.3 *Pay for manual grades in large automotive company (pesetas)*

Grade (and job example)	Gross pay (annual)	Basic pay (daily)	Productivity Incentive (daily)	Mobility (daily)	Attendance (daily)	Punc-tuality (daily)	July & Xmas bonus
Cleaner	2,152,038	2,942	2,324	436	436	436	86,942
Paintshop operative	2,176,603	2,976	2,350	441	441	441	87,935
Doorhanger	2,205,116	3,017	2,380	446	446	446	89,087
Materials handling	2,229,396	3,048	2,406	452	452	452	90,069
Engine assembler I	2,315,949	3,168	2,499	469	469	469	93,564
Engine assembler II	2,519,075	3,446	2,716	510	510	510	101,771
Welder I	2,672,768	3,665	2,886	541	541	541	107,980
Welder II	2,755,093	3,767	2,975	558	558	558	111,306
Electrician	2,879,335	3,938	3,108	583	583	583	116,325

Table 8.1.4 *Pay for technical and administrative grades (pesetas)*

Grade (and job example)	Gross annual pay	Basic pay	Productivity Incentive	Mobility	Attendance	Punc-tuality	July & Xmas bonus
Routine clerical	2,135,408	1,065,995	573,998	107,624	107,624	107,624	86,270
Typist	2,180,361	1,088,436	566,081	109,890	109,890	109,890	88,087
Secretary	3,328,197	1,162,237	625,819	117,341	117,341	117,341	94,059
Supplies coordinator	2,467,111	1,231,581	663,159	124,342	124,342	124,342	96,671
Personnel assistant	2,770,129	1,382,849	744,611	139,614	139,614	139,614	111,913
Stock control	3,194,139	1,594,513	858,584	160,985	160,985	160,985	129,043
Systems analyst	3,735,673	1,864,847	1,004,148	188,278	188,278	188,278	150,921
Compensation & benefits analyst	4,331,905	2,162,486	1,164,416	218,328	218,328	218,328	175,009

Source: IDS Ltd

The figures below are published by the Ministry of Labour (*Boletín de Estadísticas Laborales*), and show average monthly earnings for blue- and white-collar staff across different sectors. Variations across quarters are largely explained by pay rises, but also be one-off bonuses.

Table 8.1.5 *Average monthly earnings of blue- and white-collar staff by sector, 1994/95 (pesetas)*

	All sectors	Energy/ water	Chemi-icals	Metal-working	Manuf-acturing	Constr-uction	Hotel & catering	Trans-port	Financial services
White-collar									
1995 1st qtr	233,500	263,600	287,000	263,100	222,700	224,000	162,900	267,000	310,100
2nd qtr	237,300	268,200	282,000	280,400	231,100	232,800	167,100	253,000	325,200
Blue-collar									
1995 1st qtr	147,100	260,000	180,700	172,900	136,200	133,300	117,600	167,300	193,800
2nd qtr	152,500	259,100	181,300	184,300	140,900	139,500	123,000	170,700	253,400

EXECUTIVE REMUNERATION

After a decade of pay increases that vastly outstripped inflation, executive and managerial salaries have increased more slowly since 1993 (3.3 per cent in 1994; 4.6 per cent in 1995 compared with inflation of 4.3 per cent in 1994 and 4.4 per cent in 1995). More and more Spanish companies are choosing to make one pay award for the entire workforce, rather than differentiate awards for managerial and non-managerial staff as has been the norm. Compared with many other countries, Spanish executives' pay still has fewer variable elements, although this is changing. Salaries are largely determined by company size and turnover. Factors such as age, length of service and qualifications are starting to lose their importance. Nonetheless professionals under 30 can expect to earn around 25 per cent less than older staff in the same position. Firms are seeking to simplify pay structures. The company car remains the most popular executive benefit; others include supplementary pension schemes and early retirement options, medical assistance and insurance.

Table 8.1.6 *Annual remuneration in 1995 (thousands pesetas)*

	Lower quartile	Median	Upper quartile	% rel. to MD's pay
Managing Director	11,880	14,847	18,673	100
HR Director	7,541	9,615	11,797	65
Finance Director	8,153	9,900	12,002	67
Commercial Director	8,462	10,640	13,500	72
IT Director	8,239	9,804	12,048	67
Head of Sales	6,529	8,229	9,900	56
Accounts Manager	4,128	5,180	6,497	35
Systems Technician	3,999	5,400	6,566	37
Project Engineer	4,411	5,439	6,450	37
Programme Analyst	3,650	4,232	4,847	29

The figures for these tables were provided by consultancy CEINSA in Barcelona, and are reproduced with permission. (CEINSA, Córcega 329, 08037 Barcelona. Fax: +34 3 237 13 52.)

Spanish Labour Law

Alex Valls and Fraser Young,
Baker & McKenzie

THE LABOUR CONTRACT

It is important to note that any waiver of Spanish labour law or its effects by an employee is rendered null and void by operation of law.

Terms of employment

The employment contract may be either written or oral, except in respect of the following, which must be in writing:

- contracts dealing with vocational training exceeding four weeks;
- contracts dealing with employment for a fixed duration or a precise amount of work to be done;
- contracts dealing with part-time employment;
- contracts involving an employee hired in Spain to work for Spanish employers located abroad;
- relationships which one of the parties requests to be formalised in writing, even after the employment has started;
- contracts containing a non-competition covenant.

In any event, an employee is entitled to receive a document in which the main terms and conditions of his employment are set out. Labour contracts may be drawn up for limited periods in certain circumstances.

The Workers' Statute allows for the possibility of the employer and employee agreeing in writing to a trial period which, unless otherwise established in the applicable Collective Agreement, in no case may exceed:

- six months for qualified technicians;
- two months for non-qualified workers.

During a trial period both the employer and the employee are obliged to carry out the tasks which are expressed to be the subject of the trial period. The Workers' Statute contains the basic law providing for minimum rights which may be improved by the collective bargaining agreement.

Contract termination

Contracts automatically come to an end at the conclusion of their fixed term. When the duration of a fixed term contract exceeds one year, the party wishing to put an end to it must give at least 15 days' prior notice of termination. Contracts for an indefinite period may terminate for one of the following reasons:

- mutual agreement of the parties;
- reasons validly mentioned in the contract and permitted by the law;
- the wish of the employee giving notice as required in the collective agreement;
- death or absolute incapacity of the employee;
- the retirement of the employee;
- the death, retirement in those cases provided for in the social security system, or incapacity of the employer;
- *force majeure*;
- the complete shutdown of the industry, commerce or service, based on technological or economic reasons, provided that this has been duly authorised in accordance with the law;
- at the option of the employee in case of breach of his contract by the employer;
- dismissal of the employee; or
- other legally recognised objective reasons.

Under the Workers' Statute, a justified dismissal of an employee does not give rise to payment of severance compensation. Justified dismissals may be either 'disciplinary' or 'objective'.

Disciplinary dismissals may be on the following grounds:

- repeated and unjustified lack of punctuality or attendance at work;
- lack of discipline or disobedience at work;
- verbal or physical aggression to the employer, other staff or their families;
- breach of good faith and abuse of confidence in performing the job;

- intentional and continuous diminishing of regular or agreed work performance; and
- drunkenness or drug addiction, if it adversely affects the employee's work.

Disciplinary dismissals must be notified to the employee in writing, stating the facts giving rise to the dismissal and its effective date. The employee then has 20 working days as from the effective date to appeal against the dismissal. However, before the employee can request such an appeal or review of his dismissal by the Labour Court, the parties are required to attempt to settle the matter at the Mediation, Arbitration and Conciliation Institute (IMAC), an agency of the Labour Department.

If the Labour Court finds in favour of the employee, the employer may choose whether to reinstate the employee or pay severance compensation. Severance compensation is computed on the basis of 45 days' gross salary per year of employment with a maximum of 42 months. In addition, accrued salary from the effective date of dismissal to the date of the Court decision notification must also be paid to the employee. If this period exceeds 60 working days, the government may repay the company the difference.

Objective dismissals may be on the following grounds:

- an employee's incompetence that has come to light or occurred after the trial period has elapsed;
- an employee's failure to keep up with reasonable technological developments affecting his or her position (after two months from the date of implementation of the new conditions);
- the need to phase out a position in a company, due to economic, technical, organisation and/or production reasons (see further below);
- employee absence in excess of 20 per cent of working days during any consecutive two-month period, or 25 per cent of working days during any four-month period within one year.

Dismissals for any of the above causes are subject to a number of formalities. The employer must give the employee 30 days' prior written notice of the reason for the dismissal. The employer must also pay to the employee severance compensation in an amount equal to 20 days' salary for each year of service with a maximum of the equivalent of one full year's salary.

If an 'objective' dismissal is declared by a Labour Court to be illegal or null, the provisions governing disciplinary dismissals are applicable.

Contract termination caused by economic, technical, organisation and/or production reasons (collective dismissal)

The Workers' Statute Law and Royal Decree 696/1980 provide the employer with the right to terminate labour contracts for 'economic, technical, organisation and/or production reasons'. These are understood to be serious financial difficulties which necessitate the reorganisation of the company, or serious difficulties concerning the organisation of the company which puts employment in danger.

Collective dismissals may be allowed provided that, during a 90-day period, the termination affects to a minimum of:

- ten employees in companies hiring less than 100 employees;
- 10 per cent of employees in companies hiring between 100 and 300 employees;
- 30 employees in companies hiring 300 employees or more.

Contract terminations due to economic reasons are only effective if the detailed procedures established by law have been followed. These involve the employer obtaining approval from the Labour Authorities, having, if possible, reached agreement with the employees' representatives. The advantages of reaching an agreement with the employees' representatives for this kind of contract termination are substantial. Spain has a very high unemployment rate and therefore 'dismissals' will be authorised by the Labour Authorities only under very strict circumstances since the Authorities are fighting to keep down unemployment.

As far as the redundancy terms are concerned, in the absence of an agreement, the Workers' Statute Law sets compensations at 20 days' salary for each year of service. However, this must not exceed a total of 365 days' pay, providing the contract termination is authorised by the Labour Authorities. Therefore, should an agreement be reached, the terms usually exceed the mentioned compensation.

Special labour contracts

As a measure to fight unemployment, the government considerably softened labour regulations concerning the hiring of new employees by means of approving a new set of special employment contracts. The contracts offer two attractions: (i) severance pay is not applicable upon termination (the only exception being general temporary contracts); and (ii) some of the new contracts entitle the employer to certain social security exemptions and other fringe benefit cuts.

On-the-job Training Employment Contracts are available only for persons between 16 and 25 years of age who do not have a diploma. The duration period ranges from six months to three years.

The Apprenticeship Employment Contract is available to allow employees with a diploma to develop their theoretical skills and acquire certain practical experience in their fields. The duration period ranges from six months to two years and employees are required to have completed their studies within the four years immediately preceding their employment.

Part-time Employment Contracts can be entered into either on the basis of number of hours per day or per week, or number of days per week or per month. Whatever the basis for employment the total time agreed upon shall be lower than the regular daily shift. In general, part-time employment is deemed to have an indefinite duration. However, a part-time agreement may qualify as one of special limited duration, such as the ones described above.

A 'Relay' Employment Contract is defined as a part-time agreement entered into with an unemployed worker in order to substitute another worker who is partially retired and works only one half of his regular working day (eg job-sharing). The duration of this agreement is equal to the time remaining for the partially retired employee to reach official retirement age.

Special Temporary Employment Contracts fall into four categories:

- contracts for launching a new activity;
- contracts for a specific service or task;
- contracts for extraordinary production requirements;
- provisional agreements.

The Workers' Statute provides for special labour relationships which are subject to additional regulation, in particular for senior executive staff. In the so-called 'top executive contracts', the parties may establish a trial period not exceeding nine months, during which either party may terminate the labour relationship without giving rise to any severance compensation. The duration of the employment agreement is not subject to a maximum or minimum period. In the absence of a written term, the contract is deemed to be for an indefinite period of time. The executive may terminate the contract with the only requirement being a minimum three months' advance notice. Nevertheless, this period may be up to six months if it is so provided in writing in a contract entered into for an indefinite period or for a duration exceeding five years. In such cases of voluntary terminations, the executive is not entitled to any severance compensation. Persons acting in business transactions on behalf of one or more principals without assuming their risk or benefit (commercial agents – see Chapter 6.2) are also governed by the provisions of the Workers' Statute as special labour relationships.

Confidentiality and restraints against competition

Confidentiality
The law on confidentiality obligations is not particularly clear and it is therefore advisable to include a confidentiality clause in employment agreements. It should be noted that there may be difficulties in establishing an action for breach of confidentiality, since the employer will be required to prove not only actual damage suffered but also that this damage was caused by the disclosure of confidential information by the employee concerned (see Chapter 3.2).

Non-competition
The Workers' Statute provides for the enforceability of an employee's duty not to compete with the employer as a post-termination restriction. The validity of the non-competition clause is subject to various conditions:

- it must be agreed between the parties and be in writing (ie to prove its existence);
- the duration of the duty is limited to a maximum of two years for technicians and six months for other employees;
- the employer must have a genuine proprietary industrial or commercial interest which requires protection;
- the employer must pay the employee appropriate compensation. In practice, when the obligation has a two years' duration appropriate compensation will vary between one and two years' salary.

Senior managers' employment contracts are expressly excluded from the scope of the Workers' Statute Act, and are governed by Royal Decree 1382/85. The Royal Decree provides for the enforceability of a non-competition obligation subject to the same criteria as stated above. The duration of the non-competition obligation is limited to a maximum of two years.

In case of breach of the non-competition obligation, the employer is entitled to claim damages before the Labour Court. In practice it can be difficult to succeed in such a claim as Labour Courts do not like to deal with such problems and to favour the employee.

Non-solicitation of employers, suppliers, customers
An obligation not to solicit employees, suppliers or customers of one's former employer is theoretically enforceable but, in practice, is rarely found in Spanish employment contracts.

SEX DISCRIMINATION

The foundation of Spain's implementation of the Equal Treatment Directive is to be found in Article 14 of its Constitution.

Spanish law does not make a particular distinction between direct and indirect sex discrimination, but merely prohibits all forms of discrimination. Therefore there is no provision that compensation cannot be awarded in the case of indirect discrimination which is unintentional.

Where the equal treatment principle has been infringed, the employee concerned can file a claim with the Labour Magistrate having gone through the appropriate procedures first. The court has power to award compensation and there is no statutory maximum on the amount of damages that can be awarded.

The Workers' Statute reinforces the principle of equal pay by declaring void all clauses in collective agreements or employment contracts which contravene this on grounds of sex or marital status. In addition, it requires employers to give 'equal pay for equal work' with no possible grounds for sex discrimination. Pay is widely defined as including not only basic pay, but also all bonuses and supplements.

COMPANY LABOUR RELATIONS—WORK COUNCILS

Employees are represented before a company's management by labour representatives. The number of representatives depends upon the number of employees:

No of employees			No of representatives
up	to	30	1
30	to	49	3
50	to	100	5
100	to	250	9
251	to	500	13
501	to	750	17
751	to	1,000	21
over 1,000			an additional 2 per 1,000 (maximum of 75)

In companies with more than 50 employees, employees' representatives are elected by permanent employees to Work Councils (*Comites de Empresa*) for a period of four years. Members of Work Councils enjoy certain special rights with regard to sanctions and dismissals. In addition they are allowed a number of hours each month to devote to their functions as employee representatives. The number of hours allowed ranges between 15 hours per month (in companies having up to 100 employees) to 40 hours per month (in companies with more than 750 employees).

Work Councils have full authority to represent the employees in collective bargaining. They may also intervene in problems arising as a result of working conditions, and bring before the company and the labour and social security authorities, matters pertaining to health and safety requirements, social security, or any other aspects relating to the working conditions. Employers are required to disclose information on sales, production and employment status, and financial statements at the Work Council's request. Work Councils must also be allowed to give their opinion on certain situations affecting employment, such as collective reorganisations, on-the-job training, relocation, and corporate reorganisation.

Labour representatives are entitled to be informed about all employment agreements to be executed in writing by the employer. To that end, the employer is obliged to give Labour representatives a basic copy of all employment agreements within ten days of the date of execution. However, the senior executive agreements are expressly excluded from the obligation of disclosure. Should the employer fail to comply with the above-mentioned obligation, a fine of between 50,001 and 500,000 pesetas may be imposed by the Labour Authorities.

SOCIAL SECURITY

Levels of contributions and benefits vary according to the tariffs subscribed to by the beneficiary (as in the case of self-employed workers) or by fixed quantities based on salary levels. Affiliation to the system is mandatory for both parties to a labour relationship and for self-employed workers.

Social security contributions are paid by the parties to the labour relationship. Employers and employees are obliged to subscribe and, in the case of work accidents and work-related illnesses, the employer is obliged to pay the full amount. Employers have the basic responsibility to collect and pay the contributions. The employer must contribute the employer's share as well as the employee's share, which is deducted from the salary. Omission of this deduction at the time of paying salary to the employee makes the employer liable with respect to the employee's contribution.

WORK AND RESIDENCE PERMITS

Work and residence permits for non-EEC members

A foreign national entering Spain must produce a valid national passport and, with the exception of nationals of countries that have entered into bilateral agreements with Spain, a valid visa. A residence permit must be obtained by foreign nationals wishing to remain in Spain for more than 90 days. Foreign nationals (with a few exceptions) wishing to work in Spain must obtain a work permit for the same term as the resident permit.

An individual who wishes to enter Spain to work should have, prior to entry, filed an application for a residence and work visa with the Spanish consulate in the jurisdiction where the individual works or lives. Once he has obtained the residence and work visa, an application should be filed by the employer or the employee with the Spanish Employment Department in order to obtain the residence and work permits.

There is no obligation on the employer to advertise the position before a work permit will be granted. Nevertheless, it is advisable to file with the local employment office a form called *oferta de empleo* (employment offer), setting out what attributes are being sought of the employee such as languages and special qualifications. If the employment office is unable to find a Spanish person who fits these requirements, the work permit will be granted.

Companies which do not have a branch or subsidiary in Spain cannot apply for work permits. The branch or the subsidiary must be fully incorporated and registered with the social security before any application can be lodged.

Work and residence permits for EEC members

EU members do not need to apply for a work permit in order to work in Spain; however, there are certain formalities which have to be followed at the Police Headquarters to obtain Special Residence Cards (see also Chapter 9.2).

Part 9

Foreigners Moving to Work in Spain

INTRODUCTION

Doing business with Spain could involve moving personally to the country for a period of time. This naturally raises a number of questions. One of them is the tax situation, others are pension schemes, National Insurance contributions, and compliance with the requirements of the Spanish public or private healthcare systems. Contributions to all these systems vary from one country to another and the parent company may also want to study in detail the alternatives available.

Addressing these questions is the aim of the following two chapters. They are written when a general concern about the future of the public pension system is spreading in both the UK and Spain as a result of demographic pressure and the commitment to reduce the public deficit. In Spain, at the time of publication, compliance with the Maastricht treaty is a declared strategic goal for major political parties and the future of the public pensions and health systems is an important issue in the political arena. The reconciliation of all the variables involved will require some imagination, most certainly increasing the role of private insurance and pension funds.

9.1

UK Individuals Leaving the UK to Take Up Employment in Spain

David Adams, KPMG, London, and
Celso Garcia Granda, KPMG, Madrid

Before considering some specific issues in connection with UK individuals coming to Spain for employment purposes, it is worth considering a few concepts that affect an individual's liability to Spanish personal and net worth tax and to UK personal tax.

SPAIN – RESIDENCE RULES

In Spain the treatment of an individual for personal income tax and net worth tax purposes depends on the question of the individual's residence.

An individual is considered a Spanish resident for tax purposes if he remains in Spain for more than 183 days in a given calender year, or if his business or economic interests are located within Spanish territory. An individual may also be resident in Spain by virtue of his spouse or minor dependent children being resident in Spain (unless the taxpayer can prove that he is resident in another country). Having become resident, a taxpayer will be considered to have been resident for the entire tax year, and not simply from the date on which residence was taken up. Residents in Spain are taxed on a worldwide basis, regardless of the source of the income, at progressive rates ranging from 0 per cent to 56 per cent.

By contrast, in general, non-resident taxpayers are taxed at the rate of 25 per cent on income obtained in Spanish territory or which arises from Spanish sources, and at the rate of 35 per cent on capital gains arising from Spanish sources. Specific rates apply to certain other types of income, such as pensions.

THE UK – RESIDENCE RULES

For UK tax purposes, the residence and ordinary residence status of the individual is significant in determining his tax liability. Generally, all the time an individual is not resident in the UK, he may only be liable to UK tax on UK source income.

In determining an individual's residence status, three overriding basic rules apply:

- if a person is not physically present in the UK at all during a UK tax year (6 April to the following 5 April), he will not normally be regarded as resident in the UK in that year;
- if a person is physically present in the UK for a total of 183 days or more in a UK tax year, he will be regarded as UK resident in that year; and
- if a person comes to the UK to take-up employment for a period of two years or more, or to take-up permanent residence, he will be regarded as UK resident from the date of his arrival.

There is a further rule which concerns the position where an individual makes a series of visits to the UK over a number of years but may not be present in the UK for 183 days or more in any one year. Where such visits amount to an average of 91 days or more in the UK per year over ordinarily, a four-year period, the individual may be regarded as becoming UK resident. A person will be regarded as ordinarily resident in the UK if he is expected to remain in the UK on a longer-term basis.

Specific rules apply to the situation where a UK resident individual leaves the UK to work in Spain. If such an individual is going to work in Spain under a full-time contract of employment and the following conditions are met, that individual will be regarded as not resident and not ordinarily resident in the UK from the day after he leaves until the day before he returns. The conditions are:

- all of the duties of the employment are performed abroad, or any duties performed in the UK are 'purely incidental' to the overseas duties;
- the individual is absent from the UK and employed abroad for

at least a complete UK tax year (6 April to 5 April); and
- while working abroad, the individual's visits back to the UK are limited.

If all of the above conditions are **not** met, the individual is likely to be regarded as remaining resident and ordinarily resident in the UK throughout and hence liable to UK tax. However, if an individual's absence from the UK is for a period of 365 days or more and he only makes limited return visits to the UK during that time, even though he may remain UK resident throughout, his earnings may be exempt from UK tax.

Where an individual is regarded as not resident and not ordinarily resident, the emoluments of his overseas employment are not normally liable to UK tax.

UK – DOMICILE RULES

There is a third UK tax concept which has a specific bearing on expatriates in the UK. This is the concept of domicile. Broadly speaking, an individual's domicile refers to the 'state' which he regards as his homeland. Typically this is the country in which he was born and raised and is normally 'inherited' from his father. Although an individual may leave his homeland and remain overseas for a prolonged period of time spanning many years, if he retains the intention of returning to his homeland at some point, such as on his retirement, then while he is likely to be regarded as not resident in his homeland, he may continue to be regarded as domiciled there.

Generally, individuals who are resident in the UK are liable to UK tax on worldwide income and capital gains. However, where individuals are resident but not domiciled in the UK, they are generally not liable to UK tax on income (including earnings) or capital gains arising abroad, if the income or gains are not remitted to, or otherwise 'enjoyed' in, the UK, either directly or indirectly.

Spouse

The residence, ordinary residence and domicile status of an individual's spouse are determined separately.

DUAL RESIDENCE

It can be seen that a person may be resident both in Spain and in the UK under the domestic law of both countries. The person's tax residence must then be decided according to the terms of the Spain/UK double tax treaty. This treaty – which has been concluded between the two countries to avoid double taxation of taxpayers – contains a 'tie-breaker' clause which states that where an individual is considered to be resident in both countries under local law, for the purpose of the treaty he is to be treated as being resident in the country in which he has a permanent home. If he has a permanent home available in both countries, he is treated as being a resident of the state in which his 'personal and economic relationships are closer'. If it is not possible to decide residence under this test, the treaty states that the individual is to be treated as being resident in the country where he has his habitual abode and if this cannot be identified in the country of which he is a national. Lastly, if none of these tests are applicable, the treaty states that the Spanish and UK tax authorities must settle the question by mutual agreement.

MOVING TO SPAIN – EFFECT ON RESIDENCE

Broadly speaking, if a UK resident individual moves to Spain for more than 183 days in a given calendar year he will become resident in Spain under domestic law. However, he will not automatically cease to be UK resident. As previously indicated, he will be regarded as not resident and not ordinarily resident in the UK from the day he leaves until the day before he returns if certain conditions are met.

If all of the above conditions are not met and the individual remains resident and ordinarily resident in the UK, he could be dual resident in the UK and Spain under domestic law; therefore it would be necessary to look at the terms of the UK/Spain tax treaty for the avoidance of double taxation in order to decide where the individual was resident for tax purposes. This is dealt with in more detail in the section on the treaty set out below.

EFFECT OF BECOMING RESIDENT IN SPAIN

Taxes and rates

When the individual becomes resident in Spain, he will basically be subject to two direct taxes – namely, a comprehensive income tax and a net wealth tax. Other taxes include inheritance tax and gift tax. Residents are taxed on a worldwide basis, regardless of the source of the income. For the present purposes it is assumed that the individual is not also UK resident and so Spain's taxing rights are not limited by the UK/Spain tax treaty.

For 1994 and 1995 the rates start at 0 per cent and progress up to 56 per cent of taxable income for resident tax-payers.

Tax returns and compliance

The due date for filing the tax return and making payment is normally from 1 May to 20 June of each year for the income obtained in the previous year. If the tax return is not filed on time, penalties will be imposed. Married couples may choose between filing separate or joint returns.

Spanish resident employers and permanent establishments of non-residents are obliged to deduct tax from income paid to the employees. The amount of tax withheld is in accordance with a progressive scale based on the amount of taxable income and the taxpayer's number of dependent children. As of 1 January, 1992, withholding also applies to fringe benefits. The withholding tax is paid to the tax authorities on a monthly or quarterly basis and will be deducted from the final tax due. If the total amount of withholdings exceeds the taxpayer's ultimate liability, the tax authorities must refund the difference.

Individuals engaged in independent or business activities must make certain advance payments on account of the final tax liability throughout the year.

Remuneration from employment

As a general rule, all types of remuneration received by an employee for services rendered constitute taxable income, although severance payments within the limits established by the Labour Law are exempt from tax. Benefits in kind are generally taxable. Social Security contributions and a fixed deduction of 5 per cent of the gross salary up to the limit of 250,000 pesetas are deductible in calculating the total taxable employment income.

Investment and rental income

Investment income, such as dividends and interest arising from loans, bonds, bank deposits, etc is considered to be ordinary income. It is therefore added to the rest of the individual's income in order to calculate the taxable base. The administration and maintenance expenses of an investment may be deducted from taxable income, as well as a prescribed deduction of 28,000 pesetas. However the general deduction cannot be used to generate a loss.

Property rental income is also included in taxable income. The expenses related to such income, such as local taxes, fees to execute documents and depreciation at a 1.5 per cent straight-line rate, are deductible.

An individual who owns unrented urban property, wherever it is located, will be taxed on deemed income equal to 2 per cent or 1.1 per cent of the property value used for net worth tax purposes. This amount may be reduced by interest paid on a mortgage secured on the property (if it is his habitual residence) up to a limit of 800,000 pesetas (1,000,000 pesetas in the case of joint returns). (See also Chapter 10.2.)

Suppose then a person leaves the UK and becomes resident in Spain; he or she has income from investments in the UK and rental income from the house in the UK which he or she lets out while abroad. Both the investment and the rental income would have to be declared in this person's Spanish tax return. However, he or she would receive a foreign tax credit for any UK tax incurred and this could be set against Spanish tax payable on the same income within certain limits.

Capital gains

Capital gains are generally added to the taxable income base. However, the capital gain derived from the sale of an individual's main residence is tax exempt, provided that the full amount obtained is reinvested in the acquisition of a new house within a two-year period. Capital gains are also exempt when total property sales in the year do not exceed 500,000 pesetas, except in the case of capital gains arising from the sale of shares or participations in Collective Investment Institutions.

General tax credits

There are a number of tax credits which are available to resident taxpayers ranging from those based on family circumstances to certain types of donations. Other frequently claimed tax credits include the following:

- foreign tax credits in respect of foreign tax paid on income arising from non-Spanish sources;
- 15 per cent of medical, hospital and pharmaceutical expenses duly justified and documented;
- investment income: 10 per cent of life insurance premiums paid to Spanish resident insurance companies;
- investment income: 15 per cent of the investment made in the acquisition or refurbishment of a personal residence;
- employees' tax credit: taxpayers earning employment income are entitled to an employment credit of 276,000 pesetas.

Net wealth tax

Resident individuals are subject to net wealth tax in respect of their worldwide assets. For the 1995 period, a resident must file a tax return if his net wealth exceeds 17,000,000 pesetas or the value of his gross wealth exceeds 100,000,000 pesetas.

EFFECT OF CEASING TO BE UK RESIDENT

Although an individual may avoid UK tax on his overseas earnings while not resident, any other income including investment income he has arising in the UK would generally continue to be liable to UK tax. A UK citizen or a person qualifying under certain other categories, would be due UK personal allowances to set against any UK source income.

UK capital gains tax is generally only payable on capital gains realised at a time when an individual is resident or ordinarily resident in the UK.

Individuals resident and working in the UK normally pay class 1 National Insurance contributions, or social security. Where an individual is sent by his UK employer to work in Spain for a few years, exemption from Spanish Social Security payments can normally be obtained under European Union regulations so that the individual is permitted to continue contributing to the UK system.

UK/SPAIN DOUBLE TAX TREATY

If all the conditions for the cessation of UK residence set out above are not fulfilled, a UK individual who leaves the UK to work in Spain and becomes a Spanish resident may remain resident and ordinarily resident in the UK. This could be the case, for example, if the individual regularly spent four months a year in the UK and eight months in Spain.

In this case, in order to determine the individual's residence, it would be necessary to look at the terms of the UK/Spain double tax treaty. Assuming that the individual would not acquire a permanent home in Spain (as he only intends to remain in Spain for a limited period of time) and that he has a permanent home in the UK, according to the treaty he would be treated as a UK resident and not as a Spanish resident. He would therefore remain liable to UK tax on his worldwide income, including any employment income earned in Spain.

Although the individual would not be resident in Spain under the treaty, he would still be taxed as a non-resident on income obtained in Spain or which arose from Spanish sources, and on capital gains which arose from Spanish sources. The applicable domestic rates of tax are 25 per cent in respect of income and 35 per cent of capital gains. However, the rate is restricted in some cases by the tax treaty; for example, Spain could only tax interest earned in Spain at the rate of 12 per cent, but gains on the sale of real property could be taxed at the full 35 per cent rate.

As regards employment income, according to the tax treaty the UK individual's employment income would only be taxable in the UK and not in Spain if:

- he was only present in Spain for a period or periods not exceeding a total of 183 days in the fiscal year.
- the remuneration was paid by a non-Spanish resident employer; and
- the remuneration was not, basically, recharged to a Spanish branch of the employer.

If these conditions were not satisfied, the Spanish employment income would be subject to Spanish tax in full; in this case, a credit would be given in the UK against UK income tax for any Spanish tax suffered.

A non-resident with taxable Spanish income should appoint a tax representative in Spain. The tax authorities must be notified of the appointment within two months of its having been made. The non-resident individual would also remain liable to net worth tax in respect of assets situated or deemed to be situated in Spain, regardless of the values involved.

9.2

Public and Private Pension and Health Provision in Spain

Félix Soroa and Tim Reay, Aserplan

BENEFIT SYSTEMS

State scheme benefits

The Spanish Constitution guarantees the maintenance of a welfare system providing assistance and social benefits to cover all needs. The welfare system has two levels of public benefit, namely minimum welfare benefits (*asistencial*) which are available to everyone (independent of salary and contributions history) and, more importantly, earnings-related benefits (*contributivo*) which not only cover employees but also the self-employed and certain special sectors such as miners, fishermen, domestic employees etc.

Let us start by considering the state earnings-related scheme for employees, known as the Social Security General Regime ('SSGR'). This is financed by way of obligatory company contributions (of about 30 per cent) and employee contributions (of about 6.4 per cent) based on total earned remuneration, but subject to certain maxima (of about 4,400,000 pesetas or some £23,200 using an exchange rate of £1 = ptas 190) and minima depending on professional status. This amount is known as the 'contribution base'.

The benefits provided by the SSGR include health care, pensions, disability, unemployment and death cover, along with other minor benefits. Healthcare benefits can be broken down into four main groups:

(i)   general medicine: both in hospital and at the patient's home;
(ii) surgical admissions and psychiatric hospitalisation;
(iii) prescriptions: part of the cost is paid for those in active employ-
      ment and 100 per cent of the cost for pensioners (only prescrip-
      tions given by a recognised Social Security institution). Diet and
      cosmetic related products are excluded;
(iv) other services such as orthopaedics, prosthesis, etc.

All these benefits are provided to employees, pensioners and their families.

The main financial benefits of the earnings-related scheme are summarised in Table 9.2.1. The overall maximum pension for 1995 was 3.7
million pesetas (about £19,500). Table 9.2.2 shows the average state
pension benefits paid to those retiring now with full pension entitlement.

Table 9.2.1 *Main financial benefits of the earnings-related scheme*

	Retirement	**Widow and Orphans**	**Disability**
Minimum contribution period	15 years, at least 2 of which were in the last 8 years	500 days within the 5 years preceding death	Depends on whether the illness or accident is work or non-work related
Final pensionable earnings (*base reguladora*)	Average 'contribution base' over the last 8 years	Average 'contribution base' over the last 2 years	Average 'contribution base' over the last 8 years
Amount	100% of the Final Pensionable Earnings after 35 years of contributions Years % of BR 15 years 60 +1 year 2 35 years 100	*Widow:* 45% of Final Pensionable Earnings *Orphan:* 20% of Final Pensionable Earnings for each orphan. This is increased by the widow's pension if both parents die. Maximum of 100% combined widow & orphans pension	Own profession – 55% of Final Pensionable Earnings Any profession – 100% of Final Pensionable Earnings Total incapacity 150% of Final Pensionable Earnings
Beneficiary	Workers aged 65 years Early retirement from age 60 for those contributing before 1.1.1967	*Widow:* Widow or widower *Orphan:* Legitimate, legitimised or recognised natural children aged up to 18 or disabled	Employees declared disabled by INSS*

*Instituto Nacional de la Seguidad Social – the equivalent of the NHS.

Table 9.2.2 *Average state pension benefits paid to retirees with full pension entitlement*

Salary level	Retirement benefit as % of final salary
Up to 3m ptas (£15,800)	80–90
From 3m to 5m ptas (£15,800–£26,300)	60–70
From 5m to 10m ptas (£26,300–£52,600)	70–40
From 10m to 20m ptas (£52,600–£105,300)	40–20
More than 20m ptas (£105,300)	less than 20

(Using an exchange rate of £1=Ptas 190)

Funding of the state scheme

Having looked at the contributions and benefits we now turn to the financing of the social security system.

In Spain the social security system is an unfunded pay as you go system, ie benefits are paid out of the current year's contributions. As a result the ability to pay benefits depends on prevailing conditions. Such a system implies the need for certain restrictions, for example the setting of a maximum pension and the rules governing the calculation of the Final Pensionable Earnings.

We should also consider the following points which affect the ability of the social security system to meet benefit payments:

- overall levels of contributions are reducing because of a reduction in the size of the active population due to increasing unemployment, people starting their first job at later ages, early retirements and lower birth rates;
- levels of benefits are increasing, mainly due to increasing longevity.

It is clear then that there is an imbalance between benefits and financing. The picture becomes even worse when welfare benefits are introduced into the equation, particularly since these are non-contributory. Such an imbalance underlines the need for private provision on top of state benefits.

Private healthcare

Private healthcare is usually covered by means of an insurance policy, in one of the following forms:

(i) *Policy providing medical benefits*
   In return for payment of premiums the insurance company provides a series of services for the insured. These services include

visits to GPs and specialists, hospitalisation and surgery, as well as any medical tests and treatment required. The assured may choose any doctor from a list provided by the insurance company.

Prescriptions are not covered by these policies. Dental treatment is also normally excluded, although a few insurance companies do include it.

(ii) *Medical expenses policy*

In return for payment of premiums the insurance company will reimburse a specified percentage of expenses incurred in receiving medical treatment, surgery and hospitalisation.

The insured is completely free in his choice of service provider, but is required to make all payments in the first instance, a part of which may then be claimed back from the insurance company.

Limits on benefits are usually specified in terms of a limit per visit to a general practitioner, per visit to a specialist, per illness and total cost per year. Such cover is more expensive than the first type of cover mentioned above, however, it is normally more appropriate for high net worth individuals.

The insurance products described above are available either on an individual basis or on a group basis. In fact, it is very common for companies to provide this type of cover to, at least, senior management. In such situations, medical expense cover is the most common benefit.

Company sponsored schemes

As we have already seen state benefits will reduce in the future. There is an obvious need, therefore, for additional complimentary benefit systems to be established. An analysis of complimentary systems should consider both the employers' and the employees' requirements.

Clearly, from the employer's perspective the provision of additional benefits is a good human resources tool as it may be used to improve loyalty to the company. It has also become a useful means of reducing employee numbers, when necessary, in a non-traumatic way through early retirements, and without implying excessive costs to the company.

From the individual's point of view, additional benefits provide a means of long-term saving and an averaging of income over the individual's lifetime so as to ensure an acceptable level of income both during active employment and in retirement.

There are three main types of complimentary system:

(i)   *Defined benefits:* the benefits are established at the outset and the necessary contributions are determined by actuarial methods. The system or scheme may be integrated with the state scheme (meaning that the ultimate benefits either take into account or are independent of the state scheme), and dependent on salary and/or number of years' service with the company or group.

Typically in Spain private arrangements are independent of the state scheme (to avoid an increasing burden being placed on the scheme by a gradual reduction in state benefits), based on number of years' service with the company (which improves loyalty to the company), and they aim to provide benefits of the order of 50 per cent of final salary.

(ii) *Defined contributions:* in such schemes the contributions levels are set, and these contributions are then applied, together with accrued interest, to provide retirement (and other) benefits. Contributions may be salary-related, and may be subject to certain limits dependent on the results of the company.

(iii) *Mixed schemes:* as its name implies, such schemes combine the two methods mentioned above. Normally the defined benefits method is used to fund death and disability benefits and the defined contributions method to fund other benefits (such as retirement pension).

Increasingly companies are introducing such benefits to their companies; initially for senior management but in such a way that the benefits can be extended to lower levels of staff in the future.

Funding of company sponsored schemes

Finally, it is important to note that legislation passed in November 1995 requires all company sponsored schemes to be financed either by way of a Qualified Pension Plan (*Plan de Pensiones* – qualified under the 1987 pensions legislation) or by an insurance policy. Internal book reserves are prohibited by the new law (except for certain financial sectors). This provides employees with additional security about the future payment of their benefits, but also complicates the technical and fiscal considerations when establishing such a scheme.

The main characteristics of the two funding options are:

(i)   *Qualified Pension Plan:* employees are required to have majority control over the decisions affecting the Plan, although it is possible to ensure that the employer's consent is required for certain decisions. The contributions are deductible (for tax purposes) for both the employer and the employee, however the benefits are considered to be taxable income without any rebates. These plans have a high level of solvency and are regulated by state authorities.

(ii) *Insurance Policy:* this method allows greater flexibility than the Qualified Pensions Plan, but has worse tax treatment of contributions although the tax treatment of the benefits in payment is better. There is a high level of solvency, arising from the strict regulation of the insurance sector.

TRANSFERRING EMPLOYEES BETWEEN THE UK AND SPAIN

Principles

Employees who are transferred from the UK to Spain can generally be divided into three groups:

- short-term secondments (for up to a year or so);
- longer-term assignments (usually for a few years, rarely in practice more than five); and
- semi-permanent or permanent transfers (where there is no immediate expectation of return to the UK, although in many cases the individual will return at some point in the future).

When considering benefit design and financing issues, as we have seen above, it is essential to stress the importance of social security, which in Spain is in most cases more expensive than in the UK, as well as providing a considerably more generous retirement pension.

Finally, when (if) the employee returns to the UK, the accumulated benefit rights which he has 'left behind' in Spain must be considered.

Social security

Table 9.2.3 *Difference between the UK and Spanish social security systems*

	UK	Spain
Employer contribution rate (approximate)	10% on all earnings	About 30% on first £23,200 pa
Employee contribution rate (approximate)	2% on first £3,000 pa plus 10% on next £21,000 pa	6.4% on first £23,200 pa
Maximum pension	£7,000 pa	£19,500 pa

(Using an exchange rate of £1=ptas 190, and assuming contracted-in status in the UK.)

Table 9.2.3 illustrates the difference in scope between the two systems.

Social security for mobile employees in the European Union is covered by EU Regulation 1408/71. This applies to EU nationals and sets out the general principle that employees pay social security contributions, and accrue social security benefits, in the EU member state in which they are living and working, regardless of who employs them and where they are actually paid.

There are two principal exceptions to this rule:

- employees working in more than one member state (eg frontier workers, or individuals with two offices in different countries) – these are outside the scope of this chapter;
- employees on short-term secondment to another member state, who may remain in their 'home country' social security system.

In order to take advantage of this facility, an application must be made to the UK social security authorities (DSS). If the secondment is expected to last for less than 12 months, an application is made under 'Article 14' of the EU Regulation, and once the application is approved by the DSS, they issue an E101 Certificate of Continuing Liability. If the employee subsequently stays in Spain for more than 12 months (this must not have been expected at the outset), the E101 certificate is renewable for a further 12 months.

If, however, the secondment is initially expected to last longer than 12 months, an application should be made under 'Article 17' of the EU Regulation. This requires the consent of the Spanish authorities as well as the DSS, and is more a matter of negotiation, but if it can be shown that the application is in the employee's best interests and that he has been sent to Spain to carry out a particular job for which he has special skills, with the intention of returning to the UK after that job has been completed, the Spanish authorities are likely to consent to retention in the UK scheme, normally for up to five years. An E101 certificate is also delivered in this case.

Thus, a UK employee sent to work in Spain will have to pay Spanish social security contributions, unless he has an E101 certificate which allows his employer to pay him without deduction of social security contributions in Spain. In this case, the UK employer will continue to pay UK National Insurance contributions and will look to the employee to pay his share.

Turning to retirement benefits, an employee retained in the UK National Insurance system continues to accrue a UK state pension in the same way as if he had remained in the UK.

An employee who contributes to Spanish social security will earn an entitlement to benefit, even if he has not contributed for the minimum period of 15 years, as long as he has paid a total of at least 15 years' contributions to schemes within the EU. This is by virtue of the EU Regulation. In the case of an employee who has paid social security contributions in both Spain and the UK during his career, the Spanish authorities will calculate the pension he would have earned if all his contributions had been paid to their social security system, and will multiply this amount by the proportion of his total EU career which he spent in Spain. An analogous calculation is done by the UK authorities. (For example, after four years' contributions in Spain and 36 years in the UK, the employee would receive 4/40ths = 10 per cent of a Spanish pension based on 40 years' service.)

Company pensions

As far as company pensions are concerned, the employer has three main options:

- continue providing the employee with UK benefits; or
- provide the employee with Spanish company scheme benefits (if one exists); or
- provide him with a 'third country' or 'international' scale of benefits, in respect of his period of service in Spain.

Note that benefit design and financing should be considered separately: it is not strictly necessary, for example, to retain an employee in the UK scheme in order to provide him with UK-style benefits, although this is of course the most straightforward method of doing so. The benefits can be provided from other sources (eg an international pension scheme or an unfunded promise from the employer).

For an employee on short-term secondment, it is usually considered preferable to continue to provide him with UK benefits. How should these be financed? The obvious solution is to retain the employee in the UK scheme, and the Inland Revenue has recently revised its requirements for retention of such employees in UK pension schemes. Very broadly, any employee in Spain who is employed and paid by a UK company may remain in a UK scheme indefinitely, and any employee in Spain who is expected to return to the UK (even only to retire) may remain in the UK scheme for up to ten years.

However, the following three issues must also be considered:

- *social security* – if the employee is participating in Spanish social security, his UK scheme benefits should be adjusted to allow for this, to avoid unnecessarily expensive overprovision in many cases;

- *local rules* – the employee may be obliged to join a Spanish scheme, and this should be allowed for in the calculation of his UK scheme benefits as well;
- *taxation* – if he is resident in Spain he will be liable to Spanish income tax on his worldwide income including any contributions paid by his employer into the UK scheme (it not being an approved scheme in Spain). For very short secondments this may not be considered material. If it is, however, the employee may be withdrawn from the UK scheme when he goes to Spain, with a promise that when he returns to the UK he will rejoin the scheme (this avoids difficulties with the UK earnings cap). His pre- and post-secondment periods of service can be aggregated for benefit purposes, and he can be granted additional years of service corresponding to the period spent in Spain (possibly off-setting any additional benefits he has accrued in Spain), so that he is 'made whole'. The Inland Revenue limits on pension benefits may mean that this cannot be done immediately on his return.

What if it is decided that the employee should join the local Spanish scheme? This may be appropriate for longer-term transfers, or people not initially expected to return to the UK. Particularly if he is contributing to Spanish social security, he would then be treated as a local employee.

He may wish to transfer his accrued benefits from his former UK pension scheme to Spain. However, this is not permitted in most cases; he will have to receive the pension from the UK when he retires (paid in sterling, not taxed in the UK but taxed in Spain).

Finally, genuinely mobile employees may be provided with benefits through a 'third country' international scheme, perhaps in an 'offshore' location. The implications of this are very similar to those of being retained in the UK scheme, particularly from the Spanish taxation point of view (see above). The schemes are, however, more flexible than UK schemes in the benefits which they can provide and the length of time most employees can remain members while outside the UK.

Healthcare

Spain operates a national health service similar to the UK's, where treatment is provided to all residents irrespective of their social security contribution status. Therefore, the decision as to whether to contribute to UK or Spanish social security does not affect the employee's health benefits. As in the UK, the employee may wish to supplement the state system with private insurance.

Note that UK nationals on secondment to Spain may wish to take out international insurance with a private UK health insurer. Such policies typically provide for repatriation to the UK in the event of serious illness requiring hospitalisation. If the employee had private insurance before going to Spain, continuing the contributions in his absence would avoid the possibility of 'pre-existing condition' exclusion clauses if he rejoins on his return.

Return to the UK

If the employee was retained in the UK social security system throughout his service in Spain, there are no issues here; he is treated as if he had remained in the UK.

If he contributed to the Spanish social security system, he will have earned an entitlement to a Spanish benefit as described above. He must keep records of his and his employer's social security numbers (these will normally appear on payslips). This information, together with the dates of his period of service in Spain, should be sent to the DSS before he retires, so that they can organise calculation and payment of his pension. The Spanish pension will be paid from Spain, in pesetas.

As far as company pension schemes are concerned, if the employee was retained in the UK scheme, there are no issues here. If he was promised UK benefits but withdrawn from the scheme for tax purposes, he will need to be readmitted to the scheme and 'made whole' as described above.

If he has retained an entitlement in a Spanish company scheme, this will be paid to him (in pesetas) when he reaches retirement age, and the employer might wish to take this into account in setting UK scheme benefit levels. If the benefit is in a qualified pension plan in Spain, the cash value cannot be transferred to the UK.

Part 10

The Real Estate Market

INTRODUCTION

The real estate market in Spain has witnessed major developments since the late 1980s. During those years the contractual system which ruled rents and leases from the 1940s onwards, and which had survived with only minor alterations, was reformed. The old system was aimed at protecting business and residential tenants through a number of clauses which prevented a free disposition of the property of the owner and controlled rents in many central areas at minimal prices. This situation delayed the development of an efficient property market, and is the main reason for the structure of property ownership in Spain in which a vast proportion of property is owned by the same company and people who use or live in the property.

The famous *Decreto Boyer*, a decree so named after the finance minister who enforced it in 1988, was the starting point of these changes. The decree introduced some measures that facilitated the disposition of the property for its owners and eased the conditions for termination of contracts and liberalising new leases.

Economic growth during the late 1980s and early 1990s and the enforcement of the new tenancy and leasehold systems led to the construction of brand new offices and refurbishment of old ones, to be let in more favourable economic conditions. At that time, a number of foreign investors were attracted to Spain and, since then, a significant amount of foreign investment dedicated to real estate development has been coming into the country.

In this section, readers will find an assessment of the opportunities in the real estate market. For convenience it is divided into chapters concerning commercial (10.1) and residential property (10.2).

The Commercial Property Market

James Preston, Jones Lang Wootton, Madrid

INTRODUCTION

The Spanish commercial property market, as with those markets throughout southern Europe, is less mature than those of its northerly neighbours, and is lacking the same degree of transparency, liquidity, and regulation. This can lead to difficulties for investors and occupiers alike. In addition to this, cross-border activity in real estate is complicated by cultural and language difficulties, and local idiosyncrasies. At the outset, sound advice should be sought in doing property business in Spain. Most international real estate consultants are familiar with the needs of international clients, advise many such clients in other markets, and while understanding the property needs of international companies/investors are able to act locally and bridge the cultural, language, and business gaps.

INVESTMENT

The Spanish commercial real estate investment market was thin prior to 1985 on account of the urban leasing law giving tenants security of tenure, and depressed rentals.

In 1985, the *Decreto Boyer* (named after the Minister of Finance, Miguel Boyer) liberalised these rents in relation to all new tenancies, and thus introduced market forces into the real estate market. This timing coincided with Spain's entry into the EC in 1986, when it became the focus of much investment, and the economic boom of the following few years was reflected also in the commercial investment market, focused in Madrid and Barcelona – a city which also benefited considerably on account of the 1992 Olympic games.

The recent recession has led to dramatic falls in both rental and capital values, and the property market is only now emerging from recession. This is reflected in the fact that investor demand is at its strongest for a number of years, with rental growth projections being some of the strongest in Europe. However, we have yet to see the re-emergence of a liquid investment market.

High interest rates remain a dampener on the market, particularly affecting international investors who are not prepared to take the currency risks. Furthermore, there remain vast differences between vendors' and purchasers' price expectations, and one of the key reasons why vendors' price expectations remain high is on account of the relatively weak pressure, in contrast to other countries, emanating both from the Bank of Spain, and the accounting regulations, which is resulting in a number of banks and other property owners maintaining historically high book cost values in accounts and failing to write down to market values, which have fallen dramatically over the last few years.

While many vendors indicate a willingness to sell at prices which may reflect 80 per cent of their current book cost, very few are prepared to sell at market value and absorb losses which in some cases are in excess of 50 per cent. This situation will either change as a result of increasing pressure from the Bank of Spain, dramatic increases in value serving to cushion the real losses that have taken place, or simply as a result of vendors accepting the losses, releasing capital, and redeploying the capital into areas with better growth prospects.

With regard to the domestic investment market, the only significant deals that have taken place over the recent past have been from local insurance institutions, most notably Mutua Madrileña. However, domestic property investment overall is relatively thin: pension fund property investment activity is almost non-existent, and insurance company property investment activity is unpredictable and inconsistent.

A study of domestic insurance company property portfolios reveals low levels of activity, buildings with generally small lot sizes, and fairly specific investment criteria. The notable exception to the small lot size rule is Mutua Madrileña, which has been relatively active during the last few years purchasing high profile, large size buildings in prime locations.

Prime office yields lie in the region of 6.5 per cent in Madrid, and 7 per cent in Barcelona.

RETAIL

The structure of the retail market in Spain is relatively immature, and the last 10 to 15 years have witnessed many changes in the structure of retailing, and investment in retail premises.

Intense legal and planning restrictions within city centres have served to protect the interest of the independent retailers. Retailers within city centres have traditionally benefited from full security of tenure, and artificially depressed rentals, with the effect that the market has been restricted in terms of development of 'high street' retail environments, and agglomeration economies, such as those most evident within the highly-developed retail market of London – department stores and high street multiples on Oxford Street, high fashion and jewellery on Bond Street, gentlemen's tailoring on Savile Row, and shirts on Jermyn Street, for example. The ability for international retailers to gain presence within the high streets has thus been severely limited, resulting in a number of international retailers achieving a presence in the high street through representation in some of the larger stores such as El Corte Inglés and Galerias Preciados. Marks & Spencers, for example, were first represented within the Spanish store Galerias Preciados and Virgin maintained a presence within the same chain.

The consumer expenditure profile, in the meantime, suggests significant opportunities for retailers. The Spanish level of retail sales is the fifth largest in western Europe, being 2.5 per cent times that of the Netherlands. Furthermore, Spanish consumer behaviour has changed rapidly: an increase in disposable income in the last boom resulted in a greater exposure to external influences with a significant growth in convenience foods and fast foods, for example. Having said that, however, the structure of retailing within Spain varies considerably. There is a wide gulf between Madrid/Barcelona and other areas of Spain which may never change, and which are unlikely to provide significantly important markets for sophisticated retailing.

In the context of the above, the lack of modern retailing environments in city centres, combined with clear consumer demand, led to the rapid development of shopping centres in the mid 1980s onwards. These centres were initially hypermarket based, the French dominating the market, with little provision in the early years for speciality shopping. Now however there is an increasing existence of speciality malls anchored usually by a hypermarket, and following the northern European model, providing good, modern, critical mass retail environments and international retailers in such schemes include Marks & Spencers, Stefanel, C&A, Body Shop, Benetton, and Virgin, for example. We are seeing the increased presence of the multiple retailers, and though Spain still has, after Italy, the greatest number of independent retailers in Europe, the number is diminishing as the retail environment becomes led by the multiples.

Finally, a recently passed law will have the effect of phasing out the benefits granted to retailers on historic leases within city centres, and this will free the market. Though the effect of this law will be limited in the short term, in the medium to long term we would expect city centres to provide greater opportunities for retailers seeking a presence in the high street.

OFFICES

The same lease law referred to above is applied throughout the market, and the traditional centres of Madrid and Barcelona contain a relatively high proportion of office buildings which continue to be subject to historic leases. Furthermore, the effect of such leases was to dampen investment demand for real estate given the lack of opportunity to realise open market rentals. A number of major companies, therefore, constructed buildings for their own occupation and this is still a feature of the market. However, since 1985 new leases have been able to operate on the basis of open market rental levels, and this has coincided with the beginning of the strong growth of the Spanish economy. Accordingly, historic office centres have been increasingly displaced from the historic centres of both the major cities, with development taking place northwards along Paseo de la Castellana, and westward along Avenida Diagonal in Barcelona. Both of these areas now provide modern office environments. During this period cities saw, as elsewhere, business parks developed on the periphery of the city: this has further contributed to the drain of offices from historic centres. These schemes have varied in their level of success, and in the recent recession a number of developments have suffered given the amount of competition.

Both Madrid and Barcelona, during the last five years, have witnessed falls in rental and capital value second only to that of the City of London. Falls in prime rental levels have been more than 50 per cent. However, in Madrid at least, most commentators believe that rental levels have now bottomed out and office rents in both cities are some of the cheapest within European Union countries.

Total Office Stock

Estimated total office stock of the city administrative area.

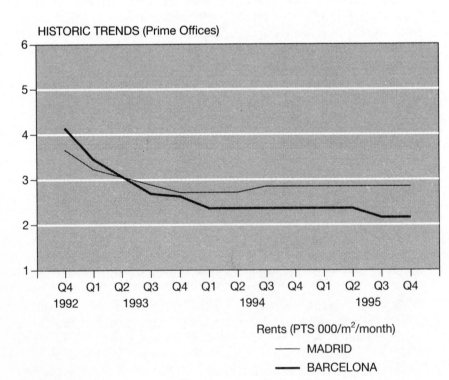

PARIS	30.6
LONDON	26.8
MUNICH	14.1
BERLIN	12.8
HAMBURG	11.4
FRANKFURT	8.5
MILAN	8.0
BRUSSELS	7.4
MADRID	7.4
STOCKHOLM	7.0
AMSTERDAM	4.8
DÜSSELDORF	4.3
LYON	3.8
THE HAGUE	3.7
BARCELONA	3.5
ROTTERDAM	2.7
GLASGOW	1.9
LUXEMBOURG	1.8
EDINBURGH	1.7
UTRECHT	1.7
ANTWERP	1.5
DUBLIN	1.3

* Office stock in the departments
of Paris, Hauts-de-Seine, Val-de-Marne
and Seine-St-Denis

Figure 10.1.1

HISTORIC TRENDS (Prime Offices)

Rents (PTS 000/m²/month)

——— MADRID

—— BARCELONA

Figure 10.1.2

Prime office rents lie in the region of 2,500 pesetas per m² per month in Madrid, and 1,800 pesetas per m² per month in Barcelona.

Prime Office Rents (ECU/m²/pa)

LONDON-WEST END	535
WARSAW	515
LONDON-CITY	505
PARIS-GOLDEN TRIANGLE	495
FRANKFURT	415
LUXEMBOURG	380
BERLIN	355
PRAGUE	355
MUNICH	320
HAMBURG	310
STOCKHOLM	295
PARIS-LA DEFENSE	295
BUDAPEST	290
PARIS-BERCY	280
PARIS-GOLDEN CRESCENT	280
EDINBURGH	270
DÜSSELDORF	255
GLASGOW	235
VIENNA	230
AMSTERDAM	220
BRUSSELS	215
MILAN	210
DUBLIN	205
MADRID	200
THE HAGUE	185
UTRECHT	155
BARCELONA	155
LYON	155
ROTTERDAM	140
ANTWERP	125

Figure 10.1.3

INDUSTRIAL

Industry accounted for about 24.4 per cent of Spanish GDP last year. Spain has developed an internationally competitive industrial sector, with firms often accountable to multinational parents. The market remains stable with a considerable supply of industrial land for development. In the last few years this market has moved away from the earlier owner occupation and is of interest to investors. Since lease terms are generally 10 years or more and with yields lying in the region of 10.5–12.5 per cent, there is considerable appeal.

The majority of demand for small units is from small- to medium-size companies wishing to owner occupy. The leasehold demand for larger units is also relatively strong, particularly from foreign companies – especially from the US and EUC – establishing or expanding their manufacturing activities in Spain.

Rents in PTS/m²/month					
Offices:					
Madrid	2700	2700	2700	2700	2700
Barcelona	2300	2300	2300	2100	2100
Retail:					
Madrid	8000–10000	8000–10000	8000–10000	10000–12000	11000–13000
Barcelona	4000–6000	4000–6000	4000–6000	3500–600	3500–600
Industrial:					
Madrid	800–900	800–900	800–900	800–900	800–900
Barcelona	600–750	600–750	600–750	600–750	600–750

Figure 10.1.4 *Letting*

% Yields					
Offices:					
Madrid	6.75–7.50	6.50–7.25	6.50–7.25	6.50–7.25	6.50–7.25
Barcelona	700–7.50	7.00–7.50	7.00–7.50	7.00–7.50	7.00–7.50
Retail:					
Madrid	7.00–8.00	6.50–7.50	6.50–7.50	6.50–7.50	6.50–7.00
Barcelona	6.50–7.50	6.50–7.50	6.50–7.50	6.50–7.50	6.50–7.50
Shopping Centres:	8.00–9.00	8.00–9.00	8.00–9.00	8.00–9.00	8.00–9.00
Madrid	10.50–11.50	10.50–11.50	10.50–11.50	10.50–11.50	10.50–11.50
Barcelona	9.00–11.00	9.00–11.00	9.00–11.00	9.00–11.00	9.00–11.00

Figure 10.1.5 *Investment*

Prime industrial rents lie in the region of 750–950 pesetas per m² per month.

10.2

The Real Estate Residential Market

Eduardo Fernández-Cuesta,
Richard Ellis Residencial SA

1990–1995

From 1990 and especially in 1992 and 1993, a crisis in the real estate sector fundamentally affected the office and industrial market. The change in prices of new homes from 1980–94 in the municipality of Madrid is shown in Figure 10.2.1.

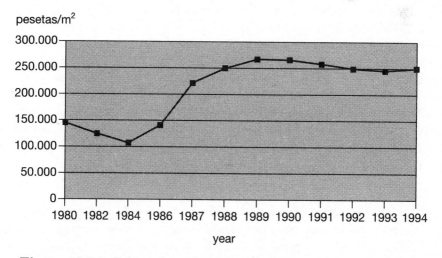

Figure 10.2.1 *Prices of new homes in the municipality of Madrid*
Source: Community of Madrid – Housing Department

It can be seen that prices, after their spectacular increase until 1990, have fallen slightly during the last four years. On the other hand the office market has suffered a decline of up to 50 per cent. The difference in behaviour was due to two main factors: (i) housing is a primary need less exposed to economic cycles; and (ii) a big reduction in the average size of homes in an attempt to maintain the price per square metre.

The change of the average usable space of new homes in Spain in the last few years can be seen from Table 10.2.1.

Table 10.2.1 *Average usable space per home*

1990 – 97,87 m²
1991 – 93,55 m²
1992 – 93,19 m²
1993 – 91,06 m²
1994 – 92,11 m²

Source: Ministerio de Obras Públicas, Transportes y Medio Ambiente

Despite this progressive reduction in the size of the home, the spectacular increase in the prices during the period 1985–90 caused an imbalance between the product offered and the purchasing power of a high percentage of families. At the same time, during this period, homes with some type of protection or grant experienced a free fall. Officially protected homes (*Viviendas de Protección Oficial* – VPO), whether privately or publicly promoted, were equally affected. Not even rented accommodation, as we shall see later, could be considered an alternative to ownership. On the contrary, since the 1960s the percentage of homes for rental has declined.

Finally, the demand for housing stock increased significantly from 1985–90 due to the baby boom of the 1960s; legal changes such as the elimination of automatic contract extension; the urban restrictions in Madrid and other cities; and easy availability of mortgages. In other words, the increases in prices from 1985–90 caused a disequilibrium in the market which has lasted until today.

The other important thing to describe, and which has been true everywhere, as much in Madrid as in Barcelona, is the movement of the population towards the popular districts on the city outskirts, as a result of the shortage and cost of homes in the city centres. We think this trend will change in the near future.

1995–2000

In 1994 the market started to show signs of recuperation as shown in Table 10.2.2.

Table 10.2.2 *Price per square metre of homes less than one year old*

Year	Madrid and hinterland	Barcelona and hinterland	Other cities with more than 500,000 inhabitants
1990	208,194	151,480	114,715
1991	225,441	179,897	128,944
1992	185,431	151,720	115,003
1993	185,922	153,821	105,736
1994	192,608	161,193	107,936

Source: Ministerio de Obras Públicas, Transportes y Medio Ambiente

In 1995 prices experienced a slight increase although less than inflation. It should also be noted that in the second half of 1995 there has been a slight fall off in sales compared to those reached in 1994. This fall off has not affected the sales of protected homes, mainly VPO. Demand has been concentrated in Madrid and Barcelona at prices of less than 15 million pesetas. In future years we do not think that the residential market will suffer excessive variations although the trend will be slightly upward. However there will continue to be a strong demand for accessible prices, 7–17 million pesetas in Madrid, and therefore a good deal of pressure on government to intervene in order to resolve this problem.

The Madrid City Council, as in Barcelona, in an attempt to promote the construction of the necessary housing is developing the following policies:

- creation of a land bank big enough to prevent the exodus of city dwellers, through reduced costs and hence lower-priced housing;
- improving the management of the land and planning of promotional campaigns.

2000–2004

The policy for the promotion of the land stock available at reduced cost and hence the price of the housing, has its greatest exponents, as we have already mentioned, in Madrid and Barcelona. Some important land developments are planned in the district of Madrid, most of these within the action programmes (*Programmas de Actuación Urbanisticos* – PAU). The most significant developments are shown in Table 10.2.3.

Table 10.2.3 *Important land developments in the district of Madrid*

Situation	Number of housing units
Monte Carmelo	8,546
Las Tablas	12,272
San Chinarro	13,568
Arroyo del Fresno	3,728
Villa de Vallecas	21,000
Carabanchel	11,350
Vicálvaro	4,900
Total	75,364

Similarly in the district of Barcelona, where land prices have been high in recent years, the following developments shown in Table 10.2.4 are planned:

Table 10.2.4 *Housing developments in Barcelona*

Situation	Number of housing units
Opening of the de la Diagonal to the sea	6,000
Outskirts	700
Sant Andreu – Sagrera	7,500
Frente Marítimo	2,400
Kepro – Diagonal Mar	1,600
Prim	465
Total	18,665

We estimate that the majority of these large real estate developments will start to offer housing accommodation for sale from 1999–2000.

The consequences of the availability of this new housing stock are as follows:

- it could produce an equilibrium between supply and demand which will lower the final price of housing, in accordance with the objectives of the Town Hall;
- today's trend for young families to move out of the city centre and live in the outskirts will be reversed in the near future.

It is expected that the new supply of housing expected in the coming years will provoke a change in the current trend, and will cause an increase in the population of the Madrid and Barcelona districts.

This brief analysis demonstrates that the development of the Spanish residential housing market is cyclical and that each period has an influence on that following it. There are obviously other conditions that influence the behaviour of the market and that are linked to the economic, political and social situation.

RENTAL ACCOMMODATION

The housing market is notable for the low quantity of rental accommodation.

The percentage of available rental accommodation is approximately 18 per cent, according to the housing survey of MOPT of 1990. The average in Europe is 36.3 per cent, although in countries such as Holland and Germany it is more than 55 per cent.

In 1991 there were 17.1 million homes in Spain, according to the data provided by the national statistics institute, of which 11.7 million were used for residential purposes. Of these, 2.2 million were classified as rental accommodation.

Until the introduction of the new law governing urban rental accommodation in Spain, *Ley de Arrendamientos Urbanos* (LAU), there were three different types of rental contracts, according to the date when they were signed:

1.   The old rental contracts signed before the law of 1965, representing scarcely 25 per cent, the second biggest.
2.   Those signed between 1965 and 1985, during which time permanent contracts were signed which permitted the revision of rents and which represent 54 per cent of the total.
3.   Those signed after 1985, when a freeing up was introduced permitting one year contracts and which make up the other 21 per cent.

The existence of these permanent rental contracts means that these approximately two million homes rented out on this basis are effectively not available in the market. The situation now is certainly positive, thanks to the supply created since 1985, although still very far from what we find in other similar countries. See Figure 10.2.2.

Spain has the lowest percentage of rental accommodation available in the European Union. The LAU (1994) tried to increase and improve the rental market by balancing the excessive protection of the old rental contracts and to reduce the tension generated since 1985 as a result of the Sr. Boyer decree freeing up the contracts and reducing tenant protection.

The high cost of rental accommodation has a number of consequences. The potential to introduce more mobility into the labour market is enormously limited. Furthermore the lack of supply pushes up prices making the rental alternative unattractive compared to purchase. See Figure 10.2.3.

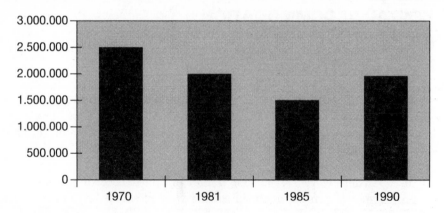

Figure 10.2.2 *Change in the Spanish rental accommodation market*

The main reason for the lack of rental accommodation has traditionally been the lack of confidence of owners and promoters to invest in a
sector where there is little protection from the law, such that the rental
of accommodation is not profitable for owners of empty apartments, nor
for the traditional promoters. The public authorities are looking at
changing this trend and promoting rental accommodation in line with
what can be found in similar countries.

The three pillars of the government policy for promoting residential
accommodation are:

1. The law governing urban rental accommodation – LAU
   (November 1994)
2. Real estate investment funds (May 1993)
3. State Housing Plan 1996–1999

The law governing urban rental accommodation

The new law has established a minimum contractual period of five
years for rented accommodation which, in principle, is binding for the
landlord, in an attempt to reach a compromise between the tenant's
need for security and stability and the rights and economic interests of
the landlord. This will pave the way for a recovery in the housing rental
index.

Real estate investment funds

The Housing Funds are collective investment institutions which benefit from tax incentives, and whose long-term aim is to collect funds for
purchasing land destined for the construction of rented housing. Once

these funds are more developed and have access to more capital, they will have the power to increase rental accommodation.

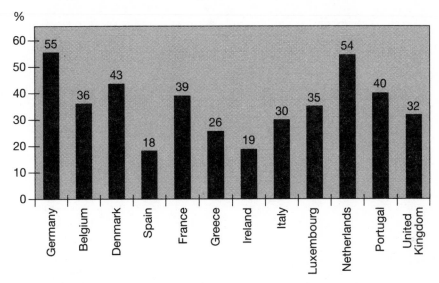

Figure 10.2.3 *The rental housing market in the European Union*

State Housing Plan 1996–1999

This lays down the main guidelines for housing policy in the immediate future. The plan is innovative in its efforts to promote the rented housing market, mainly by means of fiscal aid.

Conclusions

(i)   We are of the opinion that the market will continue on an upward trend for the next two or three years.

(ii) The most sought-after product is small to medium-sized housing in the average to lower price bracket.

(iii) As from 1999/2000, it is expected that a large supply of land will become available both in Madrid and Barcelona, which could affect residential sales prices.

(iv) The rental market will expand due to the promotion of the sector which is currently being undertaken.

Part 11

General Aspects of the Business Culture

INTRODUCTION

When conducting day to day business matters, often the way that colleagues interact has a major effect on the outcome of events. Knowing as much as you can about your business partner always works to your advantage.

Spain is a country with a distinctive character and differs from Britain in many ways. It may take a little time and patience to understand it and get used to its daily practices.

The characters described by Spanish writers such as Fernando de Rojas, Quevedo, Machado or Cela are so familiar to Spaniards but they appear strange and exotic to the British. Being aware of cultural differences is very important and keeping an open mind will enable you to enjoy an enriching experience when doing business in Spain.

The following two chapters offer guidance based on the experience of two qualified commentators, one British and one Spanish. We hope you will find them helpful in getting the best from your Spanish business experience.

11.1

Bridging the Cultural Gap

Leslie Stern, DTI Export Promoter for Spain

Coming to terms with the cultural differences of any market you are developing is an essential part of creating successful business relations. This is particularly the case in Spain, where failure to recognise cultural differences – and adapt to them – can make the difference between success and failure in your endeavours. Perhaps the essential point to remember is that you must adapt to their ways if you are trying to sell your product or service: you can only really insist on things being done your way when you are doing the buying. Above all, do not be deterred by the cultural differences you encounter. Spain is a major industrialised trading nation, and commerce does take place – the obligation is on you to understand how!

Perhaps the starting point in making contact is to remember that Spaniards have two surnames, the father's surname and mother's maiden surname, and care should be taken to use the former, which appears first if both are used, (although confusingly this is not always the case), as offence can be given by using the incorrect one. A similar potential for confusion exists with the courtesy title 'Don', used before male christian names, and 'Doña' used with female christian names. This courtesy title may be used in speech when addressing an older person, or when referring to an absent colleague, but is used principally in writing, in the abbreviated forms 'D' or 'Da'. Thus an envelope would be addressed to 'Sr D Pedro González García', but the letter would begin 'Dear Sr González'.

Some of the more obvious differences require little effort to understand or adapt to. Remember, for example, that the *siesta*, the long break during lunchtime and the afternoon, but working on into the evening, is in reality only a different timetable: just as you would adapt your timetable to contact a trading partner in the United States because of the time change, so you will need to adapt timings to be able to contact your Spanish trading partner.

Spain enjoys two more days public holiday, *fiestas,* and most Spaniards also celebrate a regional and a local *fiesta*, in all four more working days taken as holiday than the UK. Some of these *fiestas* will be carefully timed to facilitate the taking of a long weekend, just as we do. In practice, Spaniards will work around 240 days per year against around 250 in the UK. Adapting to this difference is but a minor inconvenience.

In terms of conducting business, the larger the company you are dealing with, the less you will notice the 'cultural' differences of the Spanish way of doing things. Just as at the Ford plant in Dagenham, the production line is not stopped at lunchtime, so the Ford plant in Valencia does not close down for a *siesta*. Differences are likely to be much more marked when you deal with the smaller company. Although generalisations are always potentially dangerous, you will notice that business meetings, for example, are likely to be much less structured than we are accustomed to, without a formal agenda, or formal minutes being recorded, although the meeting could well begin with more formal introductions of participants, and their professional or technical qualifications.

The love of *talking* through a problem rather than resolving matters in writing is perhaps why Spaniards are not as punctilious as we are about replying promptly to letters and faxes: provided you show patience and commitment the contract *will* be signed.

In addition to patience, recognise that you may have to wait patiently for appointments, even if pre-booked and confirmed, as Spaniards undoubtedly have a different view of punctuality to ours: your host may not even have arrived at the office at the appointed time. Your appointment schedule must allow due time for appointments to run late and for protracted negotiations: you are unlikely to accomplish as many appointments during the day as you would in the UK. Above all, do not get angry or annoyed at delayed appointments: it is unlikely to accelerate the timetable, and will not result in achieving your business objectives.

Not only commitment to the successful outcome of negotiation will be required, and your Spanish trading partner expects you to believe – and believe passionately – in your company and your product or service. This passionate belief should preclude you from criticising the UK and anything British, which could be taken as indirect criticism of yourself! Equally, you should never criticise Spain or anything Spanish, even if your Spanish trading partner does so, and comments on Spanish politics will be regarded as very 'bad form'. Whatever your feelings regarding bullfighting, a subject which does raise the most passionate feelings, common sense suggests that this subject is best avoided: it is unfortunately the way of the world that whatever side of the debate you are on, your potential trading partner will be on the other side, and you could therefore easily destroy a blossoming relationship. In the same way, the subject of Gibraltar, while not a serious obstacle to British–Spanish trade, could by its political sensitivity spoil burgeoning business relations.

Like most Latins, Spaniards are friendly, exuberant and demonstrative – probably the very antithesis of the British sang-froid: indeed, we are often thought by the Spanish to be too reserved, and to find it hard to adapt to a different business environment. It is important therefore to work hard at not being stuffy: you should not wait to be invited to join in a conversation. Spanish exuberance results in noise levels considerably higher than experienced in the UK, both in meetings and also in public places: a quiet restaurant in Spain is an empty restaurant! Noise levels do take some getting used to – taking advantage of the *siesta*, not for a sleep but to relax quietly, may be beneficial. In addition to wearing noise levels, British business people may well find the Spanish timetable exhausting, particularly if being entertained, or entertaining, in the evening, when dinner will not be before 9 pm, and could be very much later, particularly during the hotter parts of the year.

Being entertained has its own set of rules in Spain. While it would be quite normal in the UK for a foreign visitor staying in a hotel to be invited to your home for a drink or a meal, this is not common practice in Spain. If you are invited to visit a Spaniard's home, this implies a very high level of contact or friendship, and should never be refused. Observe what might be called the old-fashioned courtesies: take (or send the next day) a bunch of flowers for your hostess (but not a bottle of wine). If you are invited to lunch or dinner, your host will expect to pay, even if a woman. You should note that an essential part of Spain's return to democracy has been the emancipation of women: recognise that women now occupy senior and middle management positions in Spanish business, and rightly expect to be treated as business equals.

When entertaining, you should expect to pick up the bill if you have issued the invitation: never try to 'split' the bill. If you wish to take your Spanish trading partner for lunch or dinner, but are unsure of a suitable restaurant, ask your guest to recommend one. Your Spanish guest will almost certainly choose somewhere he would go himself and where he is likely to be seen by his peer group. As we do not come from a wine producing country, ask your guest to choose the wine!

If all the above sounds off-putting, remember that hundreds of Spanish companies already enjoy commercial relationships with British companies. Spaniards are very receptive to UK goods and services, and perceive the British as ideal partners to do business with, although somewhat unable to deliver on time and rather unwilling to treat Spain as a serious market with excellent prospects for long-term development. As the Spanish market is a highly competitive market, and extremely price sensitive, to develop those long-term relationships, there is a need to demonstrate real commitment by regular visits to and regular communication with your trading partners, and customers.

How UK Managers can Negotiate Successfully in Spain

Professor Ramón Montaner, ESADE

As Lord Chesterfield once said: 'Bad negotiators are those who just do business'. I hope that readers of this book can do more than just 'business in Spain'. This article provides some pertinent information regarding the peculiarities of negotiating in Spain.

The first thing to realise is that many people believe that their culture is the best and that the rest of civilization lives in ignorance. Many people come to Spain with this limited and high-handed attitude. They believe and even argue that their physical, social and cultural values, or even their social status, are superior and preferable to any other. Those sharing that belief will not do much business in Spain. There are two reasons for this: first, Spain is a modern country with a high level of education and services; second, the Spanish are very proud and if offended, could be motivated to find revenge!

Spain is a land of opportunity, so instead of trying to muscle in on an existing market, why not try to create a new one? It is quite possible that by taking the time to create a more lasting relationship, the rewards will be greater. If you have a good product or service and are negotiating with a potential distributor, you could limit yourself to that product or service and close the deal without further ado. However, if you are prepared to go a little bit further, you may find that your new Spanish colleague has many other business interests which other British companies could benefit from. In Spain, relationships and contacts are very valuable and it is quite likely that from an initial business deal, others will follow.

Often the British do not realise that Spain is a country of many different regions and peoples. It is important to know a little bit about these regional differences before embarking on negotiations.

Central region

These are skilful negotiators who are able to close deals quickly after rather protracted discussions.

The North-east

As well as Spanish, they also speak Catalonian. They are serious and skilled negotiators, and tend to be reticent. Meals are considered a forerunner to the negotiation meeting but the deal will be closed in the office. They are fairly time-conscious and like to be considered cosmopolitan. As negotiators, they are flexible, adaptable and straightforward.

The North

Northerners tend to be serious, experienced and taciturn. The Basque Country is part of this region and the Basques are proud of their institutions and traditions. They have traditionally done business with Britain. Normally tough negotiators, they are likely to play 'all or nothing'. If they dislike something, they will let you know.

The North-west

Very skilful people, the Galicians tend to be ambiguous and naturally cautious and their negotiation style reflects this.

The South

Andalucians are very relaxed and like to get to know you personally as well as professionally. They are flexible negotiators and love bargaining.

USEFUL TIPS

- Do not show feelings of superiority. Spaniards appreciate a detail of familiarity – try speaking Spanish;
- try to create a new market/demand: there are plenty of opportunities if you are able to explore all avenues;

- do not become obsessed by price. Look for alternatives; with just a little imagination you will find them;
- try to adopt the 'win–win' strategy during your negotiations. As we say 'let the other one get the last peseta';
- try to earn the confidence of the other party through your words and actions. You will immediately notice that negotiations proceed more smoothly;
- remember that both the personal and the professional approach is one of the keys to negotiating successfully in Spain;
- wherever possible, try to save your counterpart's face. Never damage his or her self-esteem;
- prepare your arguments in advance – Spaniards seldom do so;
- be sure of what you want to achieve. Prepare the minimum and maximum what you want to achieve and what you are prepared to offer. In every negotiation, you will always have to concede something;
- prepare your research thoroughly and be positive;
- be patient – you are in a country with different customs which should be observed;
- be careful with alcohol. Its social use is very extended and remember to be polite when rejecting drinks;
- make an effort to find a common ground, eg mutual interests etc;
- always keep your goals in mind and at the same time try to be flexible;
- be careful about closing the negotiation too swiftly; this is the most delicate point and where it is most likely to fail;
- put your agreements in writing, preferably in English. Your Spanish partners can deal with the translation;
- if the deal has gone well for you, try not to show it.

Buen viaje, compañero!

Part 12

Public Administration and Business Representatives

INTRODUCTION

This last section of the book includes a description of the structure of Spanish public administration. It also describes the role of the chambers of commerce, which Spanish law recognises as special promoters of economic activities.

There are three other articles. One refers to the role of the Confederation of Spanish Industry (CEOE) in the promotion of business in Spain. The remaining two are profiles of the sponsors of this book; the Spanish Chamber of Commerce in Great Britain and Iberia.

Spanish administration can sometimes be a little bit complex to understand since activities that used to be attributed to the central government might have been transferred to some of the 17 regional administrations or autonomies. So you might find that the body in charge of a particular function in Murcia is dependent on the national government, while in Catalonia it could be part of its regional administration.

In any case, all autonomies will have a department in their government which is concerned with the subject in which you might be interested. Contact details of all the investment offices of the regional governments are provided in the useful addresses section. They will be able to help you on any queries or put you in touch with the right institution.

The Spanish Chamber of Commerce in Britain and the chambers of commerce in Spain can also offer guidance on where to get more information or where to apply for particular projects. Finally, the Spanish Commercial Office is always a readily available source of information and guidance that you should bear in mind.

We hope that the information contained in this book together with that which the agencies of this last chapter offer may help you to understand and enjoy doing business with Spain.

12.1

Public Administration and the Role of Chambers of Commerce

Miguel Riaño, J & A Garrigues

DEFINITION OF THE PUBLIC ADMINISTRATION

Spanish positive law provides no single definition of public administration. The Spanish Constitution of 1978 designed a scheme of administrative entities, the predominant note of which is notable territorial decentralisation. Today, therefore, there are at least four types of public administration each corresponding to one of the four basic territorial levels in which Spain is organised (the state, autonomous regional governments, provinces and municipalities). Each of these four levels is governed by a political body, of an electoral nature and origin and, in turn, each of these political entities has its own administration or administrative organisation.

But the administration of the state, the 17 autonomous regional governments and the local administrations are not the only legal administrative bodies in Spain. There is also a large number of organisations and agencies which have their own legal status, are formally independent from the entity that created them but closely related to it, and whose functions are to discharge duties or render services originally attributed to the parent agency. These bodies are of great importance, since many administrative sectors are entrusted to entities of this kind, eg social security, rail and air transport, and so on. There is no one constitutional statute applicable to them all.

Two different types of organisation exist as described below.

DIRECT OR PRIMARY ORGANISATION

The prototype of this organisation is seen in the administration of the state. At the top is the government and each of the members of government, the ministers, each of whom is the head of a ministry or ministerial department, which in turn is organised by hierarchy in a pyramid. Each ministry is sub-divided internally into several under-directorates general (*ministerios* and *secretarías de estado*), these into various departments, each department into several sections and each section into various units. Naturally the organisation is much more complex than this, but this outline explains the basic model.

In the other three administrative levels, while the organisation is not so developed it is very similar. The regional governments have followed the state administration model. The higher levels of the autonomous regional governments are structured around three figures: the council of government, the president and the counsellors. The name each receives depends on the region where they govern. Most regions use the term *consejero* for the regional ministers and *presidenti* for the president. However in the Basque region the president is referred to as *lehendakari*. Under the management of the council of government and the coordination of the president, the administration is organised into boards or departments consisting of agencies ordered in a hierarchy, each dependent on the respective councillor.

The autonomous regional communities also have a major apparatus of peripheral administration, particularly the regional governments covering more than one province, in which provincial or territorial delegations are established dependent on each of the boards. In the sphere of local administration, the governmental apparatus rests with the municipality as an elected body. The plenary meeting of the municipality consists of the councillors (concejales), one of whom assumes the duties of the mayor (alcalde). The number of councillors depends on the number of inhabitants in the municipality.

Similar to what occurs in the municipality, the organisation of the apparatus of government and administration of the province consists of three bodies, all integrated in what is known as the provincial deputation: the plenary meeting, its president and the commission of government.

INSTRUMENTAL ORGANISATION, INSTITUTIONAL OR CORPORATE ADMINISTRATION

Together with the primary and direct organisation, the structure of each of these public administrations is completed with an array of organisations formally separated from but dependent on each of them.

The basic feature of these organisations is that each of them has its own legal status different from the entity that created it. The duties entrusted to these organisations could *a priori* be discharged by integrated agencies in what we have called direct or primary organisations. If they become independent and entrusted to entities with their own status, this is purely for reasons of convenience and efficient management. Their classification is supported on the fact that some have a corporate or associative base and others take the form of an institution or foundation. The latter may in turn be subdivided into three large sectors.

First, those called the public entities for management, a category which in turn includes entities of four kinds (autonomous agencies, public institutions, social security management entities and local independent services); second, publicly-owned companies, private forms of business corporation classified according to whether they belong to the state, the regional governments or local corporations; and finally what are known as public foundations, including a heterogeneous series of juridical persons in the form of private foundations belonging to the public entities.

INSTRUMENTAL ADMINISTRATION, PARTICULARLY PERSONIFICATIONS OF CORPORATE NATURE

On classifying instrumental bodies, we start from the prior differentiation between entities of corporate base and entities of foundational base.

When speaking of corporations, we refer to a group of persons organised in the common interest of them all, and participating in the group administration. These members are the holders of the interests that the group guarantees and the members themselves organise the entities, in the sense that it is their will which makes up the will of the entity through a representative procedure. Local entities are obviously the corporative entities *par excellence*. These corporations are of a purely administrative nature because their members constitute a political and not a private group. On the other hand, in institutional entities no members exist as such. Institutions are created by a founder which proposes the ends to be complied by the body created. It is the founder which provides the material means or manpower to accomplish these ends and decides with its will to set up the bodies of the entity and who therefore constitutes its will. It is on this last note, the dependence of institutions on their founder, which explains the difference between the two large types of institutions, public and private.

In public institutions, the founder is an administration which sets not only the aims of the institution but also allocates the material, personal and financial means to accomplish these aims. In Spanish law, there are numerous examples of institutions of this kind (The National Institute of Social Security, the National Institute of Industry, etc).

OFFICIAL CHAMBERS OF COMMERCE, INDUSTRY AND SHIPPING

We have stated that the corporation *par excellence* consists of local entities. However there is another type of public corporation in which persons group together because of their personal or professional qualifications to achieve common ends. This is the case of professional associations, chambers of commerce, planning compensation boards, etc.

These corporations have a hybrid nature with individual features, in so far as they render services to their members and safeguard their social and economic interests, but they also have a public dimension, since they are classified as corporations of law, and their organisation and members, their status as consultative bodies for the state and regional administrations are imposed on them, while they are also subject to the supervision of these territorial entities and, finally, they exercise public authorities in a deconcentrated or delegated way. This makes it possible for these corporations to be included within the definition of the public administration and therefore subject to the principles and forms of action described above.

Thus, although the main aim of these corporations is to assert their members' interests, the administration does not hesitate to charge them with duties of a public administrative nature, which implies their inclusion in the category of public administrations. The basic legislation governing chambers of commerce consists of Act 3/1993 of 22 March. This Act, in 25 articles, lays down the basic legal system governing the life of these corporations. The following aspects deserve particular attention:

1. They are corporations in public law to which duties of an administrative public nature are attributed by legislation or by express delegation of the administration, duties normally reserved for the public authorities. Their basic purpose is to represent, promote and defend the general interests of commerce, industry and shipping and to provide service to undertakings engaging in these activities. Thus the chambers become consultancy agencies for the public administration of the development of commerce, industry and shipping and are obliged, among other things, to:
   - issue certificates of origin and other certificates related to trade;
   - compile standard commercial customs and usages;
   - propose to the government the reforms or measures they consider necessary or desirable to promote commerce, industry and shipping;
   - develop activities to support and stimulate foreign trade;
   - cooperate with the administration in the management of practical training at working centres;
   - process public programmes for aids to undertakings;
   - keep a public census of all companies and their establishments, office and agencies located within its territory;
   - perform duties of national and international commercial arbitration;
   - promote and cooperate in the organisation of trade fairs and expositions;
   - to prepare trade statistics, etc.
2. As regards private duties, the legislator has merely recognised in general terms the private aspects of these corporations of public law, leaving it to their members, from their bodies of government and particularly from the plenary meeting of the chamber, to define the functions they are to discharge.
3. *Territorial scope* There is at least one official chamber of commerce, industry and shipping in each province; however, other chambers may exist with different territorial scope, or councils of chambers of autonomous regional scope, if this is determined in the respective autonomous regional legislation.
4. *Organisation* The governing bodies of the chambers are the plenary meeting, the executive committee and the president. The plenary meeting is the supreme body of government and representation of the chamber and consists of the number of members laid down in the Act. The executive committee is the standing body of management, administration and proposal of the chamber. The president represents the chambers, it presides over all its bodies and is responsible for implementing its resolutions.

Each chamber has its own internal regulations. These state in general terms the rules of operation of its bodies of government and the personnel in the chamber's service.

5. *Application of the principle of obligatory membership* One of the main features of corporations of this kind is the obligatory membership of individuals or corporations. This is their most controversial aspect, as a wide sector considers that the principle of obligatory membership consecrated in the Act violates the right of free association recognised in Article 22 of the Spanish Constitution. The controversy has reached the highest Spanish court (the Constitutional Court), which in a 1994 judgment declared the system of obligatory membership contemplated in the previous act on chambers of commerce to be incompatible with the Constitution. A given sector understands that this judgment would be extendible to the current act on the chambers of commerce and that therefore obligatory membership should be understood to be unconstitutional.

Thus, a question of unconstitutionality has been brought before the Spanish Constitutional Court requesting an express decision of the Constitutional Court to this effect. The chambers have always maintained that obligatory membership is not unconstitutional, arguing that the public legal duties attributed to the chambers in themselves justify the obligatory membership.

12.2

Spanish Embassy Commercial Office

Spanish Embassy in London, Commercial Office

ACTIVITIES

The Spanish Embassy Commercial Office is the official Spanish government body in London responsible for stimulating trade and investment between Spain and the UK. The Spanish Institute for Foreign Trade (ICEX) forms part of the Commercial Office, and its main object is to heighten the awareness and image of Spanish products in the UK.

Spanish products

The Commercial Office/ICEX is divided into different Departments covering various product sectors: wines, sherry, food, industrial products, and consumer goods. Their main aims are:

- to improve commercial links between Spanish and British companies by assisting manufacturers and exporters in Spain wishing to sell to the UK, and importers in Britain wishing to buy Spanish products;
- to improve British buyers' knowledge of Spanish products;
- to establish and implement marketing plans in the UK for the development of Spanish products and to monitor the performance of the market.

Our databases hold information on Spanish manufacturers, exporters and trade associations. Please write to us or send us a fax, specifying which product(s) you are interested in sourcing, and we will send you the appropriate list of companies and/or organisations you can contact.

Investment in Spain

There is also an *Investment Department* in the Commercial Office, which is responsible for providing information, advice and practical help on inward investment into Spain, joint ventures, etc.

General information

The Commercial Office can also furnish macroeconomic information and statistics on Spain and the UK, as well as business information of a more general kind relating to commerce and industry in both countries.

The Spanish Chamber of Commerce in Great Britain

The Spanish Chamber of Commerce in Great Britain

The Spanish Chamber of Commerce (Cámara Oficial de Comercio de España en Gran Bretaña) was founded in 1886 and is an association freely established by Spanish and British traders, industrialists and professional persons with the object of furthering economic and commercial relations between Spain and Great Britain. Since then, the development of legislation on Chambers of Commerce has given official recognition to its specific tasks as promoter of Spanish exports and trade relationships with Britain.

The Chamber's main aims are to promote Spanish exports to Great Britain in close collaboration with the Spanish Secretariat of State for Commerce, and to look after the interests of its members, offering them an extensive and comprehensive range of modern services including management consultancy, information and promotion.

Among the services specifically designed to support company management include: the opportunity to domicile head offices and companies; bilingual secretarial services; video conference facilities; booking service for social and cultural events; organisation of mail-shots; hire of cars and mobile phones; legal representation; its use as a liaison office and so on.

One of the most popular requests is for the provision of business and market information, which is available from the Chamber through on-line services, its existing database or tailor-made market research. The Chamber also offers a number of high quality publications such as: *Doing Business with Spain*, *The Anglo-Spanish Trade Directory*, which includes clearly-indexed information about hundreds of businesses operating in both countries, and the bi-monthly magazine *El Comercio Hispano-Británico*.

The Chamber of Commerce can also provide consultancy services in many different areas: some of the most popular are legal, fiscal and commercial guidance. It can also provide effective help in the reclamation of VAT or in cases of amicable mediation.

The Chamber of Commerce is also closely involved in the field of education and training, offering its own qualifications, a Diploma, Certificate and Introductory Certificate in Business Spanish. A number of organisations across the country offer courses leading to these examinations.

On a broader front, the Chamber promotes Spanish commercial interests by hosting a wide range of conferences, seminars and round tables. These are specifically designed to disseminate the latest available information on Spanish and British markets, economic and business trends, as well as modern management techniques.

As part of its social and business life, the Chamber also offers its centrally-located building as a venue for trade exhibitions, presentations, business meetings and lunches.

All these services and the confidence of hundreds of firms from both countries associated to it have shaped this Chamber as the natural forum of Anglo-Spanish business life.

Iberia – The Business Choice for Spain

If you are contemplating doing business in Spain, there can be no better way to get off to a flying start than with Iberia Airlines, who have been doing business between Spain and the UK for the last 50 years.

As Spain's national carrier and the fourth largest airline in Europe, Iberia serves the main Spanish business destinations of Madrid and Barcelona from London, Dublin and Manchester. With major hubs in Madrid, Miami, Buenos Aires and Caracas, the Iberia Group provides comprehensive connexions for the international business traveller to the whole of the Caribbean, Central and South America. The main leisure destinations on the Spanish mainland and the Canary Islands are also served by the Group carriers.

Building on its experience in providing a service to business travellers, Iberia has evolved a sophisticated European Business Class service which offers business travellers a range of extra services to improve the ease of their journey. Benefits include a telephone check-in, advanced boarding passes, chauffered parking services, dedicated Business Class check-in desks, priority baggage handling and access to 47 VIP lounges worldwide.

With the needs of the business traveller constantly in mind, the Iberia Group strives to achieve a consistently high record of punctuality. Iberia also has one of the most modern fleets in Europe which includes A320/200s with a maximum capacity of 147 passengers and MD87s which can seat up to 109 passengers. All the aircraft presently in use are less than five years old.

Once on board, Business Class passengers are assured the highest standard of service which includes a 35.5 inch seat pitch, a welcome drink, a large selection of complimentary daily Spanish and English newspapers, a gourmet meal and complimentary drinks. Understanding the need for business travellers to keep abreast of the news, Iberia's on-board entertainment includes Euro-news which provides a constantly updated oracle of international events. Business Class passengers also receive priority disembarkation on all flights.

To help them meet the requirements of their Business Class passengers with even great efficiency, Iberia has evolved a dedicated Business Class Service Centre. At this unique facility, First and Business Class passengers can make specific seat requests in advance and check in by phone; and boarding passes can be issued up to one month before departure. Passengers may pre-book specific meal requirements for most recognised diets. All hotel bookings for the Iberia Group's preferred partner hotels and chauffered parking at Heathrow can be arranged through the Business Class Service Centre.

The Business Class Service Centre is open seven days a week (Monday to Friday 0630–2000, and Saturday and Sunday 0900–1730). Tel: 0171-830 0066.

Of course, many business travellers choose to travel in Economy Class. With this in mind, Iberia ensures that Economy passengers also enjoy a high level of comfort and service. This includes a 32-inch seat pitch, complimentary wine and beer served with a meal, and a choice of newspapers. Passengers can watch a sophisticated audio-visual entertainment system with the latest Euronews and short documentaries.

For the busy executive travelling to Madrid, Iberia's unrivalled schedules allow a full nine hours of business in Spain's capital city. Iberia operates the

Advertising feature

first flight out of Heathrow in the morning to Madrid which leaves at 0730. Since Iberia's last flight out of Madrid to Heathrow leaves at 1955, this is particularly useful for business travellers who can spend a full working day in one of Europe's most important cities and return home the same evening.

For business travellers with appointments in Barcelona, Iberia flies direct to Barcelona three times a day from Heathrow Terminal 2, and daily from Manchester.

Developing Spain's natural link between the old and new worlds, the Iberia Group's extensive route network is particularly convenient for business travellers who wish to combine visits to North and South America. With Iberia's Amigo programme, passengers bound for South America travelling First and Business Class can enjoy a free stopover in Madrid, Miami or Buenos Aires. This includes transfers to and from the airport, one night's luxury accommodation, breakfast, lunch and dinner.

Additionally, all Viasa Business Class passengers travelling to or from Caracas and taking a connecting Viasa flight have the option of a free stopover in Caracas, including transfer to and from the airport and luxury accommodation on a half-board basis.

For business travellers who regularly fly across the Atlantic, the Latin American Business Class Circular Fare provides a fantastic opportunity to combine business in North and South America on an optimum budget. The fare entitles Business Class Passengers to travel in a circular direction from the UK to multiple destinations in North, South and Central America. This ticket provides all the comforts of travelling in Business Class, a superb range of destinations and great flexibility.

The Circular Fare provides routings via five cities in North America and a further 30 cities in Central and South America. Included in the programme are the North American cities of Montreal, Toronto, New York, Los Angeles and Miami. Latin American destinations include Aruba, Bogota, Buenos Aires, Caracas, Guatemala City, Havana, Mexico City, Rio de Janeiro, Santiago de Chile, Santo Domingo and Sao Paulo.

For journeys made in Business and First Class, the Iberia Group is keen that its frequent flyers should be rewarded in their leisure time for their loyalty. In 1991 Iberia was the first airline in Europe to introduce a frequent flyer programme, Iberia Plus. Business travellers who fly with Iberia, or the other airlines associated with the programme, can gain points that can be exchanged for free flights, hotels rooms or car hire.

Partners include Sol/Melia, Occidental and Inter Continental hotels, and car rental firms Avis and Hertz. Their inclusion ensures Iberia Plus members have access to a first-class hotel room and car hire anywhere in the world.

Travellers will always know how may points they can earn. Each company has a table specifying the points awarded for each service. These points will be increased with the special offers the Iberia Plus programme constantly brings out and which will be promoted through the newsletter or by contacting the Iberia Plus service centre.

The Iberia Group is looking forward to a positive future and to maintain its position as Spain's national carrier and Europe's fourth largest airline, continuing to provide a high-class and cost-effective service well into the next century.

Advertising feature

12.4

The Spanish Confederation of Employers' Organizations

CEOE

The *Confederación Española de Organizaciones Empresariales* (CEDE) – Spanish Confederation of Employers' Organisations – is the top-ranking business institution in Spain. Since it was founded in June, 1977, its mission has been to defend free enterprise in a market economy and represent employers and their interests to society at large.

The CEOE monitors and analyses the country's economy and labour market on an on-going basis, offering solutions and taking action that contribute to their enhancement for the advancement and welfare of society as a whole. Through some 200 regional and trade organisations and more than 2,000 local associations, the CEOE represents over one million self-employed business people and nearly 350,000 companies that employ around 95 per cent of all Spanish wage-earners. All sectors of the economy and all the regions and provinces of Spain are represented in the CEOE. Small- and medium-sized enterprises have their own specific representative circuit via the *Confederación Española de la Pequeña y Mediana Empresa* (CEPYME) – Spanish Confederation of Small- and Medium-Sized Firms – a nation-wide organisation targeting the specific interests of Spanish SMEs.

GOVERNING BODIES

The CEOE's governing bodies are made up of the representatives of its member organisations. The General Assembly is the Confederation's ultimate governing body and comprises representatives of all CEOE's member organisations, elected by the organisations themselves. The General Assembly elects a Chairman and a Board of Directors every four years which, in turn, elects the Executive Committee from among its members.

A number of research and advisory bodies under the direct aegis of the Board of Directors systematically analyses the social and economic context in which Spanish enterprises conduct their business, on both the national and international fronts. Such bodies comprise the following Commissions: economic and financial policy; taxation; environment; anti-trust; infrastructures and public administration services contracts; collective bargaining; health, social security and on-the-job safety and hygiene; labour market and training; European Union; international relations; promotion of new enterprises; and industrial and energy policy, as well as the Tourist Industry Council.

These Commissions and committees are counselled and coordinated by CEOE departments which implement the instructions issued by the Confederation's governing bodies. Such departments, which answer directly to the Secretary General, constitute the Confederation's executive machinery.

Companies belong to the CEOE through a dual membership criterion, sectorial and regional. Companies join a local association corresponding to the geographic location and trade in which they engage, which in turn belongs to two nationwide organisations, one sectorial and the other inter-sectorial (regional). It is these latter that belong directly to the CEOE.

INTERNATIONAL AFFILIATIONS

The Confederation belongs to the major international economic and employers' institutions: International Employers' Organisation (IEO); International Labour Office (ILO); Union of Industries of the European Community (UNICE); Business and Industry Advisory Committee to the OECD (BIAC); Interamerican Council for Trade and Production (CICYP) and the Association for EU/Latin American Business Cooperation (ACE).

One of the Confederation's objectives is to promote Spanish companies in foreign markets and foster the exchange of initiatives and experience with other countries; such action has given rise to various Cooperation Agreements.

Internationally-speaking, the CEOE devotes special attention to the European Union. Its delegation in Brussels maintains direct relations with Union institutions and the standing representations of Union countries in the Belgian capital. Moreover, the *Euroventanilla* (European counter) in the headquarters in Madrid guarantees speedy and specialised access to information of any kind on EU legislation.

The CEOE has established a network of offices in several countries in conjunction with the domestic employers' organisations, for the purpose of promoting, supporting and facilitating contacts and cooperation between Spanish and foreign enterprises. Foremost among these are the Washington Office, which ensures standing support for business people who wish to operate on the North American market or with international financial bodies (World Bank, Inter-American Development Bank) and the Tokyo Office which, in conjunction with CDTI, supports projects for technological cooperation with Japanese enterprises.

Part 13

Useful Addresses

OFFICIAL BODIES

The DTI
Overseas Trade Services
Spain Desk
Business in Europe Branch
Kingsgate House
66–74 Victoria Street
London SW1E 6SW
Tel: 0171 215 4768
Fax: 0171 215 5611

Spanish Embassy (Commercial Office)
The Investment Department
66, Chiltern Street
London W1M 2LS
Tel: 0171 486 0101
Fax: 0171 224 6409

The Spanish Chamber of Commerce in Great Britain
5, Cavendish Square
London W1M 0DP
Tel: 0171 637 9061
Fax: 0171 436 7188

Nacional Government Investment Office
Dirección General de Inversiones
Exteriores
Ministerio de Comercio y Turismo
P° de la Castellana, 162, P1 13
28046 Madrid
Tel: +34 1 349 36 11/ 12
Fax: +34 1 349 35 62

Investment Agencies and Bodies of the Autonomous Communities in Spain

Andalucía
IFA Instituto de Fomento de
Andalucía
Departamento de Promoción Exterior
C/ Torneo, 26
41002 Sevilla
Tel: +34 5 490 00 16
Fax: +34 5 490 63 00

Aragón
IAF Instituto Aragonés de Fomento
C/ Teniente Coronel Valenzuela, 9

50004 Zaragoza
Tel: +34 76 70 21 01
Fax: +34 76 70 21 03

Asturias
IFR Instituto de Fomento Regional
Parque Tecnológico de Asturias/
Technology Park of Asturias
33420 Llanera, Asturias
Tel: +34 8 526 00 68
Fax: +34 8 526 44 55

The Instituto de Fomento Regional
(Regional Development Agency) is the
main public body for industrial promotion in Asturias. The IFR offers advice
to set up business in Asturias and manages the regional incentives scheme
and some other programmes to support
companies.

Balearic Islands
Consejería de Economía y Hacienda
C/ Palau Reial, 17
07001 Palma de Mallorca
Tel: +34 71 176 751
Fax: +34 71 176 757

Basque Country
SPRI Sociedad para la Promoción y
Reconversión Industrial SA
C/ Gran Vía, 35 3°
48009 Bilbao
Tel: +34 4 479 70 12
Fax: +34 4 479 70 23

Canary Islands
Gobierno Autónomo Canario
Consejería de Economía y Hacienda
Dirección Gral de Promoción
Económica
C/ Tomás Miller, 38 4°
35071 Las Palmas de Gran Canaria
Tel: +34 28 22 21 21 / 22 42 12
Fax: +34 28 22 78 12

Cantabria
SODERCAN Sociedad para el
Desarrollo Regional de Cantabria
C/ Isabel II, 24
39002 Santander
Tel: +34 42 31 15 53
Fax: +34 42 31 16 53

Castille-La Mancha
Dirección General de Desarrollo
Industrial
Junta de Comunidades de Castilla –
La Mancha
Pza de Zocodovcz, 7 2°
45071 Toledo
Tel: +34 25 26 98 00
Fax: +34 25 26 78 73/2

Castille-León
Agencia de Desarrollo Económico de
Castilla y León
C/ José Cantalapiedra, s/n
47071 Valladolid
Tel: +34 83 41 18 57
Fax: +34 83 41 49 70

Catalonia
CIDEM Centro de Infornación y
Desarrollo Empresarial
Av Diagonal, 403 1ñ
08008 Barcelona
Tel: +34 3 415 11 14
Fax: +34 3 416 08 18

Extremadura
Consejería de Economía y Hacienda
Av del Guadiana, s/n Puertas C y D
06800 Mérida (Badajoz)
Tel: +34 24 38 51 61
Fax: +34 24 38 51 71

Galicia
IGAPE Instituto Gallego de Promoción
Económica
C/ Fray Rosendo Salvado, 16 Bajo
15701 Santiago de Compostela (La
Coruña)

La Rioja
IFE Instituto de Fomento Empresarial
C/ Villamediana, 17
26003 Logroño
Tel: +34 41 29 11 15
Fax: +34 41 29 11 07

Madrid
IMADE Instituto Madrileño de
Desarrollo Económico
Gran Vía, 42 1°
28013 Madrid
Tel: +34 1 580 26 00
Fax: +34 1 580 25 89

Murcia
Instituto de Fomento de la Región de
Murcia
Pza de San Agustín, 5
30005 Murcia
Tel: +34 68 36 28 00
Fax: +34 68 36 28 40

Navarre
SODENA Sociedad de Desarrollo de
Navarra
Av Carlos III, 36. 1° D.
31003 Pamplona
Tel: +34 48 23 04 00
Fax: +34 48 15 26 14
Tel: +34 81 54 11 75
Fax: +34 81 59 04 67

Valencia
IVEX Instituto Valenciano de la
Exportación
Pza, América, 2. 7°
46004 Valencia
Tel: +34 6 395 20 01
Fax: +34 6 395 28 79

BUSINESS ASSOCIATIONS AND SERVICES

Confederation of Spanish Industry
Confederación Española de
Organizaciones Empresariales
(CEOE)
Departamento de Relaciones
Internacionales
C/ Diego de León, 50
28006 Madrid
Tel: +34 1 563 94 15/563 96 41
Fax: +34 1 564 01 35

Advertising Agencies

Ogilvy
C/ Capitán Haya, 1 7°
28020 Madrid
Tel: +34 1 597 36 93
Fax: +34 1 555 09 66

Lintas SA
Pza Carlos trías Bertrán, 7
Edif Sollube
28020 Madrid
Tel: +34 1 556 77 55
Fax: +34 1 555 36 22

McCann-Erikson
P° de la Castellana, 165
28046 Madrid
Tel: 34 1 571 02 00
Fax: +34 1 270 11 16

Tandem/DDB Needham
C/ Orense, 6 1°
28020 Madrid
Tel: +34 1 597 26 25
Fax: +34 1 556 07 73

Tiempo/ BBDO
Av de Burgos, 12
28036 Madrid
Tel: +34 1 766 18 22
Fax: +34 1 766 11 80

J Walter Thompson
C/ Pedro de Valdivia, 10
28006 Madrid

Tel: +34 1 566 43 00
Fax: +34 1 566 44 00/01

Advertising Bodies

AEA Asociación Española de Anunciantes (Spanish Association of Advertisers)
P° Castellana, 121 8°, Esc C
28046 Madrid
Tel: +34 1 556 03 51
Fax: +34 1 597 04 83

OJD Oficina de Justificación de la Difucsión (Press Readership Agency)
Pza de Marqués de Salamanca, 9 4°D
28006 Madrid

EGM Estudio General de Medios (Media Research)
Asociación de Investigación de Medios
de Comunicación
C/ Capitán Haya, 61
28020 Madrid
Tel: +34 1 570 11 74
Fax: +34 1 570 20 49

Advertising Dealers

Mediaplanning
C/ General Perón, 38
28020 Madrid
Tel: +34 1 456 90 00
Fax: +34 1 555 91 23

Optimum Media (Madrid)
C/ Orense, 6 Plta 2
28020 Madrid
Tel: +34 1 597 26 25
Fax: +34 1 556 39 48

Optimum Media (Barcelona)
C/ Enrique Granados, 86–88
08008 Barcelona
Tel: +34 3 415 63 30
Fax: +34 3 415 04 47

Carat España
C/ Félix Boix, 7
28036 Madrid
Tel: +34 1 345 60 66
Fax: +34 1 350 31 07

The Media Partnership
C/ Arapiles, 13
28015 Madrid
Tel: +34 1 593 14 65
Fax: +34 1 593 31 91

Auditors and Accountants

Ernst & Young
Becket House
1, Lambeth Palace Road
London SE1 7EU
Tel: 0171 928 2000
Fax: 0171 928 1345

KPMG
PO Box 486
1, Puddle Dock
London EC4V 3PD
Tel: 0171 311 1000
Fax: 0171 311 3311

Price Waterhouse
1, London Bridge
London SE1 9OL
Tel: 0171 939 2470
Fax: 0171 403 5265

Price Waterhouse (Barcelona)
Av Diagonal, 640 Edif Cajamadrid, Pl. 7
08017 Barcelona
Tel: +34 3 253 27 00
Fax: +34 3 405 90 32

Direct Marketing Services

Paquebot
Centro de Transportes de Madrid
Cta de Villaverde a Vallecas Km 3,5
28018 Madrid
Tel: +34 1 507 03 00
Fax: +34 1 507 38 48

Crecendo SC
Ronda de Poniente, 6 Bajo Iz
28760 Tres Cantos (Madrid)
Tel: +34 1 804 02 50
Fax: +34 1 803 10 30

Dimensión Marketing Directo
Pza del Maestro Arbos, 19
Villa Cristemanal
20013 San Sebastián

Tel: +34 43 32 03 10
Fax: +34 43 27 82 76

Directing SA
C/ Jorge Manrique, 11
28006 Madrid
Tel: +34 1 562 99 92
Fax: +34 1 562 71 09

Estrategias Informáticas Marketing Directo
Gran Vía de las Cortes Catalanas, 646
Ent B
08007 Barcelona
Tel: +34 3 301 87 94
Fax: +34 3 302 08 62

Telefónica Publicidad Información
Av de Manoteras, 12
28050 Madrid
Tel: +34 1 339 60 41
Fax: +34 1 339 61 38

Grupo Tompla Sobre-Express
Carretera de Daganzo, Km 3
28806 Alcalá de Henares
Tel: +34 1 882 05 00
Fax: +34 1 882 65 52

Gupost SA
Camino Illarra, 4
20009 San Sebastián
Tel: +34 43 31 03 50
Fax: +34 43 31 03 56

MU Marketing & Ventas
C/ Orense, 39
28020 Madrid
Tel: +34 1 556 64 11
Fax: +34 1 555 41 18

PDM Marketing y Publicidad Directa
C/ Xaudaró, 7
28034 Madrid
Tel: +34 1 729 13 90
Fax: +34 1 729 07 90

Response JPS
C/ Víctor Andrés Belaúnde, 6
28016 Madrid
Tel: +34 1 457 26 03

Fax: +34 1 457 29 53

Asociación Española de Marketing Directo
Av Diagonal, 437, 5°–1
08036 Barcelona
Tel: +34 3 414 52 72
Fax: +34 3 201 29 88

Asociación Española de Titulados y Profesionales de Publicadad, Marketing y Comunicación
C/ Jardín de San Federico, 5 6°
28009 Madrid
Tel/Fax: +34 1 402 23 40

Teleaction
Edificio Teleaction
C/ Narciso Serra, 14
28007 Madrid
Tel: +34 1 322 65 00
Fax: +34 1 322 65 22

Valenvío
C/ Campos Crespo, 57
46017 Valencia
Tel: +34 6 378 93 52
Fax: +34 6 357 41 06

Headhunters and International Consultants

IVC International Venture Consultants SA
C/ Arturo Soria, 245
28033 Madrid
Tel: +34 1 350 69 05
Fax: +34 1 345 53 72/3

BMA Associates SL
C/ Capitán Haya, 3
28020 Madrid
Tel: +34 1 556 77 45
Fax: +34 1 597 04 54

Seeliger y Conde
C/ Padilla, 1
28006 Madrid
Tel: +34 1 577 99 77
Fax: +34 1 577 41 24

Montaner & Asociados
C/ Balmes, 209 2° 1.
08006 Barcelona

Tel: +34 3 415 76 00
Fax: +34 3 415 66 10

Lawyers

Baker & McKenzie (Madrid)
C/ Pinar, 18
28006 Madrid
Tel: +34 1 411 30 62
Fax: +34 1 562 24 25 – 564 60 35

Baker & McKenzie (Barcelona)
Av Diagonal, 652 Edif D, Plta 8
08034 Barcelona
Tel: +34 3 280 59 00
Fax: +34 3 205 40 59

Deloitte & Touche
D&T Estudio Jurídico y Fiscal
Torre Picasso, Plta 37
28020 Madrid
Tel: +34 1 555 02 52
Fax: +34 1 556 62 00

Gómez-Acebo & Pombo, Abogados
Paseo de la Castellana, 164
28046 Madrid
Tel: +34 1 582 91 00
Fax: +34 1 582 91 14

Despacho Ramón Hermosilla y Cia
C/ Claudio Coello, 32, Plta 1
28001 Madrid
Tel: +34 1 431 48 16
Fax: +34 1 436 63 66

L & A Garrigues
C/ José Abascal, 45
28003 Madrid
Tel: +34 1 456 98 00
Fax: +34 1 399 24 08

Uría & Menédez
Royex House
Aldermanbury Square
London EC2V 7HR
Tel: 0171 600 36 10
Fax: 0171 600 1718

Market Research Firms

Dym Panel SA
Camino Can Calders, 4
San Cugat del Vallés

08190 Barcelona
Tel: +34 3 581 94 00
Fax: +34 3 581 94 01

Research International
C/ Goya, 5 y 7
Pasaje Comercial, 2° Planta
28001 Madrid

Odec
Centro de Cálculo y Aplicaciones
Informáticas
P° de la Habana, 34 2°
28036 Madrid
Tel: +34 1 411 76 12
Fax: +34 1 562 25 82

Sigma Dos
C/ La Flora, 1 2°
28013 Madrid
Tel: +34 1 559 69 11
Fax: +34 1 547 57 15

Sofres AM
Instituto de Investigación
Pza. Carlos Trías Beltrán, 7 4°
28020 Madrid
Tel: +34 1 596 96 00
Fax: +34 1 555 72 32

IDS Income Data Services Ltd
193 St John Street
London EC1V 4LS
Tel: 0171 250 34 34
Fax: 0171 608 09 49

Personal Insurance

Aserplan
C/ Núñez de Balboa, 70 bis
28006 Madrid
Tel: +34 1 632 61 71
Fax: +34 1 576 65 30

Ports

Autoridad Portuaria de Valencia
Muelle de la Aduana s/n.
46024 Valencia
Tel: +34 6 393 95 00
Fax: +34 6 393 95 99

Printers

Mateu Cromo Artes Gráficas SA
Eurolink Business Centre
Unit 36
46 Effra Road
London SW2 1BZ
Contact: David Webster
Tel: 0171 738 7992
Fax: 0171 738 7558

Public Relations

**Alled and Asociados
Consejeros de Relaciones
Públicas**
Av Diagonal, 437 2°
08036 Barcelona

Bernard Krief SA
Av Reina Victoria, 72
28003 Madrid
Tel: +34 1 535 01 03
Fax: +34 1 534 75 48

Urzái & Urzáia y Asociados
Núñez de Balboa, 39 5°b
28001 Madrid
Tel: +34 1 435 48 85
Fax: +34 1 577 46

Real Estate & Office Rentals

Jones Lang Wootton
C/ Serrano, 21 Plta 6
28001 Madrid
Tel: +34 1 577 09 56
Fax: +34 1 431 06 60

Offiten
C/ Zorrilla, 21. 1°
28014 Madrid
Tel: +34 1 531 20 31
Fax: +34 1 521 76 88

Richard Ellis Residencial SA
Edificio Torre Picasso. Plta 9.
Plaza Pablo Ruiz Picasso s/n.
28020 Madrid
Tel: +34 1 555 88 99
Fax: +34 1 556 96 90

**Jesús Fernández, Housing State
Promoter**
C/ Sánchez Fortún, 2 8°
Apartado de Correos 10
30880 Aguilas (Murcia)
Tel: +34 68 41 01 09
Fax: +34 68 44 74 07

Jesús Fernandez Martinez is the owner
of a number of housing estates in one of
the most beautiful and friendly towns on
the Mediterranean, Aguilas. Adjacent to
the coast of Almeria and near Majacar,
Aguilas enjoys perfect summer weather
and mild winters. Jesus Fernandez
Martinez offers houses, duplexes, apartments and building lots, close to the sea
and with views.
  Aguilas is one-and-a-half hours from
the airports of Alicante and Almeria,
and is well-connected by rail to both
cities.

Seminars

**ESADE (Escuela Superior de
Administración y Dirección de
Empresas)**
Centro de Desarrollo Directivo
Avenida Pedralbes, 60–62
08034 Barcelona
Tel: +34 3 280 40 80
Fax: +34 3 204 81 05

ESTE, Universidad de Deusto
Aula de Banca
Camino de Mundaiz, 50
28080 San Sebastián
Tel: +34 43 273 100
Fax: +34 43 273 932

Instituto de Empresa
C/ María de Molina, 12
28006 Madrid
Tel: +34 1 563 93 18
Fax: +34 1 561 09 30

Trade Fairs

Feria de Madrid
IFEMA
Parque Ferial Juan Carlos I
Apdo de Correos 67067
28067 Madrid

Tel: +34 1 722 50 00
Fax: +34 1 722 57 99
Telex: 44025–41674

Feria del Campo
Av de Portugal s/n.
Casa de Campo
28011 Madrid
Tel: +34 1 463 63 34
Fax: +34 1 470 21 54

Translations

**Ibertrand Servicios Empresariales
SL**
C/ Condado de Treviño, 2
28033 Madrid
Tel: +34 1 302 91 30
Fax: +34 1 766 37 31

Tradtec
C/ Calabria, 241. Atico 2°
08029 Barcelona
Tel: +34 3 439 98 80/ 23 75
Fax: +34 3 321 83 06

REFRIGERATOR INSTRUCTIONS

Do not eat solid colds foods (bread, iced
lollyes, vergetables, etc.) since you can
get frost bits.
  Sometimes when you read a poorly
translated instructional manual or
business letter, you don't know whether
to laugh or cry. Let's face it, doing business in another country is complicated,
especially when you find out your
translation reads like this one.
  Because we understand both Spanish
and foreign marketplaces, we can provide your firm with practical solutions
to any queries involving the major languages of the European Union. Whether
you require a simple translation of a
business letter or printed brochure or
the implementation of complete devel-

there. For these firms, our services are far more complete: we are their point of contact in Spain; we do market research to pinpoint business opportunities; we handle in-country correspondence and organisation, facilitate invoicing and chase down lost goods.

So if you're thinking of doing business in Spain or your firm is presently limping along with misinterpreted faxes, poorly translated documents or a lack of solid market information, don't hesitate to contact us.

Just bear in mind these bloopers!

From an airline ticket office: We take your bags and send them in all directions.

From an Acapulco hotel: The manager has personally passed all the water served here.

Transport & Freight

Transportes Olloquiegui SA
26/27 Market Square
Dover
Kent CT16 1NG
Tel: (in Spain) +34 48 121 422
Fax: (in Spain) +34 48 121 032

Transportes Olloquiegui, a company which tranports goods by road, was founded in Pamplona in 1995. Together with its affiliate companies, it is one of the largest international road transport groups in Spain.

Transportes Olloquiegui is the parent company of three other firms: Coneuropa SA, headquartered in Madrid; Paris-Aquitaine Transports SA, which has its offices in Bordeaux; and Olloquiegui UK in Dover. All three companies are legally independent. The company also has delegations in Germany (Langenfeld), Paris and Lisbon, and ten delegations in the major Spanish cities.

Transportes Olloquiegui's group companies have a fleet of more than 310 technically advanced trucks. The 1995 turnover was more than 9.1 billion pesetas (£45 million sterling). All the trucks in the fleet are equipped with GSM mobile telephones, and by the end of 1996 some of them will be fitted out with telematic data transmission and satellite-positioning equipment (GPS).

Olloquiegui is in the final phase of filing for ISO 9002 certification and expects to receive final notification by the summer of 1996.

In 1995, Olloquiegui started road-rail combined traffic between Spain and Germany and, more recently, the company began 'Transtrailer' – bimodal traffic of special semi-trailers on bogies between Spain and the north of France, a technology in which the company played a pioneering role in Spain and Europe.

Olloguiegui maintains a very intense level of traffic with the UK, which led to the establishment of Olloquiegui, UK more than two decades ago. The company, wholly owned by Transportes, has greatly increased its traffic between the UK and Spain.

PRESS

Business Press

Grupo Negocios (London)
Bruno Giorgi
7, Montrose Court
Edgware Road
NW9 5BS
email: brun@dilcon.co.uk

Grupo Negocios (Madrid)
P° de la Castellana, 36–38
28046 Madrid
Tel: +34 1 432 76 01
Fax: +34 1 432 76 03
email: gnegocios@bitmailer.net

Export Magazines

Export & Freight (monthly)
Carn Industrial Estate
139 St Thomas St
Portadown BT62 3BE
Northern Ireland
Tel: 01762 33 42 72
Fax: 01762 351 046

Headlight (monthly)
PO Box 96
Coulsdon
Surrey CR5 2TE
Tel: 0186 660 28 11
Fax: 0181 660 28 24

Commercial Motor (weekly)
Materials Handling News (monthly)
Quadrant House
The Quadrant
Sutton
Surrey SM2 5AS
Tel: 01444 44 55 66

Removals and Storage
(British Association of Removers)
3, Churchill Court
58 Station Road
North Harrow HA2 7SA
Tel: 0181 861 33 31
Fax: 0181 861 33 32

Mundocamión
Transporte Mundial
Calle Ancora, 40
28045 Madrid
Tel: +34 1 347 01 00
Fax: +34 1 347 02 04

Publishers

Planeta Internacional SA
C/ Aribau, 185. 6°
08021 Barcelona
Tel: +34 3 209 50 99
Fax: +34 3 209 77 93

EXPORTING GOODS

Chemicals

Repsol derivados SA (oil products and plastics)
C/ Orense, 34. 3°
28020 Madrid
Tel: +34 1 348 78 00
Fax: +34 1 555 77·79

Clothes & Shoes

Bertie SL (footwear)
Carretera Murcia-Alicante, Km. 53
03205 Elche (Alicante)
Tel: +34 6 544 05 00
Fax: +34 5 544 06 50

Jesús Ferriz SL (footwear)
C/ Zaragoza s/n
03650 Pinoso (Alicante)
Tel: +34 6 697 02 46
Fax: +34 6 697 02 84

Jesús Ferriz SL manufactures and markets men, women and children's footwear made of leather and other materials. An extensive catalogue is available, which can be ordered by fax or post, including more than 100 articles.

Our designers make frequent visits to the main capitals of Europe and North America to gather information for adapting our products to our customers' design requirements.

The brands Paco Schuhmoden and Paco Ferriz provide quality guarantees for finishing, strength and material quality certified by INESCOP. They have been exported for 20 years to the most demanding European markets, such as Germany, Switzerland, Belgium, the Netherlands, Austria and Norway etc and have featured in the sector's main trade fairs.

Textils Mora SAL
C/ Lit M M Casanova, 1
46870 Onteniente (Valencia)
Tel: +34 6 291 29 56
Fax: +34 6 291 28 97

Curtidos La Doma SA (leather)
Barrio La Doma s/n
08530 La Garriga (Barcelona)
Tel: +34 3 871 71 81
Fax: +34 3 871 81 44

Dogi SA
C/ Pintor Domenech y Farré, 13–15
08320 El Masnou (Barcelona)
Tel: +34 3 540 41 50
Fax: +34 3 540 39 54

Satonja SA
Av Ramón y Cajal, s/n
46870 Onteniente (Valencia)
Tel: +34 6 291 27 00
Fax: +34 6 291 06 09

Decorative items

La Mediterránea Coop V
Camino de Albaida s/n
46850 L'olleria (Valencia)
Tel: +34 6 220 01 62
Fax: +34 6 220 14 84

Electrical Appliances

Electrodomésticos Solac SA
Polígono Industrial de Jundiz-Zuazobidea s/n
01080 Vitoria
Tel: +34 45 290 000
Fax: +34 45 290 517

Food

Cocde SA (flours)
C/ Juan Martínez Villergas, 6
47014 Valladolid
Tel: +34 83 33 48 99
Fax: +34 83 34 03 02

Francísco Hernández Vidal SA
(confectionery)
Av Gutiérrez Mellado s/n
30500 Molina de Segura (Murcia)
Tel: +34 68 611 200/ 610 532
Fax: +34 68 615 590

Industrias Lácteas Asturianas SA
(dairy products)
C/ Velázquez, 140
28006 Madrid
Tel: +34 1 411 77 66
Fax: +34 1 411 50 91

La Bella Easo (cakes)
Polígono Malpica c/b
Parcela 62–63
50016 Zaragoza
Tel: +34 76 574 885
Fax: +34 76 564 326

Pasa, Preparados Alimenticios SA
(lean cuisine)
C/ J Tarradellas, 38
08039 Barcelona
Tel: +34 3 439 54 00
Fax: +34 3 410 64 87

Nutrexpa Internacional
C/ Lepanto, 410–414
08025 Barcelona
Tel: 34 3 290 02 90

Nutrexpa, founded in 1946, is a leading group of Spanish companies, and manufactures and distributes a wide range of food products.

A household name in Spain, Nutrexpa owns several best-selling brands. These are well-established in their markets and generate high returns on shares. Some of the more famous products include Cola Cao, Granja San Francisco, Okey, Hit, Phoskitos, La Piara and Aneto.

Nutrexpa's large range of products include drinking chocolate, honey, cakes and pastries, confectionery, milkshakes, meat and fish patés, hams and other cold cuts, and baby food. Everything is produced with Nutrexpa's own facilities under the strictest operating system of quality and hygiene.

Clearly dominant in Spain, Nutrexpa also has a strong base in five continents, where they operate production facilities and commercial offices. Accustomed to working with the most important distributors, the group exports to more than 50 countries, with appropriately adapted market support.

Cámara Arrocera de Amposta
SCCL (rice)
C/ San Cristóbal, 115
43870 Amposta (Tarragona)
Tel: +34 77 701 020/ 700 054
Fax: +34 77 700 190

Dacsa, Maicerías Españolas SA
(corn)
Charles Wimble Sons and Co Ltd
Thrale House
44, Southwark Street
London SE1 1UN
Tel: 0171 378 88 22
Fax: 0171 407 69 88

Dacsa is a company engaged in maize and rice milling and their products are well received in Spain and the European countries to which they export.

Their standard products include flaking grits, brewer's grits, grits for snacks, fibres and normal and micronised meal for baby food. Their rice products include long-grain, semi-long grain and round rice, semolina and flour from coarse or selected batches.

Their maize is generally harvested in Spain (specific varieties) or imported from Argentina or the United States. Their rice is from Spain and community countries.

Dacsa is certified as a supplier by large multinationals in the food, drinks and distribution sectors, and is currently developing and implementing ISO 9002.

Dhul SA
Carretera de Málaga Km 3
18015 Granada
Tel: +34 58 27 40 50
Fax: +34 58 29 46 06

Dhul, like many large enterprises, began as a small family concern, dedicated to making a traditionally home-made dessert, egg *créme caramel*, and selling it locally.

The success of this dessert, along with *tocino de cielo*, is due not only to the natural ingredients used (fresh eggs, milk and sugar), but primarily to the very specialised way in which they are processed, *bain-marie*.

Today, Dhul markets a wide range of products, from traditional desserts to more modern products such as *créme caramel*, creamy custard, *tocino de cielo*, chocolate cup, fresh cheeses, fruit juices, biscuits and cheesecakes. The EC has granted the Dhul company the European Certificate of Quality in recognition of the efforts of the workforce in marketing tradition and quality for more than 25 years.

Onza de Oro
Lugar Riveiriña s/n.
15948 Puebla del Caramiñal (Coruña)
Tel: +34 81 83 00 08
Fax: +34 81 83 25 04

Fruit and Groceries

Danisco Foods Albacete SA
Carretera Albacete-Jaen Km 14
Apdo Correos 842
02080 Albacete
Tel: +34 6 727 01 85
Fax: +34 6 270 155

Frutos de Bétera SA
Av del Ejército, 18

46117 Bétera (Valencia)
Tel: +34 6 160 05 51
Fax: +34 6 169 17 10

Manuel Garrido Fernández
Av de la Constitución s/n
30191 Campos del Río (Murcia)
Tel: +34 68 22 11 40
Fax: +34 68 22 06 33

Hortamar S Coop And
Carretera de Alicún Km 3
04740 Roquetas de Mar (Almería)
Tel: +34 50 320 475/6
Fax: +34 50 324 314

Perales y Ferrer SL
C/ Apatel s/n
03380 Bigastro (Alicante)
Tel: +34 6 535 01 00
Fax: +34 6 535 07 19
Perales & Ferrer is a consolidated company founded in 1975, making it a young company devoted predominantly to growing and buying citrus fruits, which it then exports to all European markets, including the United Kingdom.

This company enjoys the benefits of the Spanish Levante region's excellent climate and is located in the Vega Baja del Segura district bordering the two provinces with the highest lemon production: Alicante and Murcia.

The company is managed by highly qualified professionals who are familiar with all agricultural products and can make a careful selection to guarantee quality in terms of colour, flavour and presentation.

Our brand 'La Perdiz' principally guarantees the quality of our lemons, but covers all our citrus fruits. We also have other brands: 'Charito', 'Citrivega', 'Siglo de Oro', etc, which have been well received in the Spanish and European marketplaces.

Furniture

Ferrando Guanter SL
C/ Pastor Fúster, 7
46009 Valencia
Tel: +34 6 348 28 21/ 11 75
Fax: +34 6 348 35 30

Coinma, S Coop
C/ Vitoriabildea, 4
01010 Vitoria (Alava)
Tel: +34 45 24 16 16/ 14 16
Fax: +34 45 24 06 37

Kade, Import-Export AIE
P° de Isabel la Católica, 2
50009 Zaragoza
Tel: +34 76 55 61 35
Fax: +34 76 35 79 45

Coim
Carretera de Navalón s/n
46640 Moixent (Valencia)
Tel: +34 6 226 11 58
Fax: +34 6 226 12 15

Gamamobel SA
Camino de Vereda, s/n
46469 Beniparrel (Valencia)
Tel: +34 6 120 13 58
Fax: +34 6 120 35 68

Danona S Coop
Barrio Lasao s/n
20730 Azpeitia (Guipúzcoa)
Tel: +34 43 81 59 00
Fax: +34 43 81 00 66

Industrial Fabrics

Spontex España SA
C/ Albert Einstein s/n
46500 Sagunto (Valencia)
Tel: +34 6 266 40 61
Fax: +34 6 266 56 51

Industrial Manufacturers

Sagola SA (valves, compressing machines, filters)
C/ Urartea, 6
01080 Vitoria
Tel: +34 45 241 550
Fax: +34 45 241 949

Industrial Porcelain

Azulindus & Martía SA, Cerámica
Av Manuel Escobedo, 16
12200 Onda (Castellón)
Tel: +34 6 460 02 50
Fax: +34 6 460 50 81

Porcelanas de Saneamiento SA
Ctra Madrid Valencia, 316
46370 Chiva (Valencia)
Tel: +34 6 252 08 50
Fax: +34 6 252 22 26
Porsan SA is a member of the Uralita group, and a manufacturer of vitreous china sanitaryware. Porsan also promotes other commodities, usually supplied by other factories in the Uralita group, which complement its own products: these include ABS seats and covers for lavatory pans, wastes and siphons, bath tubs of enamelled steel or acrylic sheet, asterite sinks, discharge mechanisms for cisterns, several series of traditional mixers, ceramic mounting, and single levers. All are guaranteed by Porsan for quality and reliability.

Porsan's aim is to achieve the best balance of quality and price. This is particularly evident in a range of economical products favoured by local councils constructing housing to a tight budget.

Using the latest technology, Porsan manufactures pieces in white and six different shades. Four bathroom ranges are available, from the most simple, economical model to more luxurious designs (such as the Venecia, Noa, Europa and Delta collections). Different styles of basin within each range and small ceramic accessories for the bathroom allow scope for the customer's creativity.

Gres de Nules SA
Carretera Valencia-Barcelona Km 44.300
12520 Nules (Castellón)
Tel: +34 64 672 752
Fax: +34 64 674 245

Estoli SA (toilet seats)
C/ Paises Catalanes, 18

Polígono Industrial Casanova
080730 Els Monjos (Barcelona)
Tel: +34 3 898 07 29
Fax: +34 3 898 04 62

Natural Building Materials

Asociación Gallega de Graniteros (granites)

Rúa Nova, 28 3°
15705 Santiago de Compostela
Tel: +34 81 59 64 31
Fax: +34 81 59 77 30

Galicia is an autonomous community located on the Atlantic coast of northeastern Spain and is one of the world's most important granite producers. Last year one and a half million tonnes was extracted from its quarries, which are located throughout Galicia, but are largely concentrated in the town of Porriño, in Pontevedra.

The different types of Galician granite – 'Porriño pink', 'Modáriz grey', 'pearl grey' and 'crystal white', to name just a few of the more than 20 varieties – were exported last year to Italy, France, Germany, Japan and Taiwan, among other destinations. The granite sector in Spain's most westerly autonomous community invoiced 75 billion pesetas to more than 300 companies, using more than 80 quarries and 50 factories which provide work for 2,500 people.

The rise in the sector is supported by the interest of prestigious architects such as Isozaki, Foster and Alvaro Siza in building with Galician granite; the most recent example is the 'Domus' or 'House of Man' built in La Coruña by Arata Isozaki. The Tokyo city hall itself was built entirely with Galician granite.

Nevertheless, Galician granite is now entering a new stage, oriented toward painstaking professional qualifications which make it possible for the product to reach its destination in a completely finished state.

The efforts of the sector to achieve greater competitiveness in all markets are also applied to ecology and the environment to minimise the extraction capacity and subsequently rehabilitate the spaces used. To do so, all the remains produced by extraction are transformed and ground down into aggregates. Slope studies are then done on the quarry to be rehabilitated and the project is immediately initiated.

The most important points of the entire process of production and elaboration of Galician granite are the high level of quality, the considerable technological capacity, the protection of the environment and Galicia's geographic location. By sea or by land, Galicia is in an excellent position to distribute the product to any part of the world in the shortest possible time.

Mármoles Sandoval SA (marble)

Empalme Caravaca-Calasparra s/n.
30400 Caravaca de la Cruz (Murcia)
Tel: +34 68 741 211
Fax: +34 68 741 206

Olive Oil

Ildefonso Espinosa

C/ Albercas, 14
23110 Jaen
Tel: +34 53 36 00 63
Fax: +34 53 36 02 00

Coop Nuestra Sra de los Desamparados

Av de la Estación (s) 118
14500 Puente Genil (Córdoba)
Tel: +34 57 601 262
Fax: +34 57 601 266

Paints and Coatings

Ralva SA

Carretera de Ajalvir a Torrejón de Ardoz, Km 2
C/ de la Calahorra s/n
28864 Ajalvir (Madrid)
Tel: +34 1 884 40 85
Fax: +34 1 884 41 92

Industrial Químicas Nabersa

Autovía Cartagena-Valencia Km 279
46469 Beniparrel (Valencia)

Tel: +34 6 120 04 00
Fax: +34 6 120 35 07

Railway Material and Construction

Ferrovial Group
C/ Príncipe de Vergara, 135
28002 Madrid
Tel: +34 1 586 25 00
Fax: +34 1 586 26 77

Tafesa SA
Carretera de Andalucía Km 9
Madrid
Tel: +34 1 797 86 62
Fax: +34 1 798 09 61

Traffic Control Systems

Abengoa Saínco Tráfico SA
C/ Albarracín, 21
28037 Madrid
Tel: +34 1 304 42 66
Fax: +34 1 327 02 17

Watches

Festina
Vía Layetana, 20 4°
08003 Barcelona
Tel: +34 3 268 11 66
Fax: +34 3 310 52 55

Wines & Spirits

Corporación Alimentaria Europea SA
Carretera de Santa Cruz Km 4,500
16400 Tarancón (Cuenca)
Tel: +34 69 32 51 11
Fax: +34 69 32 40 25

Grupo Bodegas Berberana
C/ Alfonso XI, 12
28014 Madrid
Tel: +34 1 531 06 09
Fax: +34 1 531 06 78

Cherubino Valsangiacomo SA
C/ Vicente Brull, 4
46011 Valencia

Tels: +34 6 367 31 02/ 31 51/ 31 59
Fax: +34 6 367 23 50

Bodegas Muga SA
Agent in Britain:
Michael Druitt Agencies
1, Lamb Walk
London SE1 3TT
Tel: 0171 403 9191
Fax: 0171 403 9393

Headquarters:
Barrio de la Estación s/n
26200 Haro (La Rioja)
Tel: +34 41 311 825
Fax: +34 41 312 867

Freixenet (DWS) Ltd
Culpitt House, 74/78
Town Centre
Hatfield
Hertfordshire AL 10 0JW
Tel: 01707 265 532
Fax: 01707 275 104

Freixenet is Spain's largest producer of Cava, with a wine distinctly recognisable by its black bottle, Freixenet Cordon Negro. The Ferrer family has been producing sparkling wine for well over a hundred years at Sant Sadurni d'Anoia, near Barcelona.

The Freixenet Cavas use the traditional grape varieties of Catalunya – Macabeo, Parellada and Xarel-lo. These are blended and the wine is fermented in bottle to produce the natural effervescence that is associated with Cava.

Freixenet's expertise in making sparkling wines has led it to establishing wineries in other parts of the world. Gloria Ferrer is produced in the Sonoma Valley of California and Sala Vive is made in Mexico. Freixenet also owns France's third oldest Champagne house, Champagne Henri Abelé.

In the UK, Freixenet established its own distribution company in the 1970s, Freixenet (DWS) Ltd. It markets and sells the full range of Freixenet Cavas and the still wines of René Barbier, DO Penedes.

Cava has become extremely successful in the UK. According to Nielsen (Stats MR), Cava now accounts for almost one in every five bottle of sparkling wine sold in the UK off trade. This is a major achievement, considering that Cava was only officially recognised as a generic wine just over a dozen years ago!

Coviñas Coop V
Av Rafael Duyos
46340 Requena (Valencia)
Tel: +34 6 230 06 80
Fax: +34 6 230 26 51

Bodegas Marqués de Cáceres (Unión Viti-vinícola SA)
Carretera de Logroño s/n
26350 Cenicero (La Rioja)
Tel: +34 41 455 064
Fax: +34 41 454 400

Bodegas Schenk SA
Av de Francia s/n
46023 Valencia
Tel: +34 6 330 09 80
Fax: +34 6 330 41 46

S Coop Ltda Santa Catalina
C/ Cooperativa, 2
13240 La Solana (Ciudad Real)
Tel: +34 26 632 194/ 631 085
Fax: +34 26 631 085

Consejo Regulador de la Denominación de Origen 'Valdepeñas'
(Valdepeñas' wine self-regulating body)
Av de la Constitución, 19
13300 Valdepeñas (Ciudad Real)
Tel: +34 26 32 27 88
Fax: +34 26 32 10 54

Bodegas Pinord SA
C/ Dr Pasteur, 6
08720 Villafranca del Penedés (Barcelona)
Tel: +34 3 890 30 66
Fax: +34 3 817 09 79

Index

Index of Display Advertisers